Editor
Gisela Lee

Managing Editor
Karen J. Goldfluss, M.S. Ed.

Editor-in-Chief
Sharon Coan, M.S. Ed.

Cover Artist
Lesley Palmer

Art Coordinator
Denice Adorno

Imaging
Alfred Lau
Rosa C. See

Product Manager
Phil Garcia

Publishers
Mary D. Smith, M.S. Ed.

Daily Skills Practice

Grades 5-6

Author

Jane Hutchison

Teacher Created Resources

Banks School Supply Inc.

☐ 11080 Irma Drive, Northglenn CO. 80233-3611 (303) 255-7173
☐ 731 Billings Street, Aurora, CO. 80011-6739 (303) 367-5737
☐ 2415 Rand Ave., Colo Springs, CO. 80906-2892 (719) 576-4011
1-800-228-2538 banksschoolsupply.com

ISBN: 978-0-7439-3303-2

©2000 Teacher Created Resources, Inc.
Reprinted, 2012
Made in U.S.A.

The classroom teacher may reproduce copies of the materials in this book for use in a single classroom only. The reproduction of any part of the book for other classrooms or for an entire school or school system is strictly prohibited. No part of this publication may be transmitted, stored, or recorded in any form without written permission from the publisher.

Table of Contents

Introduction

Daily Skills Practice: Grades 5–6 was designed to cover a wide range of skills and concepts typically introduced or reviewed during a school year. The practice pages provide a quick assessment of how a child is performing on a particular skill or with a specific concept. In addition, the activities in this book provide teachers, children, and parents with consistent, daily feedback on a child's academic progress.

How to Use the Practice Pages

In the Classroom

The daily skills pages are easily implemented in the classroom during whole-class instruction. Here are some suggestions for introducing and assigning the pages:

- To use some or all of the practice sheets for whole-class or group instruction, simply photocopy them onto overhead transparency sheets and use them throughout the year. Students will need to have a daily practice notebook to copy the exercises off the overhead. This is an excellent way to begin each morning, by having them practice sheet on an overhead ready for students when they walk into the room. The transparencies can be organized and stored for use for many years.

- Give each child a photocopy of the daily practice sheet you wish to use, or prepare a small packet for each child. Send packets home every one to two weeks. Decide how you will review and assess the children's completed work and communicate this to both the children and the parents.

At Home

The practice pages in this book make excellent reinforcement exercises at home. With over 200 daily practice pages from which to choose, a child is given the opportunity to review concepts and skills he or she already knows. For newly acquired skills, the pages provide reinforcement through practice. As pages are completed, parents and children can work together to correct the exercises using the answer key provided in the back of the book.

Practice Page Sections

Each practice page is divided into the following sections:

- **Math Practice**—Math Practice consists of a variety of math problems. Generally, there is a word problem at the end of each math section. See the Table of Contents for a list of specific skills and page numbers used in this section.

- **Language Practice**—Language Practice consists of a variety of grammar and writing skills. This is an effective way to quickly preview or review a skill. See the Table of Contents for a list of specific skills and page numbers used in this section.

- **Writing Practice**—Each day, a writing prompt is given for students to practice their writing skills. Students should be encouraged to write at least a paragraph of 5–6 sentences, yet they could write more, if they wish. Give students reading practice by letting them share their writings with the class.

(**Note:** If you wish to extend the activities by writing your own lessons, reproduce the blank skills practice form on page 206.)

Name _____

Math Practice: Writing Numbers

Write each mathematical sentence in words. Then solve problem 5.

1. 54 + 75 = 129 _____ _____ _____ _____	2. 256 − 54 = 202 _____ _____ _____ _____	3. 44 x 6 = 264 _____ _____ _____ _____

4. 390 ÷ 13 = 30 _____ _____ _____	5. The number of students in fifth grade is 15 more than last year. If there were 118 fifth graders last year, how many students are in fifth grade? _____

Language Practice: Sentences

Read each group of words. Write **S** if it is a sentence or **F** if it is a fragment.

_____ 1. Going to watch a play.

_____ 2. He trying to make a good grade on his test.

_____ 3. Dave asked if he could go to the video store.

_____ 4. Three students went to the library to research Africa.

_____ 5. The lab animals in science class.

_____ 6. Mrs. Branch had a long dress on.

_____ 7. The water fountain working now.

_____ 8. Monica prepared an apple pie for dessert.

Writing Practice: Describe a family tradition that you have.

Math Practice: Writing Numbers

Write each mathematical sentence in numbers. Then solve problem 5.

1. Forty-five plus twelve equals fifty-seven. _____	2. Seventy minus twenty equals fifty. _____	3. Eight times thirty equals two hundred forty. _____
4. Ninety-eight divided by two equals forty-nine. _____	5. Rex had a dozen oranges and ate four. How many did he have left? Write a mathematical sentence using the information given. Then solve the problem. _____	

Language Practice: Nouns

Write each noun in the blanks provided. (**Note:** Pronouns should not be included.)

1. These two guys will give a speech.

   _____   _____

2. Crossing a river on a swinging bridge is dangerous.

   _____   _____

3. People can do anything when they work together.

   _____   _____

4. They can take the bus and go home after school.

   _____   _____

5. Crissie wore her blue shirt to church.

   _____   _____

6. The girls' basketball team won first place.

   _____   _____

 Writing Practice: What would your life be like if you were a king or queen of a country? Write a descriptive paragraph.

Math Practice: Number Properties

Identify whether each problem is an example of the *commutative property* or the *associative property*. Then solve problem 5.

1.	2.	3.
$43 + 10 = 10 + 43$	$3 \times (2 \times 6) = (3 \times 2) \times 6$	$(30 + 9) + 4 = 30 + (9 + 4)$
_____	_____	_____

4.	5.
$11 \times 4 = 4 \times 11$	Skip has collected baseball caps for the past three years. He had 10 the first year, 14 last year, then added 12 this year. Write a number sentence using the associative property. Then solve.
_____	_____

Language Practice: Verbs

Underline the verb in each sentence.

1. Only one student made a passing grade on the test.

2. Jets travel fast.

3. Their dinner consisted of ham and potatoes.

4. She hardly touched her food.

5. Nikki spent the night with her friend.

6. Coleman put seven candles on his brother's cake.

Writing Practice: You get to plan your own birthday party. Write a paragraph about how you would plan it and what you would like to happen during the party.

Math Practice: Patterns

Complete each pattern by filling in the blanks and then solve problem 5.

1. A, B, B, C, C, C, D, D, D, D, ____, ____, ____, ____, ____.	**2.** 1, 2, 4, 7, 11, ____, ____, ____.	**3.** AB, BC, CD, DE, ____, ____, ____, ____.
4. 2, 4, 8, 16, ____, ____, ____.	**5.** Mrs. Johnston traveled to 12 cities on her summer vacation. She brought four brochures from each city. How many brochures did she bring back? _____

Language Practice: Subjects

Find the simple subject in each sentence. Write it in the space provided.

_____ 1. She sang "Happy Birthday" to her friend.

_____ 2. Rain poured from the sky.

_____ 3. Is your baby sister walking yet?

_____ 4. You will feel better when your fever goes down.

_____ 5. Dave played the flute in the school band.

_____ 6. We watched a movie called *Return to Oz*.

 Writing Practice: You have been asked to design a logo for your school T-shirt. Write what you would do, then draw the design you created.

Name _____

Math Practice: Chart

Using the information in the chart, answer the following questions below.

1. How many more dogs were owned in 2000 than 1990?	2. What was the total number of cats and dogs owned in 2000?	3. Which pet had the smallest increase?
_____	_____	_____

4. How many pets were owned in 1990? In 2000?	Pet Population		
1990: _____ 2000: _____	Pet	1990	2000
	Cat	540	718
	Dog	622	962
	Bird	83	110
	Fish	51	79

Language Practice: Sentences

Rewrite each sentence to make more sense.

1. Under the table were her shoes.

   _____

2. For the party I had to pick her up.

   _____

3. Across the room sat Miss Michaels.

   _____

4. Near the couch was the baby's toy.

   _____

5. For quietly just a moment she sat.

   _____

6. Faster and faster came the runners.

   _____

 Writing Practice: Write a paragraph about a pet you have or a pet you've always wanted.

Math Practice: Estimation

Estimate each answer.

1. About how much more money would you need to buy a sweater that cost $29.95 if you have $15.00? _____	2. You want to buy paper and 2 pencils for $1.89 and you have $5.00. About how much would your change be? _____	3. What is the estimated total of students in your class if there are 18 girls and 13 boys? _____
4. How many movie tickets could you buy with a ten dollar bill if each ticket cost $4.00? _____	5. Sue bought 10 stamps that cost 32¢ each. Estimate how much she paid for her stamps. _____	

Language Practice: Punctuation

Add punctuation marks where needed in the following paragraph.

My mother took me to a picnic on Memorial Day
There were so many people there so we had to
park far away We ate the following foods hot
dogs hamburgers potato salad and baked beans
Then it started to rain so we had to go home

 Writing Practice: What do you think life would be like if people were invisible?

Name _____

Math Practice: Place Value

Write each number in standard form and then solve problem 5.

1. one thousand, four hundred three _____	2. two hundred thirty-seven thousand, nine hundred seventy _____	3. 2 thousands, 2 hundreds, 2 ones _____
4. 80 thousands, 9 hundreds, 1 ten, 8 ones _____	5. Kasey bought a present for her mother. She gave the cashier 4 tens and 7 ones. How much did it cost if she had the exact amount? _____	

Language Practice: Verbs

Write the correct form of the verb *see* in each sentence.

1. I looked out the window and _____ snow falling.

2. I hope I _____ _____ snow tomorrow.

3. Hey, I _____ the sun shining!

4. Last winter we _____ snow at Christmas time.

5. Maybe next winter we _____ _____ snow again.

 Writing Practice: Write a persuasive paragraph describing why everyone should like milk.

Math Practice: Place Value

Write each number in expanded form and then solve problem 5.

1. 1,256,753	2. 38,281	3. twenty-two thousand, six hundred
_____	_____	_____
_____	_____	_____
_____	_____	_____
_____	_____	_____
_____		

4. eight hundred forty thousand, three	5. Grant wants to buy a CD for $16.99. If he saves $4.00 a week, how many weeks will it take him to save enough money to buy the CD?
_____	
_____	
_____	
_____	_____

Language Practice: Sentences

Determine what kind of sentence each one is. Write *declarative, imperative, interrogative,* or *exclamatory.* Then add the correct punctuation.

_____ 1. What is your name

_____ 2. My name is Josiah Brown

_____ 3. Shut the door, Josiah

_____ 4. Where are you going with Sandy

_____ 5. What a great friend Sandy is

_____ 6. Please go check the mail

 Writing Practice: If you could make a movie or write a book, what kind of story and characters would you create? Write a descriptive paragraph.

Math Practice: Comparing Numbers

Which number is greater, **A** or **B**? Circle the correct answer. Then solve problem 5.

1.	2.	3.
A. 625,834,222 B. 624,843,222	A. 354,827 B. 354,287	A. 9,268,925 B. 9,269,625

4.

   A. 800,000 x 3

   B. 300,000 x 7

5. A toy company made 1,000,000 dolls in one year. They also made 10 times as many stuffed animals as dolls. How many stuffed animals did they make?

_____

Language Practice: Punctuation

Rewrite each sentence with correct capital letters and punctuation marks.

1. your letter is in the mail   _____

2. please do your homework tom   _____

3. i bought a hamburger at Mcdonald's   _____

4. what a great game it was   _____

5. when will we go on our field trip   _____

6. the 4-h club meets every tuesday   _____

 Writing Practice: Use this writing prompt to write a short paragraph:

Our school picnic was so much fun until . . .

Math Practice: Comparing Numbers

For problems 1–4, circle the correct answer (or answers). Then solve problem 5.

1. Which number is greater than 442,823?	2. Which number is less than 30,000?	3. Which number is between 195,000 and 305,000?
439,203 21,982 42,187 219,823 30,001 453,000 328,445 45,300	439,203 21,982 42,187 219,823 30,001 453,000 328,445 45,300	439,203 21,982 42,187 219,823 30,001 453,000 328,445 45,300

4. Which number is greater than 32,000 but lower than 54,850?	5. Manny has to read 91 pages in his novel before next week. How many pages must he read every day for 7 days to get it all read?
439,203 21,982 42,187 219,823 30,001 453,000 328,445 45,300	_____

Language Practice: Verbs

Choose between *come* and *came*. Write the correct word in the space provided.

1. Yesterday, the rain _____ after the sunshine.

2. The sunshine had _____ and gone.

3. The mailman had _____ before noon yesterday.

4. He _____ after 1:00 P.M. today.

5. My brother _____ home late last night.

6. Have you _____ over to work on homework?

 Writing Practice: Everyone likes to get gifts, but how about giving them? What gift would you like to give someone? Write a paragraph describing your idea.

Name

Math Practice: Comparing Numbers

Write < or > for each pair of numbers. Then solve problem 5.

1. 345 thousand ◯ 354,000	2. 12,878 ◯ 12,787	3. 49 billion ◯ 490,000,000

4. 62,357 ◯ 62,375	5. Todd ran in a 50-mile race. His first stop was 15 miles. His second stop was 10 miles before the end of the race. How many miles did he travel between both stops? _____

Language Practice: Plurals

Write the plural of these animals.

1. pony   _____

2. dog   _____

3. ox   _____

4. cow   _____

5. deer   _____

6. buffalo _____

7. sheep   _____

8. fish   _____

 Writing Practice: In your opinion, what traits make a good friend? Write a descriptive paragraph.

Math Practice: Rounding

For problems 1–4, round **428,146** to the nearest value shown. Then solve problem 5.

1. nearest hundred	2. nearest thousand	3. nearest ten
_____	_____	_____

4. nearest hundred thousand	5. The population of a southern city was 61,822. What rounded number would be used if a brochure about the city was printed?
_____	_____

Language Practice: Subjects

Circle the simple subject in each sentence.

1. Only Lena had her homework.

2. Ivan said, "That homework was difficult."

3. The sick children stayed home from school.

4. You play the piano well.

5. Our uncle came to visit us.

6. Can we play a game of jacks?

 Writing Practice: Describe your favorite television show.

Name _____

Math Practice: Variables

Find the value of each expression. Then solve problem 5.

1. $x - 12 = 88$	2. $7 \times z = 49$	3. $144 \div y = 12$
$x =$ _____	$z =$ _____	$y =$ _____

4. $n + 120 = 241$	5. On the way to Mrs. Ward's classroom, the new student will pass five rooms. Mrs. Proctor's room is next to Mrs. Baker's room. Mrs. Morgan's room is between Mrs. Proctor's and Mrs. Prince's room. Mrs. Prince's room is not next to Mrs. Ward's room. Which classroom is beside Mrs. Ward's room?
$n =$ _____	_____

Language Practice: Nouns

Write the following nouns under the correct heading. Use capitalization where needed.

- playground
- book
- elm street
- athlete
- detroit
- caddie woodlawn
- aunt
- england

Common Nouns	Proper Nouns

 Writing Practice: Write a short story about your class at school. Underline each common noun and circle each proper noun.

Math Practice: Multiplication

Solve the problems below.

1.	2.	3.
39.37 x .21	11.89 x .33	91.44 x .16

4.	5. Kareem is two years older than his brother, Javier, but is 5 years younger than his sister, Janis. If Janis is 19, how old are Kareem and Javier?
40.47 x .25	Kareem is _____. Javier is _____.

Language Practice: Alphabetical Order

Write these mathematical terms in alphabetical order.

perimeter _____

ratio _____

multiply _____

percent _____

division _____

place value _____

decimals _____

geometry _____

 Writing Practice: What is your favorite food dish? Why? What is your least favorite food dish? Why?

Name _____

Math Practice: Fractions

Circle the correct answer that is equivalent to the given fraction. Then, solve problem 5.

1. $\dfrac{4}{5}$ $\dfrac{10}{18}$ $\dfrac{8}{10}$ $\dfrac{12}{22}$	2. $\dfrac{3}{7}$ $\dfrac{15}{35}$ $\dfrac{5}{14}$ $\dfrac{6}{12}$	3. $\dfrac{2}{3}$ $\dfrac{10}{16}$ $\dfrac{12}{20}$ $\dfrac{8}{12}$
4. $\dfrac{3}{4}$ $\dfrac{25}{30}$ $\dfrac{21}{28}$ $\dfrac{15}{18}$	5. Sharon wanted to buy a dress for her school dance. She had only $30.15, but the dress cost $59.87. How much more money does she need? _____	

Language Practice: Verbs

Write sentences using these vivid verbs.

1. sobbed: _____

2. mumbled: _____

3. moaned: _____

4. protested: _____

5. gasped: _____

6. insisted: _____

 Writing Practice: Use this writing prompt to write a short paragraph:

I began my time travels by . . .

Math Practice: Division

Solve these division problems. Then solve problem 5.

1. $6\overline{)39}$	2. $4\overline{)97}$	3. $7\overline{)590}$

4. $5\overline{)641}$	5. At the bookstore, paperback books cost $3.00 and hardback books cost $7.00. What is the total cost of 3 paperback and 4 hardback books? _____

Language Practice: Syllables

Divide these words into syllables.

1. hardy _____

2. palomino _____

3. material _____

4. phonograph _____

5. appoint _____

6. chili _____

7. sideline _____

8. umbrella _____

9. computer _____

10. movie _____

 Writing Practice: If a relative gave you $500.00 to buy anything you wanted, what would or wouldn't you buy?

Name _____

Math Practice: Variables

Solve for *x*. Then, solve problem 5.

1. $52 + 6 = x + 12$ $x = 46$	2. $18 + 7 = 22 + x$ $x = 5$	3. $61 - 6 = 73 - x$ $x = 17$

4. $82 - 8 = x - 12$ $x = 62$	5. Marty paid for a new jacket. The jacket cost $21.99. His change was $18.01. How much money did he give the clerk? 3.98

Language Practice: Synonyms

Write a synonym for each word.

1. chimpanzee   marty
2. mountain   Peak
3. beautiful   hasome
4. surprise   _____
5. small   finey

6. soft   _____
7. trash   _____
8. exhausted   _____
9. boat   _____
10. miniature   _____

Writing Practice: Use this writing prompt to write a short paragraph:

I was home one night when I heard a noise on the front porch.

Math Practice: Subtraction

Solve each problem below.

1. 82 − 36	2. 503 − 88	3. 2,000 − 392
4. 30,415 − 4,776	5. A passenger car on a train can carry 67 passengers. How many passengers can a train with 12 passenger cars carry? _____	

Language Practice: Pronouns

Rewrite the underlined words with a pronoun.

1. The girl and her friend played on a soccer team.   _____

2. Jonah said, "Jonah like to eat corn on the cob."   _____

3. My mother used to live in South Carolina.   _____

4. Why don't the children play outside?   _____

5. The rabbit ate the rabbit's food.   _____

6. Katie and I share the same birthday.   _____

7. The next day Emilio and Caren walked home together.   _____

8. Rubert found a watch in his backyard.   _____

 Writing Practice: Describe an eventful day at school and the different things that you did.

Math Practice: Geometry

Determine whether the figure is plane or solid and then solve problem 5.

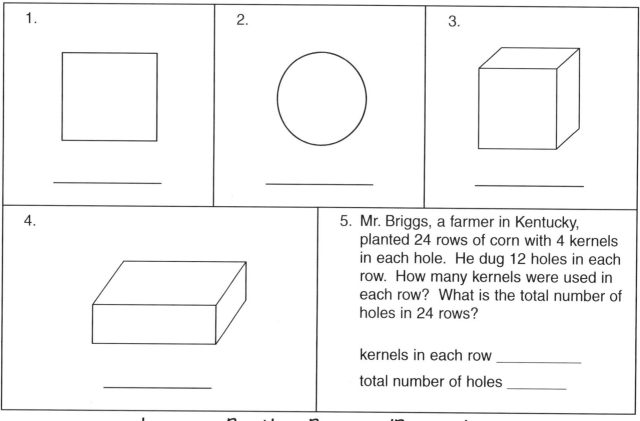

1. _____

2. _____

3. _____

4. _____

5. Mr. Briggs, a farmer in Kentucky, planted 24 rows of corn with 4 kernels in each hole. He dug 12 holes in each row. How many kernels were used in each row? What is the total number of holes in 24 rows?

kernels in each row _____

total number of holes _____

Language Practice: Pronouns/Possessives

Use *its* or *it's* correctly in the following sentences.

1. My father says _____ too early to go to school.

2. The prairie dog makes _____ home in a burrow.

3. _____ not going to matter if it rains today.

4. The tractor did _____ work on the farm.

5. _____ almost ten o'clock.

6. If _____ raining, be sure to take your umbrella.

7. He got off his bicycle to check _____ tires.

8. The fish swam in _____ aquarium.

 Writing Practice: Many children have best friends. Write a paragraph describing your best friend. What makes this person your best friend? If you don't have a best friend, write about one of your good friends.

                   ©Teacher Created Resources, Inc.

Math Practice: Place Value

Write the number from the list of numbers that has the digit 6 in the specified place holder.

1. 6,000 _____	2. 60,000 _____	3. 6,000,000 _____

4. 600,000 _____	670,749 76,900,012 45,836,808 60,087,521 167,222 247,186

Language Practice: Possessives

Write a possessive noun in the blank that will complete the sentence.

1. Kory is on the team. Mom saw _____ team play yesterday.

2. My sister has a Barbie™ doll. My _____ Barbie™ doll is new.

3. The children ran in a race. Where did the _____ race take place?

4. Kenisha has a pair of ice skates. _____ skates are white.

5. The students moved their desks. Where did the _____ desks get moved?

6. The toys belonged to her sisters. Her _____ toys were all over the floor.

✍ **Writing Practice:** How important do you think it is to know one's family history? Why?

Name _____

Math Practice: Number Order

Write the numbers in order from least to greatest and then solve probem 5.

1. 201,800 208,100
   202,788 202,877
	2. 431,559 431.559
	   4,315.59 43,155.9
		3. 5,643 5,346
		   5,436 5,634

_____ _____ _____ _____	_____ _____ _____ _____	_____ _____ _____ _____

4. 99,960 96,990 99,690 99,909	5. The Red Cross had a weekend blood drive. On Friday 120 people gave blood. On Saturday 191 gave blood, and on Sunday 85 people gave blood. By rounding each number to the nearest ten, estimate how many people gave blood during the weekend blood drive.
_____ _____ _____ _____	_____

Language Practice: Pronouns

Read the first sentence. Write a pronoun in the second sentence that describes the first sentence.

1. Brook is my neighbor. _____ has two brothers.

2. Stephan likes to play baseball. _____ plays every week.

3. Ted and Jo made a volcano. _____ made it for science.

4. Sammy is Joella's brother. _____ is three years older than Joella.

5. The tiger is dangerous. Don't go near _____.

6. Most people don't like spiders or snakes. _____ are creepy animals.

Writing Practice: Write a paragraph describing how you feel about insects.

Math Practice: Addition

Solve each problem below.

1. $\begin{array}{r} 69 \\ + 96 \\ \hline \end{array}$	2. $\begin{array}{r} 459 \\ + 391 \\ \hline \end{array}$	3. $\begin{array}{r} 6{,}765 \\ + 4{,}364 \\ \hline \end{array}$
4. $\begin{array}{r} 47{,}889 \\ + 52{,}093 \\ \hline \end{array}$	5. An ice cream store had 2 pints of ice cream for $5.00. How many pints would you get for $20.00? _____	

Language Practice: Friendly Letters

Match the part of the friendly letter with its name.

_____ 1. Dear Julie,   a. heading

_____ 2. the thoughts and ideas of your letter   b. greeting

_____ 3. January 1, 2001   c. body

_____ 4. the name of person writing the letter   d. closing

_____ 5. Your friend,   e. signature

 Writing Practice: Write a friendly letter to a friend or a relative about something interesting happening in your life.

Name _____

Math Practice: Estimation

Estimate each answer.

1. 769 → _____ + 4,364 → _____	2. 691 → _____ + 189 → _____	3. 345 → _____ + 707 → _____
4. 6927 → _____ + 18,350 → _____	5. 25,467 → _____ + 8,649 → _____	

Language Practice: Subject

Write a subject part for each sentence.

1. _____ were going to watch television.

2. _____ was hard to do.

3. _____ had been reading their books.

4. _____ is painting a picture.

5. _____ uses a blue ink pen.

6. _____ likes to swim.

 Writing Practice: Use this writing prompt to write a short paragraph:

We went to the circus to watch the lions and tigers. Suddenly, things got out of hand...

Math Practice: Geometry

Determine if the pair of figures is congruent or similar and then solve problem 5.

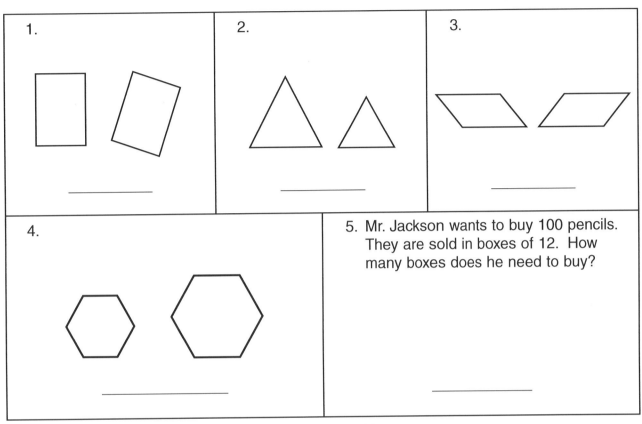

5. Mr. Jackson wants to buy 100 pencils. They are sold in boxes of 12. How many boxes does he need to buy?

Language Practice: Homonyms

Circle the correct homonym to complete each sentence.

buy   by   1. Mom drove _____ Janet house.

break   brake   2. How did you _____ your pencil?

piece   peace   3. Countries need to have _____ with each other.

There   Their   4. _____ suitcase was packed for their vacation.

To   Too   5. _____ many people live in the city.

flee   flea   6. He swatted at the _____ on his arm.

Writing Practice: If you were in charge of the school cafeteria, what kinds of changes would you make?

Name Diego

Math Practice: Money

List the fewest coins and paper money you would receive as change in the following problems and then solve problem 5.

1. If a customer spent $0.84 and paid with a dollar bill, how much change will the customer receive?	2. If a customer spent $1.73 and paid with two dollar bills, how much change will the customer receive?	3. If a customer spent $3.22 and paid with a five dollar bill, how much change will the customer receive?

1. 0.13

2. 2.00
173
.27
(.27)

3. 5.11
4.00
3.22
(1.89)

4. If a customer spent $16.55 and paid with a twenty dollar bill, how much change will the customer receive?

_____

_____

_____

5. George spent 1 dollar, 2 quarters, 3 dimes, and 1 nickel on candy. His friend spent 1 dollar, 3 quarters, and 1 nickel. How much did each spend and who spent more?

George _____

George's friend _____

Who spent more? _____

Language Practice: Adverbs

Choose the right adverb to complete each sentence.

1. The play ended _____.   carefully

2. They acted _____ in the mall.   quickly

3. Jorge plays football very _____.   badly

4. She _____ hiked up the mountain.   suddenly

5. The sunset was _____ seen.   well

6. Mrs. Johnson walked _____ to her car.   clearly

 Writing Practice: Write a paragraph about how you feel you're doing in school this year.

Name _____

Math Practice: Time

If 60 seconds (sec) equals 1 minute (min) and if 60 minutes (min) equals 1 hour (hr), calculate the times in the problems below and then solve problem 5.

1. 93 sec = _____ min _____ sec	2. 76 min = _____ min _____ sec	3. 12 hrs = _____ min
4. 41 min = _____ sec	5. Michelle walks 45 minutes everyday. How many total hours and minutes does she walk in one week? _____ hrs _____ min	

Language Practice: Proofreading

Copy each sentence correctly.

1. didn't they put on a play in november

_____

2. there class saw two playes this year

_____

3. have you ever ben to cape canaveral

_____

4. next yeare bobs aunt will work for the post office

_____

5. the olympics is fun too watch

_____

6. I like the knew sport called snowboarding

_____

 Writing Practice: Describe a sporting event you would like to compete in during an upcoming Olympics. What kind of training would be involved? What kind of time and dedication would you have to give towards your training?

Name _____

Math Practice: Rounding

Solve the problems below.

1. Round 71,845 to the nearest hundred. _____	2. Round 459,056 to the nearest ten. _____	3. Round 6,752,653 to the nearest million. _____
4. Round 495, 056 to the nearest hundred thousand. _____	5. Mr. Paul bought 20 assignment books for his classroom. They cost $0.49 each. Can he pay for them with a $10 bill? How do you know? Write a number sentence to show the answer. _____	

Language Practice: Clauses

Underline the clause in each sentence.

1. While Toby waited for the school bus, he read a book.

2. The baby yawned when she was ready for a nap.

3. We will have P. E. outside unless it rains today.

4. Until the clock strikes noon, we will work on science.

5. He received a good grade on his test although he missed three problems.

✏️ **Writing Practice:** Write a paragraph about how you could be famous one day.

Math Practice: Mixed Computation/Money

Solve the problems below.

1. $4.82 + 6.58	2. $30.40 − 18.23	3. $8.74 x 21
4. 6) 25.16	5. Miko and his father traveled to San Francisco on a train. The total cost was $96.00. However, Miko's ticket was $32.00 less than his dad's ticket. How much was his dad's ticket? _____	

Language Practice: Dictionary Skills

Circle all words you would find on a dictionary page with these guide words.

intermission   irrigate

interplay	interlock	inward
inventory	irritate	itch
intense	interval	intrude
install	interim	invest

 Writing Practice: What kind of hobbies do you have? Write a descriptive paragraph about your favorite hobby/hobbies.

Name _____

Math Practice: Perimeter

Find the perimeter for each problem and then solve problem 5.

1.

5 cm

P = _____

2.

72 m

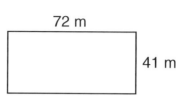

41 m

P = _____

3.

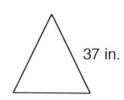

37 in.

P = _____

4.

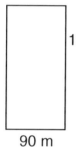

120 m

90 m

P = _____

5. The perimeter of a square is 6.20 inches. What is the length of each side?

_____

Language Practice: Contractions

Write the two words for each contraction.

1. I've   _____   _____

2. won't   _____   _____

3. you'll   _____   _____

4. he'd   _____   _____

5. haven't   _____   _____

6. isn't   _____   _____

7. aren't   _____   _____

8. she'd   _____   _____

 Writing Practice: Write a paragraph about a place where you'd like to go on vacation. Circle all contractions.

Name _____

Math Practice: Fractions

Write the mixed number represented by each picture and then solve problem 5.

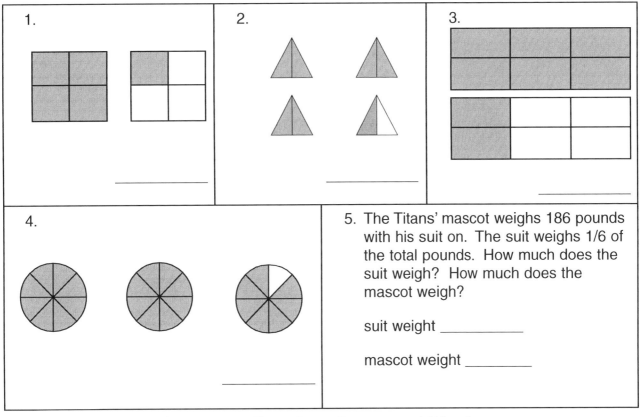

1.

_____

2.

_____

3.

_____

4.

_____

5. The Titans' mascot weighs 186 pounds with his suit on. The suit weighs 1/6 of the total pounds. How much does the suit weigh? How much does the mascot weigh?

suit weight _____

mascot weight _____

Language Practice: Compound Words

Use the following words to make compound words.

life	apple	to	same
light	saver	search	board
self	morrow	your	light
side	self	pine	house

_____   _____

_____   _____

_____   _____

_____   _____

 Writing Practice: Use this writing prompt to write a short story:

I went camping with my family. Everything was going fine until we heard a loud growl...

Math Practice: Decimals/Writing Numbers

Write out each number in words and then create your own problem 5.

1. 3.379	2. 0.92	3. 1,201.6
_____	_____	_____
_____	_____	_____
_____	_____	_____
_____	_____	_____

4. 5.002	5. Make up your own story problem using the numbers 4, 6, and 24.
_____	_____
_____	_____
_____	_____
	_____
	_____

Language Practice: Verbs

Complete each sentence with a verb or verb phrase.

1. The girls in the classroom _____.

2. The clerk in the store _____.

3. The dog at the vet's office _____.

4. The woods around the corner _____.

5. Children playing on a playground _____.

6. Soldiers fighting in a war _____.

Writing Practice: While watching television one evening, the show you were watching was interrupted with a "Special Report." Describe the breaking news.

Math Practice: Rounding

Round to the nearest hundred and thousand and then solve problem 5.

1. 23,329 hundred: _____ thousand: _____	2. 3,574 hundred: _____ thousand: _____	3. 4,725,210 hundred: _____ thousand: _____

4. 165,372 hundred: _____ thousand: _____	5. Andy's family drove a total of 1,793 miles during their two-week vacation. About how many miles did they travel each day? _____

Language Practice: Alphabetical Order

Write the names of these Civil Rights leaders in alphabetical order by last name.

Martin Luther King, Jr. _____

Mary McCloud Bethune _____

Harriet Tubman _____

Rosa Parks _____

A. Philip Randolph _____

Thurgood Marshall _____

Oliver Brown _____

Frederick Douglass _____

Jesse Jackson _____

Sojourner Truth _____

Writing Practice: Write a paragraph about what you could do to help people get along with each other.

Math Practice: Mean

Figure each bowler's average. Then solve problem 5.

1. Thurman	2. Donna	3. Kevin
176	142	133
198	129	160
215	153	121
average = _____	average = _____	average = _____

4. Jane	5. Jevon bowled 4 games at $2.40 per game. He rented shoes for $1.25. How much did it cost him to bowl?
154	
162	
188	
average = _____	_____

Language Practice: Antonyms

Match each word with its opposite.

_____ 1. entrance   a. young

_____ 2. indoors   b. outside

_____ 3. mountain   c. underneath

_____ 4. overhead   d. release

_____ 5. soothe   e. valley

_____ 6. ancient   f. exit

_____ 7. sieze   g. faithful

_____ 8. disloyal   h. agitate

 Writing Practice: You and your family have won a trip to Hawaii. Write a story about your adventures.

Name _____

Math Practice: Measurement/Estimation

Estimate the degrees of each angle and then solve problem 5.

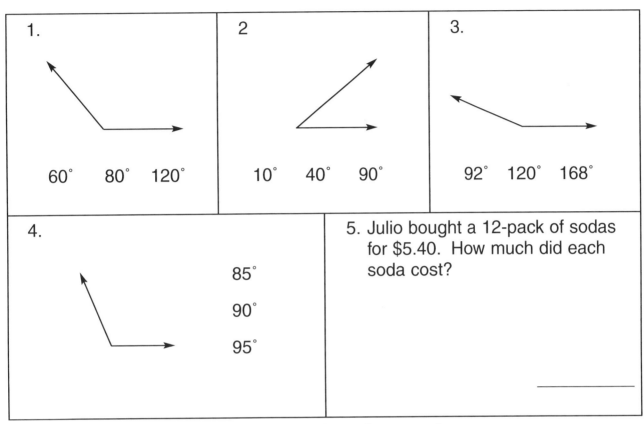

1.

60°   80°   120°

2

10°   40°   90°

3.

92°   120°   168°

4.

85°

90°

95°

5. Julio bought a 12-pack of sodas for $5.40. How much did each soda cost?

_____

Language Practice: Punctuation

Circle the colon (:) or semicolon (;) to make each sentence complete.

1. Ryan decided to stay after school (:   ;) I decided to go home.

2. I like to eat the following foods (:   ;) pancakes, bacon, and eggs.

3. At 6 (:   ;) 00 P.M. we eat dinner.

4. She won the race (:   ;) her teammate came in second.

5. Mr. Diaz asked the students to do three things (:   ;) listen, work quietly, and respect others.

6. It wasn't long till school would begin (:   ;) I was almost late.

 Writing Practice: National Children's Book Week is in November. Write a paragraph describing your favorite book.

Math Practice: Fractions

Add or subtract each pair of fractions and then simplify. Then solve problem 5.

1.	2.	3.
$\dfrac{5}{12} + \dfrac{6}{12} =$	$\dfrac{15}{16} + \dfrac{8}{16} =$	$16\dfrac{7}{8} + 5\dfrac{1}{8} =$

4.

$$9\frac{13}{15} - 3\frac{7}{15} =$$

5. In a fraction, the denominator is 6 more than the numerator. If you add the numerator and the denominator together, you get 28. What is the fraction?

_____

Language Practice: Verbs

Write whether the verb is linking or action.

1. Carrie feels sick.   _____

   Carrie feels the dog's fur.   _____

2. The baby's diaper smells bad.   _____

   The baby smells the baby powder.   _____

3. My sister turned ten today.   _____

   My sister turned her ankle playing basketball. _____

4. Pizza tastes delicious.   _____

   Caroline tastes pizza.   _____

 Writing Practice: Write a story using this title:

Hurray! The circus is coming to town!

Name _____

Math Practice: Measurement/Perimeter

Measure the following objects in your classroom to find the perimeter of each. Then solve problem 5.

1.

P = _____

2.

P = _____

3.

P = _____

4.

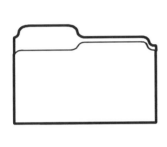

P = _____

5. How many different ways could students W, X, Y, and Z be paired in cooperative groups? Write the different combinations.

_____

Language Practice: Homonyms/Synonyms

Complete the chart by filling in each blank.

	Homonym	Synonym
1. plane		
2. peace		
3. ate		
4. see		
5. ewe		
6. pain		
7. made		
8. hay		

Writing Practice: Write a story using this title:

The Mystery of the Missing Snowman

Name _____

Math Practice: Graphs/Charts

Use the information in the chart to answer the questions below about the different mountain ranges.

1. Which mountain is the tallest?	2. Which mountain is only 20 ft. taller than Clingman's Dome?	**Mountain**	**Elevation**
_____	_____	Mt. Rainier	14,410 ft.
		Clingman's Dome	6,642 ft.
3. Which mountain is the shortest?	4. Which mountain is 300 ft. shorter than Mt. Rainier?	Mt. Hood	6,225 ft.
		Mt. Mitchell	6,662 ft.
		Mt. Lassen	10,446 ft.
_____	_____	Pike's Peak	14,110 ft.

Language Practice: Alphabetical Order

Write the names of these patriots in alphabetical order.

Thomas Paine   _____

Paul Revere   _____

Deborah Sampson   _____

Nathan Hale   _____

Patrick Henry   _____

Mary Ludwig Hays   _____

Crispus Attucks   _____

John Paul Jones   _____

Samuel Adams   _____

Baron Friedrich von Steuben   _____

 Writing Practice: National Grandparent's Day is in September. Write a descriptive paragraph about your grandparents.

Math Practice: Fractions/Decimals

Write the decimal equivalent of each fraction and then solve problem 5.

1. $\frac{1}{3} =$ _____	**2.** $\frac{2}{3} =$ _____	**3.** $\frac{3}{4} =$ _____

4. $\frac{1}{5} =$ _____

5. Look in your math book. Multiply the number of pages by the number of students in your math class. What number did you get?

_____

Language Practice: Verbs

Write a verb for as many letters of the alphabet as you can.

A _____   N _____
B _____   O _____
C _____   P _____
D _____   Q _____
E _____   R _____
F _____   S _____
G _____   T _____
H _____   U _____
I _____   V _____
J _____   W _____
K _____   X _____
L _____   Y _____
M _____   Z _____

 Writing Practice: You've been asked to plan your school's lunch each Friday. Write a paragraph about what you would plan and why you would choose each food.

Name

Math Practice: Geometry

Identify each type of triangle (right, scalene, equilateral, obtuse). Then solve problem 5.

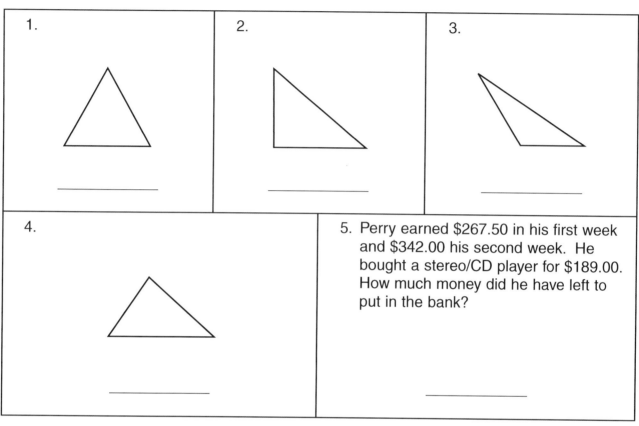

1.

_____

2.

_____

3.

_____

4.

_____

5. Perry earned $267.50 in his first week and $342.00 his second week. He bought a stereo/CD player for $189.00. How much money did he have left to put in the bank?

_____

Language Practice: Compare/Contrast

Decide if the sentence is comparing or contrasting. Write compare or contrast by each sentence.

_____ 1. Texas and Oklahoma are states in the Southwest U. S.

_____ 2. Like South Carolina, Virginia is also located on the east coast.

_____ 3. Michigan has cold winters, but Florida has mild winters.

_____ 4. Unlike Hawaii, Tennessee is surrounded by land on every side.

_____ 5. All the states in the U. S. have a governor who helps lead the affairs of the state.

_____ 6. Instead of bordering Mexico, Montana borders Canada.

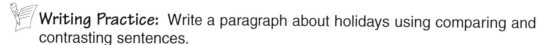**Writing Practice:** Write a paragraph about holidays using comparing and contrasting sentences.

Math Practice: Geometry

Label each figure with its geometric name—rectangular prism, pyramid, sphere, cone, or cylinder.

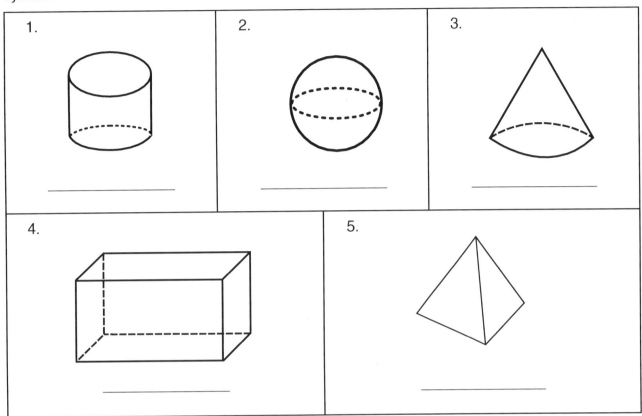

1. _____

2. _____

3. _____

4. _____

5. _____

Language Practice: Punctuation

Correct each sentence by underlining or adding quotation marks around each title.

1. The Firebird is a story in our reading book.

2. I like the poem The Road Not Taken by Robert Frost.

3. Did Amanda read the book Holes by Louis Sachar?

4. Frances Scott Key wrote The Star Spangled Banner.

5. The news reporter wrote an article called Education News in the daily paper The Globe.

6. Sports Illustrated has many articles about famous football players.

Writing Practice: If you were asked to design a new amusement park, what kind of rides and attractions would you put in it?

Math Practice: Decimals/Writing Numbers

Write out the word name for each number and then solve problem 5.

1. 0.372 _____ _____ _____	2. 2.54 _____ _____ _____	3. 6.004 _____ _____ _____
4. 3.861 _____ _____ _____	5. Kendall's time in the 100 meter run was 58.538 seconds. The winning time was 58.508 seconds. By how many seconds did Kendall lose the race? _____	

Language Practice: Writing Practice

Write a creative and descriptive Haiku poem in the space provided below.

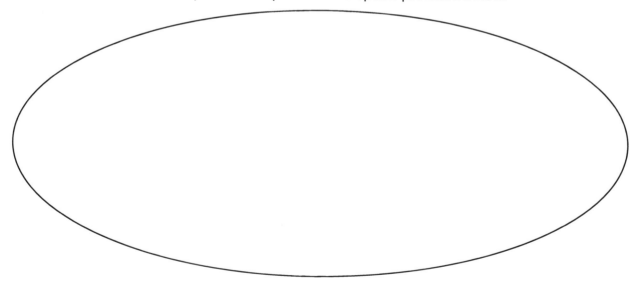

Writing Practice: Describe what your dream house would look like on the inside and outside.

Math Practice: Rounding/Decimals

Round to the nearest underlined digit and then solve problem 5.

1. 4.<u>3</u>16 _____	2. 2.1<u>5</u>7 _____	3. 0.<u>8</u>11 _____
4. 16.0<u>9</u>3 _____	5. Ryan is three years older than his sister, Julia. The sum of their ages is 21. How old is each child? Ryan: _____ Julia: _____	

Language Practice: Figurative Language

Write **S** if the sentence uses a simile or **M** if it uses a metaphor.

_____ 1. He was as quiet as a mouse.

_____ 2. It was as hot as fire!

_____ 3. He's a dog!

_____ 4. The sheets were as white as cotton.

_____ 5. Her baby is an angel.

_____ 6. Cody was as funny as Billy Crystal.

Writing Practice: Fire Prevention week is in October. Write a speech and then design a poster to use when you give your speech.

Math Practice: Table/Money

Use the information in the chart to answer the questions below.

1. You have $50.00 to spend. Which two items would you buy if your change was $10.00? _____ _____	2. You have $50.00 to spend. Which two items would you buy if your change was $3.00? _____ _____	**Item**	**Price**
		shirt	$15.00
		shoes	$36.00
		blouse	$17.00
		necklace	$9.00
3. You have $50.00 to spend. Which two items would you buy if your change was $11.00? _____ _____	4. You have $50.00 to spend. Which two items would you buy if your change was $21.00? _____ _____	jeans	$25.00
		watch	$20.00
		skirt	$30.00
		socks	$3.00

Language Practice: Figurative Language

Rewrite each sentence using literal language.

1. I'm dead!

   _____

2. It's raining cats and dogs.

   _____

3. We're like two ships that pass in the night.

   _____

4. She cried a bucket of tears.

   _____

5. He's blind as a bat.

   _____

6. Stanley has a chip on his shoulder.

   _____

 Writing Practice: The 19th Amendment to the Constitution of the United States gave women the right to vote. If you could add an amendment for children, what would it be and why?

Math Practice: Measurement

Find the volume of each object. (Remember, V = l x w x h.) Then solve problem 5.

1.

book

l = 10 in.
w = 2 in.
h = 6 in.

V = _____

2.

juice box

l = 6 in.
w = 1 in.
h = 4 in.

V = _____

3.

wallet

l = 5 in.
w = 2 in.
h = 5 in.

V = _____

4.

desk

l = 20 in.
w = 10 in.
h = 25 in.

V = _____

5. Annie traveled 722 miles in 2 days. If she traveled the same distance both days, how many miles did she travel each day?

_____

Language Practice: Antonyms

Write an antonym for each word.

1. miniature _____

2. powerless _____

3. never _____

4. least _____

5. depart _____

6. race _____

7. different _____

8. ignore _____

Writing Practice: Use this writing prompt to write a short paragraph:

The wind sounded eerie late in the night when...

Name _____

Math Practice: Roman Numerals

Write the Roman numeral for each number and then solve problem 5.

1. 206 _____	2. 64 _____	3. 29 _____

4. 1,858 _____	5. The track team ran in a 10-mile race. Tom came in last. Andre finished ahead of Benji. If Benji was ahead of Joel, and Gregg was just behind Joel, who came in third? _____

Language Practice: Nouns

Underline each noun.

1. The telephone has changed over the years; now we have phones in cars.

2. Children watch too much television when they come home from school.

3. Gardening is a great hobby for people who like to spend time outdoors.

4. You will need paper, pencils, or a pen to use with your journal.

5. My cousin is better at typing than I am, but I am better at reading.

6. This year's school election was held last Thursday in the cafeteria.

Writing Practice: If you could change anything about school, what would it be and why? Write a paragraph describing your ideas.

Math Practice: Roman Numerals

Write the number for each Roman numeral and then solve problem 5.

1. MCMLIX _____	2. DCXIII _____	3. CLX _____
4. XCIX _____	5. Tricia and her dad are putting up a fence around a rectangular area of 10 feet wide by 20 feet long. If they put a post every 6 feet, how many posts will they need? _____	

Language Practice: Adjectives

Write an adjective before each noun.

1. _____ cat

2. _____ student

3. _____ candy

4. _____ school

5. _____ stories

6. _____ pictures

7. _____ movie

8. _____ picnic

Writing Practice: What kind of career do you want for yourself in the future? Why?

Name _____

Math Practice: Geometry

Find the area of each figure. (Remember, A = l x w.) Then solve problem 5.

1. l = 12 cm w = 32 cm A = _____	**2.** l = 18 in w = 16.5 in A = _____	**3.** l = 4 ft. w = 4 ft. A = _____

4. l = 25 in. w = 5 in. A = _____	**5.** Marcos bought a pair of jeans at the department store for $19.99. He has to pay a 6% sales tax. What is the tax? What is his total cost? tax: _____ total: _____

Language Practice: Dictionary Skills

Match the correct definition of the word *mine* that goes with each sentence.

_____ 1. My friend's father mined coal in Kentucky.

_____ 2. During World War II, there were many minefields in Europe.

_____ 3. The pen he has is really mine.

_____ 4. Would you like to work in a diamond mine?

_____ 5. The coal miner has a dangerous job.

a. *pron.* my own

b. *n.* excavation for coal and mineral

c. *n.* buried or floating bomb

d. *v.* dig for a coal or mineral

e. *v.* one who works in a mine

 Writing Practice: Become a detective and write a mystery.

Math Practice: Multiplication

Use the information about the different symbols provided on the chart to solve each problem.

1. ✪ X ☐ _____	2. ◗ X ✿ _____	☆ = 5 ◗ = 30 ♡ = 10 ◆ = 35 ☐ = 15 ✿ = 40 △ = 20 ✪ = 45 ○ = 25 ✦ = 50
3. △ ◆ X ○ _____	4. ☆ ✦ X ♡ _____	

Language Practice: Adverbs

Cross out every third letter to find the names of adverbs. Write the adverb in the space provided, then write a sentence with it.

1. somftaly _____

2. menrreilay _____

3. fuyrimoukslpy _____

4. bepaudtilfusllcy _____

5. thderae _____

 Writing Practice: If you combined two fruits or vegetables into a new product, how would you advertise this new product?

Math Practice: Multiplication

Write the answer to each multiplication problem below.

1. 9 x 20 x 5	2. 12 x 9 x 7	3. 3 x 8 x 2 x 11
4. 8 x 15 x 3	5. 3 x 4 x 6 x 10	

Language Practice: Word Order

Rearrange the words in each group to make a complete sentence. Write each sentence.

1. Sweep   The   the   class   Toning   wanted   story   to   the   hear

_____

2. grades   good   get   classwork   do   have   You   to   your   to

_____

3. Marcia   best   and   friends   Barbie   in   were   grade   sixth

_____

4. anything   try   be   can   you   You   if   want   you

_____

5. Yesterday   school   to   player   CD   a   brought   Alex

_____

Writing Practice: Write about a family vacation that you are going to take or have already taken.

               ©Teacher Created Resources, Inc.

Name _____

Math Practice: Chart

Use the information provided in the chart to answer the questions below.

| 1. How many more electoral votes do Florida and North Carolina have than Georgia and Tennessee? | 2. Which 2 states' total electoral votes are equal to Florida? _____ _____ | 3. What is the total number of electoral votes in all 8 states? _____ |

4. Find the average of the total electoral votes. _____	**Electoral Votes**

Electoral Votes

Alabama	9	Mississippi	7
Florida	25	North Carolina	14
Georgia	13	South Carolina	8
Louisiana	9	Tennessee	11

Language Practice: Context Clues

Look at how the underlined Australian word is used. Write what you think the word means.

1. My mom will <u>flog</u> our dog's puppies when they get older. _____

2. The <u>jackaroo</u> worked on a ranch in Texas. _____

3. Our <u>chalkie</u> gave us <u>yakka</u> to do in class. _____

4. The <u>bloke</u> and <u>sheila</u> jogged around the block. _____

5. He bought new <u>clobbers</u> at the department store. _____

 Writing Practice: If you could create a new holiday, what would it be and why? Be sure to describe when it would be celebrated and anything special that will happen on this day.

Name _____

Math Practice: Mixed Computation

Solve each problem below.

1. Find the sum of 358 and 479. _____	2. Find the product of 461 and 52. _____	3. Find the difference between 3,650 and 1,296. _____
4. Find the quotient of 296 divided by 2. _____	5. Four players on the basketball team scored 25, 16, 15, and 8 points. Mike scored 25. Jerry did not score 8. Jeff scored less than Jerry but more than Rob. How many points did Jerry, Jeff, and Rob score? Jerry: _____ Jeff: _____ Rob: _____	

Language Practice: Adjectives

Write a sentence using these vivid adjectives.

1. gleaming _____

2. frightening _____

3. generous _____

4. invaluable _____

5. pleasant _____

6. glaring _____

 Writing Practice: Write the steps that are involved in planting a garden in your backyard.

Math Practice: Fractions

Find the LCD (Lowest Common Denominator) of each pair of fractions and then solve problem 5.

1.	2.	3.
$\dfrac{1}{3}\ \dfrac{1}{4}$ _____	$\dfrac{1}{6}\ \dfrac{1}{7}$ _____	$\dfrac{2}{3}\ \dfrac{3}{21}$ _____

4.	5. At a ballgame, there was one empty seat for every three seats. If there were 52 seats, how many were empty?
$\dfrac{11}{15}\ \dfrac{12}{20}$ _____	_____

Language Practice: Suffix/Prefix

With each word (*read* and *like*) add two suffixes and prefixes to them to make new words. Write the new words.

prefix

_____

_____

read

suffix

_____

_____

prefix

_____

_____

like

suffix

_____

_____

Writing Practice: If you could have three wishes like Aladdin had with his magic lamp, what would you wish for? Why?

Name _____

Math Practice: Fractions

Cross out the fraction that is NOT equivalent to the first fraction. Then solve problem 5.

1. $\frac{4}{5}$	2. $\frac{5}{6}$	3. $\frac{2}{3}$
$\frac{16}{20}$ $\frac{20}{25}$ $\frac{18}{30}$ $\frac{12}{15}$	$\frac{10}{12}$ $\frac{20}{24}$ $\frac{30}{36}$ $\frac{15}{16}$	$\frac{4}{6}$ $\frac{10}{15}$ $\frac{16}{24}$ $\frac{8}{18}$

4. $\frac{3}{4}$

$\frac{9}{12}$ $\frac{18}{24}$ $\frac{12}{20}$ $\frac{24}{32}$

5. After 3 minutes into a basketball game, the score was 12 to 8. If this pattern continues, what would the score be after 12 minutes?

_____

Language Practice: Dictionary Skills

Look at the pronunciation of each pair of words. Circle the correct pronunciation that matches the definition.

1. con´ test   con test´   *competition or fight*

2. pro´ duce   pro duce´   *bring into existence*

3. re bel´   reb´ el   *person who rebels*

4. graj´ u āt   graj´ u it   *person who finishes school*

5. prez´ ent   pri zent´   *gift*

6. ob´ jekt   ob jekt´   *protest*

 Writing Practice: If you were to create a charity to help others, how would it benefit your community and what would its purpose be?

Math Practice: Geometry

Use the diagram to solve the problems.

1. △ ABC is congruent to △ _____.	**2.** $\overline{ED}$ is equal to _____.	**3.** ∠BEC is equal to ∠ _____.

4. $\overline{AB}$ is parallel to _____.

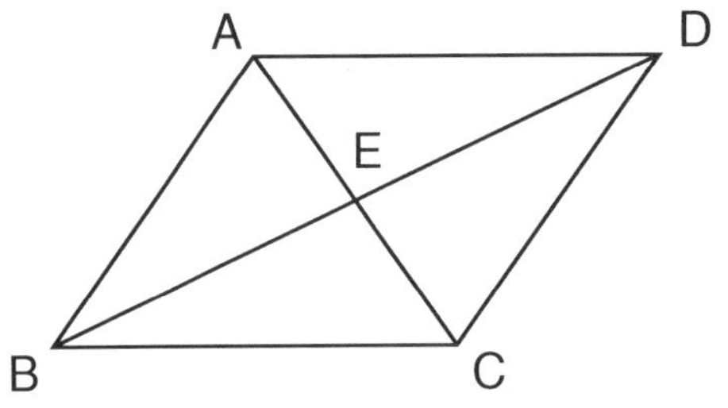

Language Practice: Adjectives

Fill in the acrostic with adjectives describing parents.

P _____

A _____

R _____

E _____

N _____

T _____

S _____

✍ **Writing Practice:** Write a story using this title:

The Birthday I'll Never Forget

Name _____

Math Practice: Money

Use the information provided in the chart and add the letters together to get the value of each word.

1. recess	2. height	a = 12¢	n = 14¢
		c = 16¢	o = 5¢
		e = 10¢	p = 22¢
		g = 25¢	r = 11¢
3. sheep	4. popcorn	h = 15¢	s = 18¢
		i = 20¢	t = 8¢
		k = 9¢	w = 26¢

Language Practice: Spelling

Rewrite each capital of the following states correctly.

1. Baton Rogue, LA _____

2. Colombia, SC _____

3. Olimpia, WA _____

4. Raliegh, NC _____

5. Sante Fe, NM _____

6. Provedence, RI _____

7. Tallahasse, FL _____

8. Lincon, NE _____

 Writing Practice: If you invented a new toy or game, describe how it works/is played. Describe what it looks like.

Math Practice: Multiply with Decimals

Solve each problem.

1.	2.	3.
9.34 x 10	0.5 x 1,000	.98 x 100

4.	5. Nicole earned $8.50. She spent $3.75 at the store and saved $3.00 in her piggy bank. How much money does she have left to spend?
76.4 x 10	_____

Language Practice: Sentences

Write four sentences about any fairy tale using each kind of sentence.

1. Declarative

_____

_____

2. Imperative

_____

_____

3. Interrogative

_____

_____

4. Exclamatory

_____

_____

 Writing Practice: Write a letter to a new pen pal describing yourself.

Math Practice: Divide with Decimals

Solve each problem.

1. $6\overline{)1.38}$	2. $5\overline{)49.5}$	3. $16\overline{)1.44}$
4. $32\overline{)2.88}$	5. Rope is 30¢ a meter. What is the cost for 1.8 meters of rope? _____	

Language Practice: Sentences

Identify each sentence with an **S** (Simple Sentence) or with a **C** (Compound Sentence).

_____ 1. My sister and her friend like to ski.

_____ 2. JoAnn is my favorite skier, but she hasn't won a medal.

_____ 3. The competition was crowded, but we found a seat near the middle.

_____ 4. Jackson and JoAnn skied in the Olympics.

_____ 5. Someday I want to ski in the Olympics and win a medal.

_____ 6. Jackson was in a race, and he won the silver medal.

Writing Practice: Imagine you were in a race and won. Write a news report about your victory.

Math Practice: Place Value

Write the place value of each problem. Then solve problem 5.

1. two places right of thousands _____	2. four places left of hundreds _____	3. one place left of thousands _____

4. one place right of millions _____	5. Don spends an average of 10¢ a minute. How much does he spend in one hour? one day? one 30-day month? one year? hour: _____ day: _____ month: _____ year: _____

Language Practice: Cause/Effect

Circle the cause in each sentence.

1. Because I fell off my scooter, I scraped my knee.

2. Since I practice swimming every day, my strokes have improved.

3. I woke up when the alarm rang.

4. I earned an A on my history test because I studied hard.

5. We decided not to go to the movies because the snow was falling heavily.

6. She laughed when the comedian told a joke.

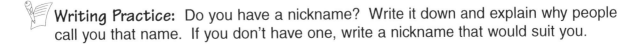 **Writing Practice:** Do you have a nickname? Write it down and explain why people call you that name. If you don't have one, write a nickname that would suit you.

Name _____

Math Practice: Writing Numbers

Match the written form with the standard form. Then solve problem 5.

1. forty-seven billion, five million
 	
  a. 47,005,000
 	
  b. 47,005,000,000
	2. three billion, twenty-two million, six thousand
	
	  a. 3,022,006,000
	
	  b. 3,022,600,000
		3. 16,000,000
		
		  a. sixteen thousand
		
		  b. sixteen million

4. 11,001,000,300
 	
  a. eleven billion, one thousand, three hundred
 	
  b. eleven billion, one million, three hundred
	5. Stella earned $1,042.00 last summer. Franklin earned $27.68 more than Stella. How much did Franklin earn?
	
	  _____	

Language Practice: Plurals

Write the plural form of the following nouns in a sentence.

1. strawberry_____

2. bush _____

3. dress_____

4. baby _____

5. beach _____

6. day _____

✎ **Writing Practice:** Write a story about someone you consider your hero or heroine.

Name _____

Math Practice: Number Properties

Circle the example that illustrates each property and then solve problem 5.

1. Commutative	2. Property of Zero	3. Associative
4 + 6 = 6 + 4	0 + 3 = 3 + 0	7 + 9 = 9 + 7
4 x 1 = 4	3 x 0 = 0	9 x 0 = 0
(4 + 6) + 1 = 4 + (6 + 1)	8 + (3 + 0) = (8 + 3) + 0	(7 + 9) + 6 = 7 + (9 + 6)

4. Identity	5. Three thousand boxes of cookies arrived at the store. One thousand sixty-seven boxes were sent back because they were damaged. How many boxes did the store keep?
11 + 0 = 0 + 11	
11 x 1 = 11	
(11 + 0) + 1 = 11 + (0 + 1)	_____

Language Practice: Nouns

Underline each noun. Write a **C** (common noun) or **P** (proper noun) above each noun.

1. My friend Eugene lives in Connecticut.

2. We drove through the state of Wyoming.

3. Our students visited the museum.

4. Saturday will be a day of nice weather.

5. Thomas Edison was a famous inventor from Ohio.

6. The first bicycle was invented in France.

Writing Practice: Using the 5 W's (who, what, when, where, why), describe a time in history.

Math Practice: Graph

Using the graph provided, answer the questions below.

1. How many people visited the Fitness Club in March?	2. How much did the visits to the gym decrease from March to April?	3. During what month did the number of visits increase to over 250?

4. Do people visit more in the winter or fall of the year?

Visits to the Fitness Club

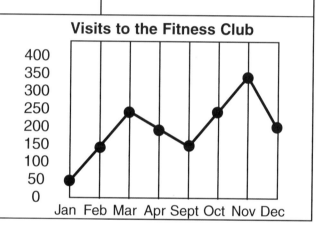

Language Practice: Abbreviations

Write the abbreviation above each underlined word.

1. <u>Doctor</u> John Miller is my mother's doctor.

2. On <u>Monday,</u> <u>January</u> 29, I visited <u>Mister</u> Serra's house.

3. She lives on 44 Jacob <u>Street</u> in Boston, <u>Massachusetts</u>.

4. We will meet for lunch at 12:00 <u>post</u> <u>meridian</u> on <u>Tuesday</u>.

5. The T. F. Hall <u>Company</u> is located on Rosswell <u>Boulevard</u>.

6. The <u>Department</u> of Agriculture had their meeting last <u>November</u>.

Writing Practice: If you could be president of the United States, what kind of changes would you make to better the country?

Name _____

Math Practice: Roman Numerals

Solve each problem below. Write your answers using standard numbers.

1. VII + XIX = _____	2. LXVIII + CXV = _____	3. XXXVI + XVIII = _____
4. CCLVI + CDV = _____	5. What is the greatest number you can write in Roman numerals without repeating a symbol? Write the number it represents. _____	

Language Practice: Possessives

Change the underlined words to possessive nouns by writing each possessive noun above the underlined words.

1. The teacher of Carrie read Caldecott Medal books to the class.

2. I saw the cat of Julia run down the street toward my house.

3. The homework of the students was turned in late.

4. The pencils that belong to Beth had her name engraved on them.

5. The classes of next year will begin 30 minutes earlier.

6. My mom knows the mother of my friend; they went to college together.

Writing Practice: You've been asked to create a flag for your school. Write a paragraph describing it and then draw a picture of it.

Math Practice: Chart/Money

Use the sales tax chart to determine the amount of tax on each amount below. Write the tax below the amount. Then add for the total.

1. $14.09 tax: _____ total: _____	2. $11.33 tax: _____ total: _____	**Tax Chart**

Amount	**Tax**
$9.00–9.49	56¢
$9.50–9.99	57¢
$10.00–10.49	58¢
$10.50–10.99	59¢
$11.00–11.49	60¢
$11.50–11.99	61¢
$12.00–12.49	62¢
$12.50–12.99	63¢
$13.00–13.49	64¢
$13.50–13.99	65¢
$14.00–14.49	66¢
$14.50–14.99	67¢
$15.00–15.49	68¢
$15.50–15.99	69¢

3. $9.72   tax: _____   total: _____

4. $12.18   tax: _____   total: _____

Language Practice: Compound Words

Underline the open compound words in each sentence.

1. He ate lunch on a picnic table in the park.

2. Mom opened up a savings account for my sister and me.

3. My friend, Antonio, became the president of the sixth grade.

4. I was the flower girl in my aunt's wedding.

5. Our Girl Scout troop had fun swimming at our neighbor's swimming pool.

6. We learned about the largest mountain range in Alaska.

Writing Practice: Write a story using the following compound words: fire engine, vice president, parking lot, and open house.

Name _____

Math Practice: Subtraction

Use subtraction to find the time difference between each event.

1. First permanent English settlement/end of World War II _____	2. 1st president/the new millennium _____	3. Declaration of Independence/end of Civil War _____

4. The ending of the two wars _____	**Historical Events** 1607—First permanent English settlement 1776—Declaration of Independence 1789—George Washington 1st President 1865—Civil War ended 1945—World War II ended 2000—The new millennium

Language Practice: Compare/Contrast

Fill in the chart below. Describe how each pair of words is alike and different.

	Alike	Different
1. cat and dog	_____	_____
2. book and movie	_____	_____
3. green beans and green peas	_____	_____
4. apples and oranges	_____	_____
5. 4th grade and 5th grade math teachers	_____	_____
6. bird and insect	_____	_____

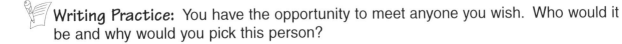 **Writing Practice:** You have the opportunity to meet anyone you wish. Who would it be and why would you pick this person?

Math Practice: Addition

Solve each problem below.

1.	2.	3.
723 588 + 396	71,259 55,169 + 543	4,635,640 3,550,518 + 1,756,170

4.	5. Kevin and Kimberly are going to Spain to visit their aunt. They estimate their cost at $690.00 each. They've saved only half. How much have they each saved?
215,705 376,156 + 89,912	_____

Language Practice: Pronouns

Choose the correct reflective pronoun that makes each sentence complete.

_____ 1. Dan taught _____ how to ride a bike.

_____ 2. We made _____ sick from eating too much candy.

_____ 3. The students are setting high goals for _____.

_____ 4. "Help _____ to a cookie after dinner," said Mom.

_____ 5. I couldn't help _____ from falling asleep.

_____ 6. The tree seemed to lean _____ toward the sky.

a. ourselves

b. myself

c. yourself

d. himself

e. itself

f. themselves

 Writing Practice: Choose an object in the room. Write five clues that would help someone discover what it is.

Name _____

Math Practice: Subtraction

Write the missing addend to complete each problem.

1. 20,482 + _____ 55,169	**2.** $67.31 + _____ $108.90	**3.** 73,281 + _____ 89,046

4. 3,807 + _____ 8,331	**5.** Mrs. Patten ordered 73 fiction, 51 nonfiction, and 38 biographies for the library. How many books did she order? _____

Language Practice: Fact or Opinion

Write **F** if the statement is a fact or **O** if the statement is an opinion.

_____ 1. Every child should have a pet dog.

_____ 2. We should all brush our teeth to keep them healthy.

_____ 3. November has 30 days.

_____ 4. Ice cream is the most popular dessert.

_____ 5. Peanut butter and jelly sandwiches are delicious.

_____ 6. School is a place where children learn.

Writing Practice: You've been given an unusual gift from your aunt. What is it? Write her a thank you note.

Name _____

Math Practice: Multiplication

Multiply the number in the center by each point. Write the answer by the point. Then solve problem 5.

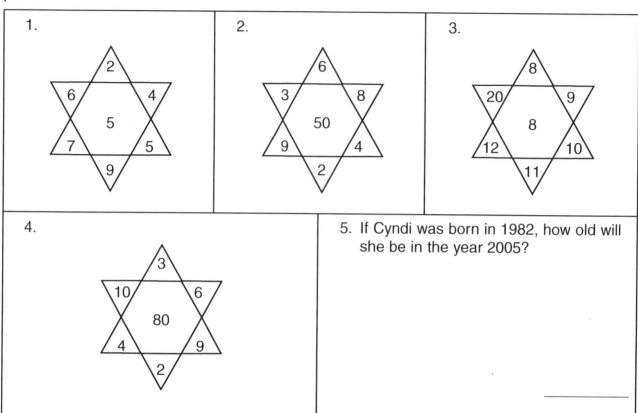

1.

2.

3.

4.

5. If Cyndi was born in 1982, how old will she be in the year 2005?

_____

Language Practice: Subject/Verb

Add a simple subject or a simple predicate (verb) to each sentence.

1. My younger _____ was born last week.

2. Barry _____ his homework to his Algebra teacher.

3. Pedro _____ a snake in a tree in his backyard.

4. The _____ of the tree slowly fell to the ground.

5. Elizabeth _____ her hand to answer the teacher's question.

6. _____ were found at the space center.

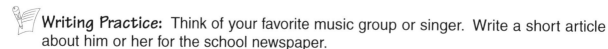 **Writing Practice:** Think of your favorite music group or singer. Write a short article about him or her for the school newspaper.

Math Practice: Mental Math/Multiplication

Solve each problem.

1. $\begin{array}{r} 300 \\ \times\ 50 \\ \hline \end{array}$	2. $\begin{array}{r} 1{,}000 \\ \times\ 800 \\ \hline \end{array}$	3. $\begin{array}{r} 100 \\ \times\ 600 \\ \hline \end{array}$
4. $\begin{array}{r} 4{,}000 \\ \times\ 70 \\ \hline \end{array}$	5. Mr. Jones buys three shirts at $12.00 each and 1 pair of jeans for $28.00. What is his change from $75.00? _____	

Language Practice: Verbs

Write the correct form of the verb in parentheses to complete each sentence.

1. We _____ at a hotel on vacation. (*stay*)

2. Mom _____ my sister in a blanket because she was cold. (*wrap*)

3. Our class _____ for our history test. (*study*)

4. Timothy _____ to remember his spelling words for the test. (*try*)

5. Juanita _____ all of our basketball games. (*attend*)

6. The hummingbird _____ her eggs in a nest last week. (*lay*)

 Writing Practice: Write a story about how a teacher has helped you. Create an award you would present to him or her.

Name _____

Math Practice: Mean

Find the average monthly earning for cutting grass for each student last summer and then solve problem 5.

1. **Joe** $768 $541 + $582 average: _____	2. **Luke** $808 $712 + $500 average: _____	3. **Hans** $692 $377 + $640 average: _____

4. **Kobe** $724 $700 + $483 average: _____	5. If you burn 520 calories an hour playing basketball, how many calories would you burn in a three-hour game? _____

Language Practice: Nouns

Fill in the chart with five nouns in each category.

Sight	Sound	Smell	Taste	Touch
_____	_____	_____	_____	_____
_____	_____	_____	_____	_____
_____	_____	_____	_____	_____
_____	_____	_____	_____	_____
_____	_____	_____	_____	_____

 Writing Practice: Imagine you are a reporter for the school newspaper. Interview one of your classmates and write a student spotlight.

Math Practice: Division with Exponents

Solve each problem below.

1. $5^2 \div 5 =$ _____	2. $4^3 \div 8 =$ _____	3. $6^2 \div 2^3 =$ _____
4. $18^2 \div 2^2 =$ _____	5. Captain Stephens has flown an average of 120 people on each of his 2,840 flights. About how many people have been on his flights? _____	

Language Practice: Pronouns

Circle the correct pronoun in each sentence.

1. (We, Us) read a book called *Heaven.*

2. (I, Me) like to visit the downtown library.

3. There are so many books for (we, us) to use.

4. Our librarian, Mrs. Sayers, is an inspiration to (I, me).

5. Jack went with (I, me) back to our classroom.

6. (He, Him) is in my language class.

 Writing Practice: Think of something you know how to do. Write a paragraph explaining how it is done.

Math Practice: Mixed Computation

Columbus discovered the West Indies in 1492. Calculate the following from the current year. Then solve problem 5.

1. Number of years passed since then. _____	2. Number of centuries passed since then. _____	3. Number of months passed since then. _____
4. Number of decades passed since then. _____	5. A circus tent weighs 508 lbs. more than the strong man can lift. If he can lift 322 lbs., how much does the tent weigh? _____	

Language Practice: Synonyms/Antonyms

Identify whether each pair of words is a synonym (**S**) or antonym (**A**).

_____ 1. peculiar / odd _____ 5. verdict / judgment

_____ 2. abrupt / sudden _____ 6. save / spend

_____ 3. allow / refuse _____ 7. prohibit / allow

_____ 4. ambitious / lazy _____ 8. alone / solitary

 Writing Practice: Write a paragraph using these pairs of antonyms: early/late, heavy/light, before/after.

Math Practice: Multiplication

Circle each correct problem. Then solve problem 5.

1. 49 x 9 = 421	2. 338 x 7 = 2,366	3. 742 x 36 = 25,712
4. 482 x 65 = 31,330	5. A dog fell in a 12-foot well. Everyday, he climbed up 3 feet and slipped back 2 feet. How many days did it take him to reach the top? _____	

Language Practice: Adjective

Write two adjectives to describe the noun. Be sure they begin with the same letter as the noun.

1. children

_____

_____

2. pie

_____

_____

3. book

_____

_____

4. leaf

_____

_____

5. sister

_____

_____

6. dog

_____

_____

 Writing Practice: If you were a fashion designer, what kind of clothing and shoes would you design? Write a short descriptive paragraph about your fashion collection.

Math Practice: Multiplication

Find the LCM of each pair of numbers. Then solve problem 5.

1. 4, 7 _____	2. 6, 9 _____	3. 5, 8 _____
4. 3, 5 _____	5. If 1 inch equals 2.54 cm, how many centimeters would 1 foot equal? _____	

Language Practice: Interjections

Add an interjection to each sentence.

1. _____ Look how far away California is.

2. _____ I finally found my wallet.

3. _____ You are so right.

4. _____ We won the game!

5. _____ She has 8 brothers and sisters.

6. _____ That baby is so tiny!

Writing Practice: Write some safety rules that people should abide by when they are swimming at the beach or at a pool.

Name _____

Math Practice: Addition/Subtraction

Write three numbers that when added together will equal the top of the pyramid. Then solve problem 5.

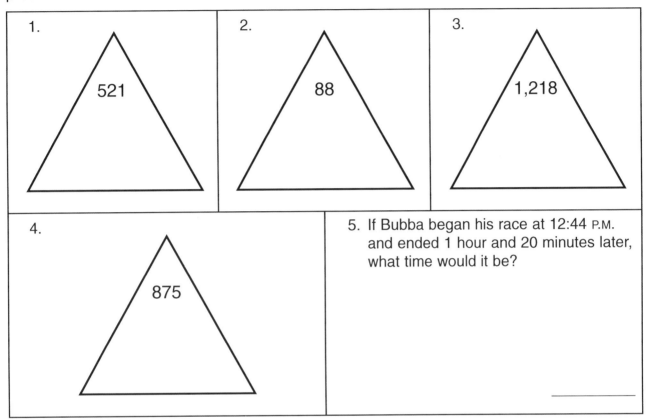

1. 521

2. 88

3. 1,218

4. 875

5. If Bubba began his race at 12:44 P.M. and ended 1 hour and 20 minutes later, what time would it be?

_____

Language Practice: Prepositional Phrases

Put parentheses around each prepositional phrase.

1. We went to a birthday party at Sue's house.

2. LuAnn came from Mexico to the United States.

3. She lived across the street from her aunt.

4. Their family speaks English, except their mother.

5. Mom got up at 7:00 A.M. and left the house before 9:00 A.M.

6. The snow continued throughout the afternoon.

 Writing Practice: Write a story about being stuck at school in a snowstorm. Underline each prepositional phrase.

Name _____

Math Practice: Mixed Computation

Using the basic operations (+, −, x, or ÷), solve each problem.

1. $3 + 3 - 3 \times 3 = $ _____	2. $(3 \times 3) + 3 + 3 = $ _____	3. $(3 \div 3) + 3 - 3 = $ _____
4. $(3 \times 3) + 3 \div 3 = $ _____	5. Using all the basic operations and the number 4, find which operations you'd use to get the answer 16. _____	

Language Practice: Direct Object

Circle the direct object in each sentence.

1. Pete completed his homework.

2. I carry a flashlight when I go camping.

3. Eskimos made homes out of frozen ice.

4. Randall read the story to his sister.

5. The punter kicked the ball over the goal post.

✍ **Writing Practice:** Describe a game you like to play. Explain how to play it.

Math Practice: Multiplication

Looking at each domino, calculate (a) the product, and (b) the LCM. Then solve problem 5.

1.

a. _____

b. _____

2.

a. _____

b. _____

3.

a. _____

b. _____

4.

a. _____

b. _____

5. How many leaves does a tree have if it has 43 leaves on each of 37 branches?

_____

Language Practice: Contractions

Rewrite the italicized words as contractions.

1. He *will not* listen to my question.

_____

2. You *must not* be late, or *I will* tell mom.

_____

3. *It is* raining, so we *cannot* go outside.

_____

4. *You will* be able to see the stars in the sky.

_____

5. They *should not* have tried to wade in the pond.

_____

6. Dr. Jackson wishes *he had* gone to France.

_____

Writing Practice: You've won a trip to outer space. Write about where you would go, what you would pack, and what you would do.

Name _____

Math Practice: Measurement

Calculate the correct equivalent measurement for each problem and then solve problem 5.

1. $\frac{1}{2}$ gal. = _____ qt.	2. 2 pt. = _____ qt.	3. $\frac{1}{2}$ c. = _____ fl. oz.

4.

$\frac{1}{2}$ qt. = _____ pt.

5. Monkeys in a zoo eat 796 bananas and 283 cans of peanuts per day. How much do they eat in 1 week?

bananas _____

cans of peanuts _____

Language Practice: Prefix

Replace the italicized words with a prefix and a base word.

1. The girl *wrote again* her science report. _____

2. She *read incorrectly* the instructions on the list. _____

3. Mom likes to drink a big glass of *not fat* milk. _____

4. Dad *planned ahead* our trip to the Grand Canyon. _____

5. The baseball game was *scheduled again*. _____

6. I had some *opposite of comfort* after my leg broke. _____

 Writing Practice: Write about the best dream that you've ever had or can remember.

Math Practice: Fractions

Add or subtract and reduce to the lowest term. Then solve problem 5.

1. $\dfrac{3}{4}$ $+\,6\dfrac{3}{8}$ _____	2. 22 $-\,7\dfrac{4}{10}$ _____	3. $11\dfrac{1}{2}$ $+\;\dfrac{9}{12}$ _____
4. 28 $-\,3\dfrac{3}{5}$ _____	5. Jessie Blanks set a record in the long jump of 7 ft. The old record was only $6\dfrac{3}{4}$ ft. By how much did he break the record? _____	

Language Practice: Suffix

Rewrite the italicized words with a suffix and a base word.

1. An act of *quality of being kind* will never be forgotten.   _____

2. The policeman was *without fear* in his daily duties.   _____

3. She was *full of care* not to spill her milk.   _____

4. The *one who skis* flew down the slope.   _____

5. Her new outfit was *able to be in comfort*.   _____

6. The students were *having worth* of a special treat.   _____

 Writing Practice: Design a futuristic car. Describe how it looks and what makes it run.

Math Practice: Mean

Find the average for each set of numbers. Then solve problem 5.

1. 25, 29, 36	2. 256, 392, 462	3. 48, 56, 82
	_____	_____	_____

4. 1,237, 1,747, 1,006	5. If Sally jogs 25 miles each week, and jogs 3 miles each on Monday, Tuesday, and Wednesday, how many miles would she jog on the remaining days?
_____	_____

Language Practice: Verbs

Circle the past tense of each verb in the puzzle.

fly	tear	begin	speak
say	run	see	go

```
k   d   a   f   l   e   w   e   s
x   i   n   m   o   r   k   n   s
n   a   g   e   b   o   d   l   a
r   s   b   t   p   t   n   e   w
p   f   c   s   s   c   k   z   p
```

Writing Practice: Use this writing prompt to write a short paragraph:

I was walking on the beach, and when I looked down, I saw...

       ©Teacher Created Resources, Inc.

Math Practice: Median

Find the median for each set of numbers and then solve problem 5.

1. 17, 24, 34, 28, 16 _____	2. 215, 219, 225, 200, 231 _____	3. 48, 68, 51, 65, 55 _____
4. $3.63, $4.74, $3.59, $4.62, $3.48 _____	5. Mrs. Forrest gave a questionnaire to her math class of 12 boys and 13 girls. 7 boys and 7 girls returned their questionnaires. How many will she still need to get back from the boys? from the girls? boys _____ girls _____

Language Practice: Proofreading

Rewrite each sentence correctly.

1. the temperature in the woods were below freezing and i got two cold

_____

2. the story about dr. terry were interesting

_____

3. last tuesday i go to see the movie the patriot

_____

4. canada be on the border of the united states

_____

5. do you like to ate shrimp

_____

Writing Practice: Write a story for a newspaper with the title "Whale Survives Oil Spill."

Math Practice: Mode

Find the mode for each set of numbers. Then solve problem 5.

1. $20, $12, $16, $12, $30	2. 46, 39, 28, 27, 39	3. 100, 200, 100, 600, 300
_____	_____	_____

4. 75, 85, 95, 65, 75	5. The 5th and 6th graders sold 98 candy bars. 12 more were sold by the 6th grade than 5th grade. How many did each grade sell?
_____	5th grade _____ 6th grade _____

Language Practice: Adverbs

Underline each adverb. Then circle where, when, or how to indicate what each adverb describes.

1. Stand there beside the tree.   where   when   how

2. Swiftly he ran toward the fence.   where   when   how

3. A man waited eagerly for his letter.   where   when   how

4. "It should arrive soon," said Mary.   where   when   how

5. The pitcher threw the ball down.   where   when   how

6. The umpire suddenly shouted for him to stop.   where   when   how

Writing Practice: What is your favorite commercial on television? Why?

Name _____

Math Practice: Comparing Numbers/Rounding

For problems 1 and 2, circle which number is less than the number given. For problems 3 and 4, circle the whole number that the given number rounds up/down to. Then solve problem 5.

1. **385,281**	2. **7,327**	3. **3.49**
385,282 385,279 385,309	7,328 7,330 7,326	4 5 3

4. **12.08**	5. Feed for the petting zoo costs $6 for 2 bags. What would 12 bags cost?
12 11 13	_____

Language Practice: Study Skills

What type of book is each item listed below? Write **R** (reference), **B** (biography), **N** (nonfiction), or **F** (fiction).

_____ 1. encyclopedia article about spiders

_____ 2. life story of Rosa Parks

_____ 3. book about space travel

_____ 4. book called *The White House*

_____ 5. novel about a time traveler

_____ 6. a recent dictionary

Writing Practice: Write a paragraph suggesting solutions to the problem of trash on the roads and highways.

Name _____

Math Practice: Addition with Decimals

Solve each problem below.

1.	2.	3.
46.8 + 9.6	8.982 + 24.83	0.84 + 0.67

4.	5. The cost of 2 books is $10.50. One cost $2.50 more than the other. What is the cost of each book?
36.341 + 22.8	Book 1 _____ Book 2 _____

Language Practice: Nouns

Underline 11 common nouns in the paragraph about whales.

> Whales are one of the most intelligent animals. They are mammals,
>
> which mean they give birth to live young and use lungs to breathe.
>
> They migrate thousands of miles each year. When there isn't much
>
> food, they can live off their blubber.

 Writing Practice: October is National Clock Month. Write about a time you lost track of time and were late for an important event/appointment.

Math Practice: Subtraction/Money

Solve each problem below.

1. $4.60 − $1.80	2. $0.90 − $0.42	3. $542.46 − $267.95
4. $13.82 − $9.40	5. The distance around a field is 59.81 meters. The total length of three sides is 37.05 meters. What is the length of the other side? _____	

Language Practice: Sequencing

Put the steps of this recipe in order from 1 to 8.

Ham Omelet

_____ Then chop up the ham into small pieces.

_____ Serve with orange juice and toast.

_____ Before you start, break the eggs in a bowl.

_____ Flip one side over the other side.

_____ Whip the eggs with a wire whisk.

_____ Add the chopped ham in the skillet.

_____ Turn with a spatula to lightly brown the other side.

_____ Pour the eggs in the skillet.

Writing Practice: Write a short descriptive paragraph about the current President of the United States and what this person has accomplished.

Name _____

Math Practice: Multiplication

Solve each problem below.

1. 1,962 x 53 _____	2. 638 x 86 _____	3. 302 x 95 _____
4. 3,509 x 72 _____	5. Kari had $34.98 left of her birthday money. She saw a sweater for $15.88 and a pair of shoes for $24.69. How much more money does she need to buy both items? _____	

Language Practice: Comprehension

Answer the questions after reading the paragraph.

The Nobel Prize is awarded annually for outstanding works in science, literature, and world peace. It was named after Alfred Nobel, a Swedish chemist. He was best known for his invention of dynamite. When he died, he left almost 10 million dollars to fund future awards. Americans like Woodrow Wilson and Martin Luther King, Jr. have won the Nobel Prize.

1. Who is the Nobel Prize named after? _____

2. What did he invent? _____

3. Name the three fields that the Nobel Prize is awarded._____

_____

4. What was the money that Nobel left used for? _____

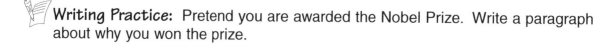

Writing Practice: Pretend you are awarded the Nobel Prize. Write a paragraph about why you won the prize.

Name _____

Math Practice: Division

Solve each problem below.

1. $9\overline{)327}$	2. $5\overline{)199}$	3. $18\overline{)2,965}$
4. $22\overline{)5,392}$	5. Art supplies for 5 girls cost $295.00. What is the cost for each girl? _____	

Language Practice: Writing Practice

Write a creative limerick in the space provided below.

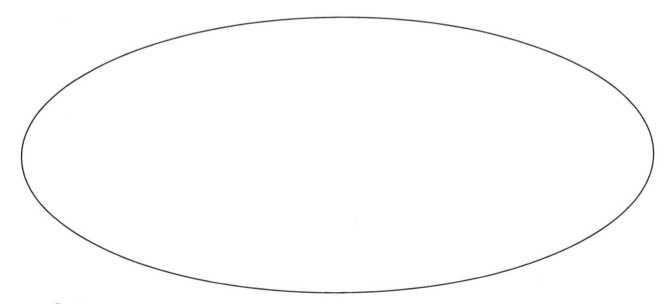

Writing Practice: December 15 is Bill of Rights Day. Write a list of rights you think all kids should have.

Math Practice: Variables

Solve for n. Then solve problem 5.

1. $48 - 12 = 6 \times n$ _____	2. $26 \times 3 = 122 - n$ _____	3. $23 + 15 = 40 - n$ _____
4. $72 \div 9 = 100 - n$ _____	5. Frances Drake explored California in 1579 and 28 years later, Jamestown was settled by Captain John Smith. What year was that? _____	

Language Practice: Synonyms

Complete the Venn diagram by writing the words (listed below) in each category.

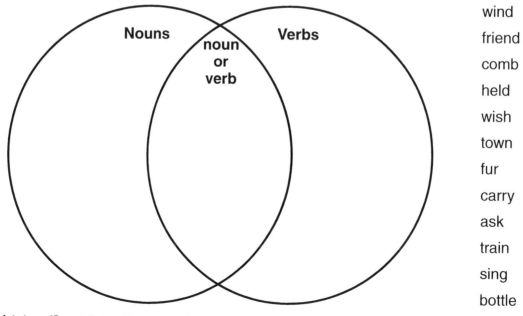

wind

friend

comb

held

wish

town

fur

carry

ask

train

sing

bottle

Writing Practice: If you could wish upon a star, what would you wish for?

Math Practice: Measurement

Write the unit (in., ft., yd., mi.) you would use to measure the items listed below. Then solve problem 5.

1. height of a light pole _____	2. length of a school bus _____	3. distance between east and west coast _____
4. length of your arm _____	5. Toni owed her sister 75¢. She paid her with a combination of 5 coins. What coins did she give to her sister? _____	

Language Practice: Synonyms

Circle the best synonym for each boldfaced word.

1. **drill**	train	useful	lifted
2. **drab**	stylish	dreary	oppressed
3. **duty**	requirement	doubtful	created
4. **doodle**	unsteady	enhance	scribble
5. **desert**	gained	cake	abandon
6. **dainty**	courteous	delicate	helpful

Writing Practice: Write a story using this title:

The Strangest Place I've Ever Been

Math Practice: Measurement

Write the correct measurements. Then solve problem 5.

1.	2.	3.
___ ounces in a pound	___ fluid ounces in a cup	___ quarts in a gallon

4.	5. If you add Yolanda and Wanda's ages, you get a total of 21 years. If you multiply their ages, you get 110. What age is each girl? (Yolanda is older than Wanda.)
___ cups in a pint	Yolanda: _____ Wanda: _____

Language Practice: Punctuation

Write a sentence that is an example of each punctuation rule.

1. Place quotation marks before and after a person's spoken words.

   _____

2. Underline the title of a book or newspaper.

   _____

3. Place an exclamation mark at the end of an exclamatory sentence.

   _____

4. Place a comma between the city and state.

   _____

5. Place a colon between the hour and minute in time.

   _____

6. Place a period after the abbreviated title in a person's name.

   _____

Writing Practice: You wake up one morning and find that your skin has turned purple. Write a story about it.

Math Practice: Multiplication/Fractions

Use multiplication to solve the problems below.

1.	2.	3.
$\frac{1}{5}$ x 40 = _____	$\frac{2}{3}$ x 12 = _____	8 x $\frac{3}{4}$ = _____

4.	5. Of 60 5th grade students, 2/3 of them are in choir. How many are in choir?
45 x $\frac{2}{9}$ = _____	_____

Language Practice: Alphabetical Order

Write the names of these famous American women in alphabetical order by last name.

Amelia Earhart   _____

Sally Ride   _____

Dorothea Dix   _____

Sandra Day O'Connor   _____

Coretta Scott King   _____

Annie Oakley   _____

Sacagawea   _____

Emily Dickinson   _____

Wilma Rudolph   _____

Elizabeth Cady Stanton _____

 Writing Practice: Rewrite a classic fairy tale with a different ending and from a different point of view.

Math Practice: Subtraction with Zeros

Solve each problem below.

1.	2.	3.
32,000 − 8,671	1,000,000 − 537,112	9,000 − 5,523

4.

7,040,200
−   64,344

5. A whale eats an average of 800 pounds of fish a day. How many would he eat in one week? One month?

week _____

month _____

Language Practice: Dictionary Skills

Write each vocabulary word with its definition. Use the dictionary, if needed.

1. leave ship or aircraft ___ ___ ___ ___ ___ ___ ___ ___ ___

2. unhappy ___ ___ ___ ___ ___ ___ ___ ___ ___ ___ ___

3. break up ___ ___ ___ ___ ___ ___ ___

4. offend ___ ___ ___ ___ ___ ___ ___

5. show unjust favor ___ ___ ___ ___ ___ ___ ___ ___ ___ ___ ___

6. release ___ ___ ___ ___ ___ ___ ___ ___ ___

| disband | disembark | disgust |
| disconsolate | discharge | discriminate |

 Writing Practice: October 15 is National Grouch Day. Write a list of 5 things that make you grouchy. Then write 5 things to do that will help you to not be grouchy.

Math Practice: Money

Use the information in the chart to answer the questions.

1. How much would it cost for 2 small ornaments and 1 large ornament?	2. Would it cost more for 1 regular set of lights or 2 boxes of cards?	**Christmas Sale**	
		ornaments	
		small	2/$3.00
		large	2/$5.00
		lights	
		regular	$4.89
3. Will $5.00 be enough to purchase 1 roll of wrapping paper, 3 bags of bows, and 1 small ornament?	4. What would the total cost be if you purchased 1 of each item?	icicle	$5.89
		cards	$2.25 box
		wrapping paper	$1.99/roll
		bows in bag	$0.59/bag 2 bags/$1.00

Language Practice: Verbs

Underline any verb and helping verb in each sentence.

1. It seemed colder yesterday.

2. We were walking down the street.

3. Bob was going to play football.

4. It began to snow heavily.

5. It was so cold, so I went inside.

6. Maybe tomorrow it will be warmer.

 Writing Practice: Write a persuasive paragraph explaining your position on students going to school for nine months versus year-round school.

Math Practice: Geometry

Write **S** if the figure is symmetrical or **N** if it is not symmetrical. Then solve problem 5.

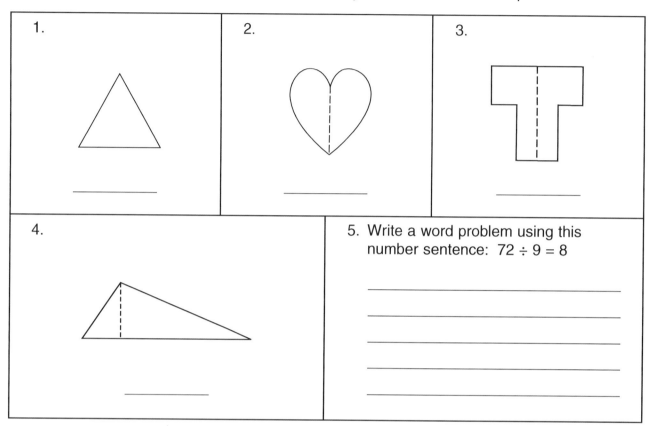

1.

_____

2.

_____

3.

_____

4.

_____

5. Write a word problem using this number sentence: $72 \div 9 = 8$

_____

_____

_____

_____

_____

_____

Language Practice: Abbreviation

Write the abbreviation for each state.

1. Idaho   _____

2. Montana   _____

3. California   _____

4. Arizona   _____

5. Utah   _____

6. Washington   _____

7. Wyoming   _____

8. New Mexico   _____

 Writing Practice: Write a travel brochure about your home state and the sites and attractions it offers visitors/tourists.

Math Practice: Addition/Subtraction

Use the map provided to answer the questions.

1. What is the difference in miles between Memphis and Chattanooga and between Memphis and Nashville?	2. Which city is the closest from Nashville— Chattanooga or Knoxville? By how much?	3. What is the distance from Knoxville to Nashville to Memphis?

4. Would it be closer to travel to the Tri-Cities from Memphis by way of Nashville, or Chattanooga and Knoxville?

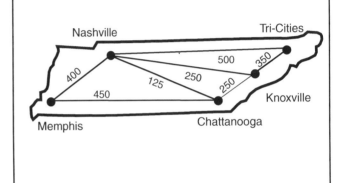

Language Practice: Study Skills

Determine if you would find the following information in an atlas, thesaurus, or almanac.

1. Which country is north of Spain? _____

2. What is a synonym for the word program? _____

3. Which continent is an island? _____

4. Which state has more tornadoes than any other? _____

5. Which state population is larger—Georgia or Alabama? _____

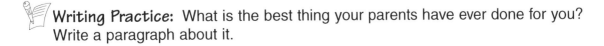 **Writing Practice:** What is the best thing your parents have ever done for you? Write a paragraph about it.

Math Practice: Addition/Subtraction

Find the dates of these events in African American history. Then solve problem 5.

1. Beginning of slavery in America (25 years before 1644) _____	2. Slavery is abolished. (246 years after #1) _____	3. African Americans are granted the right to vote. (5 years after #2) _____
4. Civil Rights Act was signed in Washington (99 years after #2) _____	5. Marcus bought a super burger for $1.59, fries for $0.89 and a soda for $0.69. What is his change from $5.00? _____	

Language Practice: Adjective/Adverbs

Fill in the chart with an adjective and adverb that begins with the same letter.

	adjective	adverb
1. a	_____	_____
2. d	_____	_____
3. g	_____	_____
4. l	_____	_____
5. n	_____	_____
6. r	_____	_____

 Writing Practice: What happened after "happily ever after"? Write a continuation story of a fairy tale. (For example, after Cinderella and Prince Charming got married, what happened afterwards?)

 ©Teacher Created Resources, Inc.

Math Practice: Division/Money

Circle the price which is the best bargain for each product. Then solve problem 5.

1. 2/69¢ or 4/$1.09	2. 3/$1.00 or 2/59¢	3. 6/$1.59 or 8/$2.39

4. 8 oz./89¢ or 16 oz./$1.69	5. The video that Jane bought was 1/3 off. If it originally cost $27.99, what would the sale price be? _____

Language Practice: Compare and Contrast

Describe how each is the same and different.

	same	different
1. rectangle and square	_____	_____
2. acute angle and obtuse angle	_____	_____
3. notebook paper and computer paper	_____	_____
4. math book and language book	_____	_____
5. your math teacher and your P. E. teacher	_____	_____
6. you and your best friend	_____	_____

 Writing Practice: How useful are computers and the Internet? Describe several ways how they help you today.

Name _____

Math Practice: Mixed Computation/Decimals

Solve each problem below.

1.	2.	3.
3,461.8 + 88.75	2.4 − 1.63	6.03 x 8.4

4.	5. Write any number down. Add 10. Multiply by 4. Add 200. Divide by 4. Subtract the number you write down. What answer did you get? Everyone's answer should be the same.
2.3) 31.05	_____

Language Practice: Context Clues

Write the meaning of each underlined word by seeing how it is used in each sentence.

1. He <u>bellowed</u> with a loud voice.

   _____

2. I was <u>flabbergasted</u> at the outcome of the game.

   _____

3. Bradley <u>grimaced</u> with pain after he broke his foot.

   _____

4. The <u>massive</u> ship held 2,500 passengers.

   _____

5. Mom was <u>bewildered</u> when her watch wouldn't work.

   _____

6. The <u>replica</u> of the original flag was almost exact.

   _____

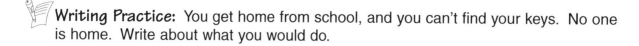 **Writing Practice:** You get home from school, and you can't find your keys. No one is home. Write about what you would do.

Name _____

Math Practice: Division

Solve the problems below.

1. $72\overline{)3,520}$	2. $40\overline{)290}$	3. $26\overline{)9,224}$
4. $44\overline{)386}$	5. If Bobby eats pizza 3 days each week at school, how many days does he eat pizza the whole school year? (36 weeks in a school year) _____	

Language Practice: Figurative Language

Complete each simile with a noun. You may add *a*, *an*, or *the* before each noun.

1. as soft as _____

2. as clear as _____

3. as little as _____

4. as bright as _____

5. as sweet as _____

6. as hard as _____

 **Writing Practice:** Would you rather be around a person who says what they think or a person who is a good listener? Write a paragraph describing why.

Name _____

Math Practice: Fractions

Add these fractions. Reduce to lowest terms. Then solve problem 5.

1. $\frac{2}{3} + \frac{4}{9} =$	2. $7\frac{7}{12} + 2\frac{4}{24} =$	3. $\frac{6}{10} + \frac{6}{12} =$

4.

$12\frac{6}{7} + 4\frac{11}{21} =$

5. If it's March 1 and Felicia's birthday is 6 months and 8 days away, when is her birthday?

_____

Language Practice: Sentences

Write S for sentence, F for fragment, or R for run-on.

_____ 1. Jane reads a book I read it, too.

_____ 2. Her sister sings songs and dances.

_____ 3. Sitting quietly while she watches television.

_____ 4. Many sisters in the house.

_____ 5. Jane had a pet it was a cat.

_____ 6. Her cat was a yellow striped tabby.

 Writing Practice: Write what qualities you think would make a good teacher and a good student.

Name _____

Math Practice: Comparing Numbers

Write these numbers from lowest to highest. Then solve problem 5.

1. 7.68, 7.49, 7.65, 7.78, 7.42	2. 1,001, 1,101, 1,100, 1,010, 1,110	3. 49.55, 44.2, 49.52, 54.27, 44.18
_____	_____	_____
_____	_____	_____
_____	_____	_____
_____	_____	_____

4. 2,422.2, 242.22, 24,222, 24.222, 2.4222	5. The Johnsons are going on vacation 2 months and 18 days after school is out on May 26. When will their vacation start?
_____	
_____	
_____	
	_____

Language Practice: Proofreading

Rewrite each sentence correctly.

1. Her and her teacher mrs jenkins walk to lunch

   _____

2. Does you know what she be having for lunch

   _____

3. mario want to write a article for the school paper

   _____

4. he like to right stories about reptile

   _____

5. mrs jenkins is take her class to the public libraries

   _____

6. there we will do research on a countries in europe

   _____

 Writing Practice: Write a paragraph about which day is your favorite day of the week and why.

Math Practice: Geometry

Calculate the volume for each problem. (Remember, V= l x w x h.) Then solve problem 5.

1. 5 in. long 2 in. wide 7 in. high V = _____	**2.** 10 cm long 4 cm wide 15 cm high V = _____	**3.** 31 ft. long 6 ft. wide 20 ft. high V = _____

4. 12 yd. long 13 yd. wide 14 yd. high V = _____	**5.** Eddie earns $5.37 an hour after school. He worked 17 hours last week. How much did he earn? _____

Language Practice: Main Idea

Choose the sentence that would go in a paragraph with the main idea.

1. Yellowstone National Park is a place of beautiful scenery.
   a. We camped outside in the park.
   b. The trees were tall and green.

2. There were some interesting animals at the zoo.
   a. The bengal tiger roared loudly.
   b. I enjoyed walking through the zoo.

3. The Christmas Parade had colorful floats.
   a. It was so cold that we watched it on television.
   b. The best float had Santa Claus sitting on top.

4. Yahtzee® is a fun game to play.
   a. You roll the dice to get points.
   b. I beat my brother three times.

 Writing Practice: Write a persuasive paragraph explaining why you need a computer in your bedroom.

Math Practice: Time

Calculate how much time has passed in each problem. Then solve problem 5.

1. 8:10 A.M. to 3:40 P.M. _____	2. 12:46 P.M. to 9:06 P.M. _____	3. 5:28 A.M. to 12:00 P.M. _____
4. 10:37 P.M. to 9:00 A.M. _____	5. It's 38° at 7:00 A.M. By 3:00 P.M. it is 52°. How much did the temperature rise? _____	

Language Practice: Possessives

Fill in the chart with the correct possessive nouns.

Noun	Singular Possessive	Plural Possessive
class		
town		
child		
beach		
whale		

 Writing Practice: Write a letter to your local newspaper expressing your concerns and views about an issue (examples: pollution, driving safety, pet adoption, etc.) that you feel needs some attention.

Name _____

Math Practice: Graph

Use the pie chart provided to determine what percent of each berry was harvested.

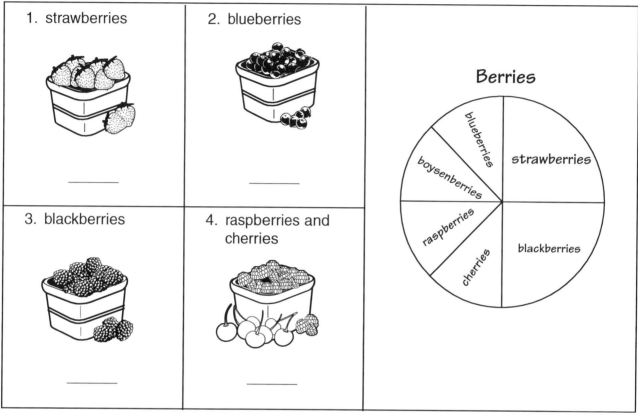

1. strawberries _____

2. blueberries _____

3. blackberries _____

4. raspberries and cherries _____

Berries

Language Practice: Plurals

Circle the correct plural of the boldfaced noun.

1. trout
   a. trout
   b. troutes

2. ox
   a. oxen
   b. oxens

3. alley
   a. allies
   b. alleys

4. brush
   a. brushes
   b. brushs

5. story
   a. storys
   b. stories

6. man
   a. mans
   b. men

7. sheep
   a. sheeps
   b. sheep

8. knife
   a. knifes
   b. knives

9. flower
   a. flowers
   b. floweres

 Writing Practice: What does it mean when people vote in elections?

Math Practice: Graph

Use the information provided in the bar graph to answer the questions below.

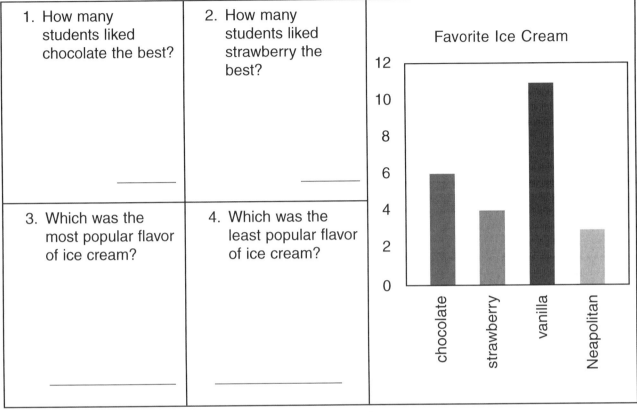

1. How many students liked chocolate the best?	2. How many students liked strawberry the best?
_____	_____
3. Which was the most popular flavor of ice cream?	4. Which was the least popular flavor of ice cream?
_____	_____

Favorite Ice Cream

chocolate   strawberry   vanilla   Neapolitan

Language Practice: Sentences

Rewrite each pair of sentences to form a compound sentence.

1. The python and the jaguar are both wild animals. They live in the rainforest.

   _____

   _____

2. The canopy is a layer of the rainforest. It is below the emergent layer.

   _____

   _____

3. Mice are members of the rodent family. Most people don't like them.

   _____

   _____

 Writing Practice: Imagine you are the school principal for one day. What changes would you make in the school?

Name _____

Math Practice: Addition

Find the minuend of each subtraction problem by using the numbers already given. Then solve problem 5.

1.
$$\begin{array}{r} \boxed{} \\ -\ 73{,}281 \\ \hline 115{,}765 \end{array}$$

2.
$$\begin{array}{r} \boxed{} \\ -\ \ \ \ \ 48 \\ \hline 26{,}154 \end{array}$$

3.
$$\begin{array}{r} \boxed{} \\ -\ 45{,}439 \\ \hline 72{,}786 \end{array}$$

4.
$$\begin{array}{r} \boxed{} \\ -\ 1{,}764 \\ \hline 5{,}783 \end{array}$$

5. After spending $342.80 for a television, D. J. had $186.20 left. How much did she have before she bought the television?

_____

Language Practice: Nouns

Fill in each blank with a common (C) or proper (P) noun.

1. _____ was born in the _____ of May.
   (P)   (C)

2. The _____ visited the _____ Zoo.
       (C)   (P)

3. On _____ we will take a spelling _____ .
      (P)   (C)

4. _____ sold magazines to his _____ .
   (P)   (C)

5. Our _____ is named _____ School.
       (C)   (P)

6. We drove through the _____ in the beautiful state of _____ .
                        (C)   (P)

Writing Practice: Describe what your life would be like if you lived underwater.

Name _____

Math Practice: Addition

Solve each problem below.

1.	2.	3.
26,407 389 1,683 + 42	705 3,060 129 + 5,783	5,863 19,700 85,708 + 635

4.	5. During the month of November, Shawn spent $42.00 for lunches, $14.00 for movies, and $67.23 for clothes. How much did he spend in all?
595 1,460 3,790 + 295	_____

Language Practice: Figurative Language

Tell what you think each figurative statement really means.

1. He's all ears! _____

2. Get off my back! _____

3. Lend me your ear. _____

4. Give me a hand. _____

5. Who let the cat out of the bag? _____

6. I've got my eye on you. _____

Writing Practice: Write a "how-to" paragraph on how to make a ham sandwich.

Name

Math Practice: Rounding

Round each number to the nearest thousand. Then solve problem 5.

1. 703	2. 28,619	3. 14,005,221
_____	_____	_____

4. 340,530	5. Irene made a 97, 73, 82, and 91 on her tests in biology. How much higher was her best score than her lowest?
_____	_____

Language Practice: Sentences

Rewrite these fragments as complete sentences.

1. burning leaves

_____

2. ran to the door

_____

3. caught in the escalator

_____

4. the famous man

_____

5. a noise outside

_____

6. with his homework

_____

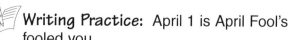 **Writing Practice:** April 1 is April Fool's Day. Describe a time when someone really fooled you.

Math Practice: Roman Numerals

Circle the number that stands for each Roman Numeral. Then solve problem 5.

1. LXI	2. CLIV	3. XCIX
a. 56 b. 66 c. 61	a. 155 b. 154 c. 164	a. 91 b. 99 c. 109

4. MCMXLV	5. If 2,982,123,000 pounds of chocolate were made into candy bars in 1985 and 2,306,582,000 pounds of chocolate were made into candy bars in 1995, how many more pounds of chocolate were used in 1985 than in 1995?
a. 1,945 b. 1,055 c. 1,155	

Language Practice: Verbs

Finish each sentence with a compound verb.

1. At the store, Mom _____.

2. During the basketball game, Marty _____.

3. On our vacation, my family _____.

4. The animals in the zoo _____.

5. The children _____.

6. The visitors at school _____.

 Writing Practice: President's Day is in February. What would you do if you were president of your class?

Name _____

Math Practice: Multiplication

Fill in the missing factors for each set of multiplication problems. Then solve problem 5.

1.	2.	3.

1.

5 x ___ = 30

___ x 8 = 48

7 x 9 = ___

2.

10 x 2 = ___

9 x ___ = 81

___ x 5 = 15

3.

4 x ___ = 32

___ x 9 = 36

___ x 5 = 25

4.

2 x ___ = 24

___ x 3 = 45

9 x ___ = 99

5. Jessica saved $92 last month and $120 this month. She spent $125 on clothes. How much does she have left?

_____

Language Practice: Word Order

Rearrange the words in each sentence to make a complete sentence.

1. speaker We a special in had library. the

_____

2. Theodor She a read story to Geisel. our about class

_____

3. Geisel Seuss. is Theodor known as Dr. also

_____

4. 1904. in born was He

_____

5. favorite he book is *and Green* My *Eggs Ham.* wrote

_____

6. writing wonder why I he use name his when real didn't books?

_____

 Writing Practice: You have been given the chance to create and publish your own magazine. What kind of articles and stories would it feature? What kind of magazine would it be?

Math Practice: Number Properties

Identify which property of multiplication that each problem is an example of.

1. a x (b x c) = (a x b) x c _____	2. k x 1 = k _____	3. 0 x q = 0 _____

4. f x g x h x i = f x h x g x i _____	Commutative Zero Associative Identity

Language Practice: Spelling

Circle the correct spelling of each word.

1. congradulations   congratulations
2. kindergarten   kindergarden
3. elevater   elevator
4. vegatable   vegetable
5. temperature   temperture
6. governor   govenor
7. beleive   believe
8. suprise   surprise

 Writing Practice: Describe how dogs and cats are different and alike.

Name _____

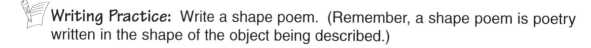

Math Practice: Patterns

Look for a pattern to figure out each answer. Then solve problem 5.

1.	2.	3.
888,888 x 2 = 1,777,776 888,888 x 3 = 2,666,664 888,888 x 4 = 3,555,552 888,888 x 5 = ? _____	55 x 2 = 110 55 x 3 = 165 55 x 4 = 220 55 x 5 = 275 55 x 6 = ? _____	1221 x 1 = 1221 1221 x 2 = 2442 1221 x 3 = 3663 1221 x 4 = ? _____

4.	5. During a weekend sale, a clothes store sold 84 pairs of jeans at $24.99 each. How much money did the store take in from the sale?
999 x 2 = 1998 999 x 3 = 2997 999 x 4 = 3996 999 x 5 = 4995 999 x 6 = ? _____	_____

Language Practice: Subject/Verb

Circle the correct verb that goes with each subject.

1. Every day Janet (watch, watches) her daughter get on the bus.

2. Beans (grow, grows) well in warm weather.

3. My sister and I (laugh, laughs) a lot when we are together.

4. Cathy (like, likes) to work in her garden.

5. The spectators (cheer, cheers) for the runners in the race.

6. The girls in my class (enjoy, enjoys) shopping at the mall.

Writing Practice: Write a shape poem. (Remember, a shape poem is poetry written in the shape of the object being described.)

Math Practice: Writing Numbers

For problems 1 and 2, write each answer in standard form. For problems 3 and 4, write the answer in expanded form. Then solve problem 5.

1.	2.	3. 2,301,450
80,000 + 4,000 + 9 =	700,000 + 80,000 + 300 + 6 =	_____
		_____
_____	_____	_____
		_____
		_____

4. 50,600	5. Two hundred fourteen people are employed at the food court in the mall. The average salary per day is $40. How much does the food court pay in salaries per day for all employees?
_____	
_____	
_____	
_____	
_____	_____

Language Practice: Word Usage

Choose the correct word to make each sentence correct.

1. Doesn't (nobody, anybody) want to play kickball?

2. Those boys have (anything, nothing) better to do.

3. Haven't you (never, ever) been to her house?

4. There isn't (any, none) food left for us to eat.

5. I guess no one (is, isn't) coming over today.

6. There weren't (any, no) prizes left for June.

Writing Practice: What is your favorite thing to do? Why?

Math Practice: Measurement

Solve each problem by using the conversion chart provided.

1. 35 cm = _____ mm	2. 652 m = _____ cm	3. 15 g = _____ mg

4. 32,000 mg = _____ g	conversion chart 1 cm = 10 mm 1 m = 100 cm 1 g = 1,000 mg

Language Practice: Dictionary Skills

Match the correct definition of the word *course* as used in the sentences below.

_____ 1. Dessert is the best *course*.   a. direction

_____ 2. I took a *course* in Spanish.   b. lessons or classes

_____ 3. The ship sailed on course to Fiji.   c. part of a meal

Match the correct definition of the word *low* as used in the sentences below.

_____ 4. Speak in a *low* voice in the hall.   a. nearly used up

_____ 5. The price of the wallet was *low*.   b. soft

_____ 6. The battery was *low* on my CD player. c. less than usual

 Writing Practice: Use this writing prompt to write a short paragraph:

I feel good about myself when ...

Math Practice: Exponents

Solve the problems below.

1. $16^2 =$ _____	2. $7^4 =$ _____	3. $22^3 =$ _____
4. $9^4 =$ _____	5. The theater has 155 rows of seats with 35 seats in each row. How many seats are in the theater? _____	

Language Practice: Prefixes

Match each numerical prefix to its meaning.

_____ 1. bi   a. one

_____ 2. uni   b. two

_____ 3. omni   c. half or partly

_____ 4. deca   d. three

_____ 5. semi   e. all

_____ 6. tri   f. ten

✎ **Writing Practice:** What would you do if you could be a teacher for a day?

Name _____

Math Practice: Mental Math/Division

Circle the correct answer by dividing mentally. Then solve problem 5.

1.	2.	3.
$8,000 \div 20 = ?$	$24,000 \div 3,000 = ?$	$250,000 \div 5 = ?$
4	8	500
400	800	5,000
40	80	50,000

4.	5. Mrs. Hill bought tickets for a ballgame. Each ticket was $12.25. The total was $110.25. How many tickets did she buy?
$34,000 \div 200 = ?$	
17	
170	
1,700	_____

Language Practice: Word Usage

Write the meaning of each word.

1. If *hydro* means water and *phobia* means fear, what does *hydrophobia* mean?

_____

2. If *insect* means bugs and *cide* means kill, what does *insecticide* mean?

_____

3. If *bio* means life and *ology* means field of study, what does *biology* mean?

_____

4. If *thermo* means temperature and *meter* means a device for measuring, what does *thermometer* mean? _____

5. If *home* means place to live and *less* means without, what does *homeless* mean?

_____

6. If *tele* means at a distance and *scope* means an instrument for seeing, what does *telescope* mean? _____

Writing Practice: Write a persuasive paragraph to convince someone to not take drugs.

Math Practice: Geometry

Match each name with the correct symbol.

1. line AB	2. ray AB	3. line segment AB
_____	_____	_____

4. vertex AB	
	a. $\overrightarrow{AB}$ c. $\overline{AB}$
	b. $\overleftrightarrow{AB}$ d. AB
_____	

Language Practice: Homonyms

Circle the correct homonym in each sentence.

1. Charlton was the first actor to come (forth, fourth) on stage.

2. "The weather (vain, vane) looks like a rooster," said Meryl.

3. Sarah is (dying, dyeing) her dress green.

4. Margaret had a (miner, minor) part in the school play.

5. The (principal, principle) of the school made the morning announcements.

6. We (new, knew) right away that we didn't belong in the meeting.

✍ **Writing Practice:** Write a persuasive paragraph to convince someone to recycle.

Name _____

Math Practice: Geometry

Circle the correct measurement for each angle. Then solve problem 5.

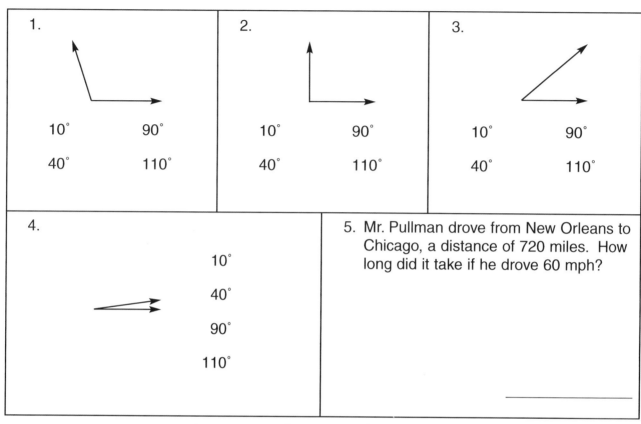

1.

10°   90°

40°   110°

2.

10°   90°

40°   110°

3.

10°   90°

40°   110°

4.

10°

40°

90°

110°

5. Mr. Pullman drove from New Orleans to Chicago, a distance of 720 miles. How long did it take if he drove 60 mph?

_____

Language Practice: Adjectives

Write the correct form of each adjective in the sentences below.

Good

1. The last quarter was the _____ of all.

2. She was a _____ student than her sister.

3. Alex is a very _____ reader.

Bad

4. I did _____ on this test than the one last week.

5. Benjamin felt _____ when he broke the window.

6. It was the _____ day in my life!

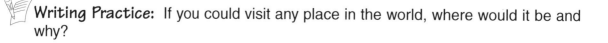

Writing Practice: If you could visit any place in the world, where would it be and why?

Math Practice: Geometry

Circle each pair of congruent figures. Then solve problem 5.

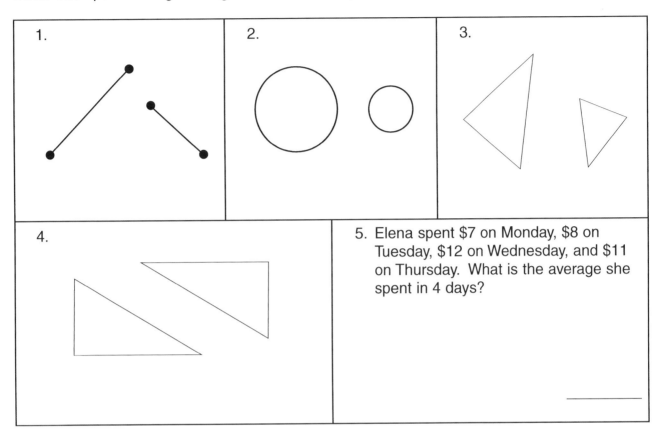

1.

2.

3.

4.

5. Elena spent $7 on Monday, $8 on Tuesday, $12 on Wednesday, and $11 on Thursday. What is the average she spent in 4 days?

_____

Language Practice: Verbs

Write the correct form of each verb in the sentences below.

Drink

1. Everyone _____ their milk.

2. Ellen _____ hers too fast.

3. I like to _____ mine slowly.

Take

4. Someone has _____ my book.

5. Our class _____ a trip to the museum.

6. Will you _____ me again next Tuesday?

 Writing Practice: Write a new commercial ad for your favorite product.

Math Practice: Geometry

Define the geometry terms listed below. Then solve problem 5.

1. parallel	2. segment	3. plane

4. vertex	Raisins are sold in boxes of 12¢ each or in a package of 8 for $1.00. Which would be cheaper?
	_____

Language Practice: Syllables

Circle the word which is correctly divided into syllables.

1. member	me-mber	mem-ber
2. memory	mem-o-ry	memo-ry
3. measure	mea-sure	meas-ure
4. matron	mat-ron	ma-tron
5. mayor	ma-yor	may-or
6. meditate	med-i-tate	me-di-tate

Writing Practice: Write a "how-to" paragraph on how to make a banana split.

Name _____

Math Practice: Geometry

Write T for true and F for false about the geometry statements below. Then solve problem 5.

1. A scalene triangle has 2 congruent sides. _____	2. A rectangle is a parallelogram. _____	3. A trapezoid is a parallelogram. _____
4. A square is a rhombus with all sides equal. _____	5. A triangle has angles that measure 34° and 79°. Find the measure of the third angle. _____	

Language Practice: Addressing Envelopes

Address the envelope correctly.

Return Address
Joy Smith
50 S. Oliver Street
Wichita, KS 65210

Mailing Address
Jane Bryant
421 Bay Street
Statesville, NC 28501

Writing Practice: Write a letter to a relative you haven't seen in awhile.

Math Practice: Ordered Pairs

Write the ordered pairs of each point on the grid.

1. A = (,)	2. B = (,)	
3. C = (,)	4. D = (,)	

Language Practice: Prepositions

Circle all prepositions in the sentences below.

1. Carol visited her sister near Chicago.

2. In the early 1900s, the telephone was invented.

3. Immigrants came to America to seek a better life.

4. The squirrel crawled through the hollow tree and onto the branch.

5. He went without playing baseball for two weeks.

6. The student sat between her friend and the principal during the program.

Writing Practice: You only have one television at home and you and your siblings all want to watch something different. What do you do?

Name _____

Math Practice: Money

Calculate the correct change. Then solve problem 5.

1. pizza $1.50	2. pencil $0.25	3. shampoo $1.89
soda $0.75	paper $1.89	conditioner $2.09
cookies $0.35	notebook $7.69	comb/brush $1.49
money given $10.00	money given $20.00	money given $10.02
change _____	change _____	change _____

4. magazine $2.50	5. Mr. Douglas needs $500.00 for a down payment on his car. He earns $275.00 a week and has saved $426.00. How much does he still need to save?
lip gloss $1.68	
gel pens $4.72	
money given $20.00	
change _____	_____

Language Practice: Main Idea

Fill in the web with details to go along with the main idea.

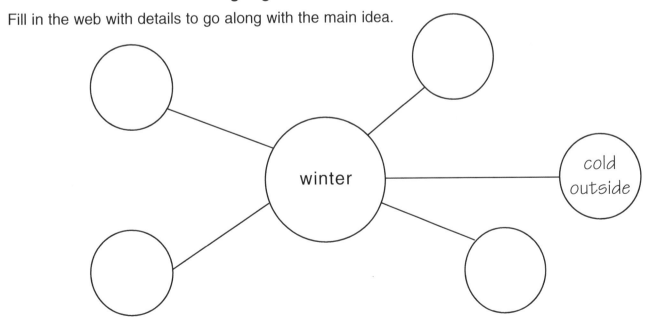

![Web diagram with "winter" in the center circle connected to five empty circles and one circle labeled "cold outside"]

✏️ **Writing Practice:** Now write a paragraph about winter using the details you wrote in the above web.

Math Practice: Mixed Review

Solve each problem.

1. Write the word name for the number below. 372,432.03 _____ _____ _____ _____	2. Put the numerals in order from least to greatest. 365,321 _____ 3,653.21 _____ 36,532.1 _____ 365.321 _____	3. $14.8 - 8.56 =$ _____
4. $8.64 + 13.4 + 2.59 =$ _____	5. Your teacher wanted you to divide all these numbers by the same number, and the answers would all come out even. The numbers are 24, 68, 104, and 80. What number can you divide into all four numbers? _____	

Language Practice: Adverbs

Circle the adverb in each sentence.

1. Janet plays the flute well.

2. Harold ran quickly to the game.

3. She spoke softly to her dog.

4. He is a very good reader.

5. The moon shone brightly over the water.

6. The police officer handles his gun carefully.

7. She wisely completed all of her homework.

Writing Practice: Do you have a favorite song? Write what your favorite song is and tell why it is your favorite.

Math Practice: Rounding/Decimals

Solve each problem by rounding. Then solve problem 5.

1. Round 3.916 to the nearest ones place. _____	2. Round 6.052 to the nearest tenths place. _____	3. Round 12.273 to the nearest hundredths place. _____
4. Round 8.619 to the nearest ones place. _____	5. Tennis balls come 3 to a can. If 25 people on the tennis team need a ball, how many cans do they have to buy? _____	

Language Practice: Clauses

Write if the clause is dependent (D) or independent (I).

_____1. the soldiers were winning the war

_____2. unless it rains today

_____3. when the door opened

_____4. with the grace and strength of a deer

_____5. she dug in her backpack for a pencil

_____6. her friend slipped on the ice

Writing Practice: Describe an invention that you would like to create and how it would be useful for people.

Math Practice: Fractions

Write the correct fraction expressed by the shaded part. Then solve problem 5.

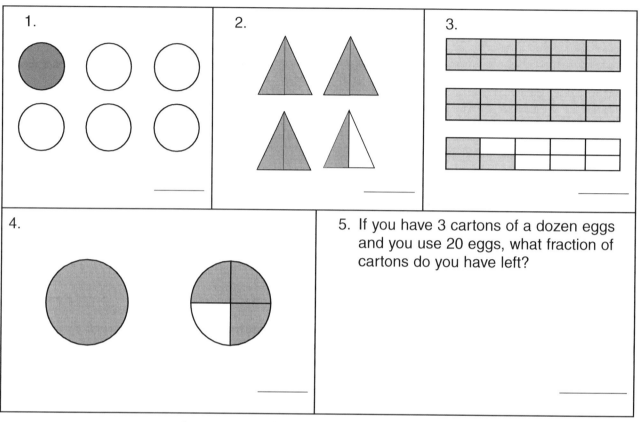

1.

2.

3.

4.

5. If you have 3 cartons of a dozen eggs and you use 20 eggs, what fraction of cartons do you have left?

Language Practice: Word Usage

Each word begins with the prefix *re*. Try to figure out the root word for each problem.

1. r e _____ _____ _____ _____ *(take from somewhere)*

2. r e _____ _____ _____ _____ _____ _____ *(to make as if new)*

3. r e _____ _____ _____ _____ *(to fix)*

4. r e _____ _____ _____ _____ _____ *(to have high regard for)*

5. r e _____ _____ _____ *(give answer)*

6. r e _____ _____ _____ _____ *(keeping; hold back)*

> Riddle: What does one do at night when he or she goes to bed?
>
> r e _____ _____ _____ _____ _____

 Writing Practice: If you had a million toothpicks, what would you build?

Math Practice: Rounding

Round each number and then solve problem 5.

1. Round 459,056 to the nearest hundred thousand. _____	2. Round 71,845 to the nearest ten thousand. _____	3. Round 6,572,653 to the nearest hundred. _____
4. Round 4,867,890 to the nearest million. _____	5. Pablo drove 521 miles in two days. He drove 67 more miles the first day than on the second day. How many miles did he drive on the second day? _____	

Language Practice: Fact or Opinion

Write *fact* or *opinion* beside each statement.

_____ 1. My school has 22 teachers.

_____ 2. My teacher is the best in the school.

_____ 3. There are 27 students in my class.

_____ 4. Our gym is larger than any classroom.

_____ 5. Our basketball team has the coolest uniforms.

_____ 6. The team's record is 11–3.

Writing Practice: Write a short story with the title:

A Terrific Day

Math Practice: Fractions

Multiply fractions. Reduce to lowest terms. Then solve problem 5.

1. $\dfrac{7}{8} \times \dfrac{2}{7} =$	2. $\dfrac{2}{5} \times \dfrac{3}{10} =$	3. $\dfrac{9}{14} \times \dfrac{7}{9} =$
4. $\dfrac{16}{24} \times \dfrac{6}{8} =$		5. If Bob ate 2/6 of the cake and John ate 1/3 of the cake, who ate more? _____

Language Practice: Analogies

Complete each analogy.

1. read is to library as worship is to _____

2. laugh is to cry as lively is to _____

3. students are to school as patients are to _____

4. antonym is to synonym as big is to _____

5. pickle is to jar as egg is to _____

6. fake is to real as hot is to _____

 Writing Practice: Use this writing prompt to write a short paragraph:

The best day at school was...

Math Practice: Fractions

Divide the fractions and reduce to lowest terms. Then solve problem 5.

1. $$\frac{3}{5} \div \frac{8}{9} =$$	2. $$\frac{2}{7} \div \frac{4}{5} =$$	3. $$\frac{7}{8} \div \frac{2}{7} =$$

4.

$$\frac{12}{14} \div \frac{3}{4} =$$

5. Basset School needs two 48-seat buses to take the football team to the playoffs. They will have only 6 vacant seats. How many people will be riding the bus?

_____

Language Practice: Alphabetical Order

Write each group of words in alphabetical order.

1. prohibit, probate, proud, proclaim

_____

2. further, fuel, fuzz, furlough

_____

3. commune, communicate, commotion, community

_____

4. span, spatter, space, spacious

_____

5. receipt, realize, react, reason

_____

6. overlay, overlook, overhaul, overseas

_____

 Writing Practice: When does a rainbow appear? Why does it appear?

Math Practice: Measurement

Match the unit of measure with its equivalent. Circle the answers then solve problem 5.

1. deci	2. deka	3. kilo
a. 100	a. 100	a. 100
b. 0.1	b. 0.1	b. 0.1
c. 1,000	c. 1,000	c. 1,000
d. 10	d. 10	d. 10

4. hecto

a. 100   c. 1,000

b. 0.1   d. 10

5. Ten campers signed up for 1 week of camp. The total amount paid was $2,025.00. How much did each camper have to pay?

_____

Language Practice: Word Usage

Use the code to find out famous authors.

code	z	y	x	w	v	u	t	s	r	q	p	o	n
letter	a	b	c	d	e	f	g	h	i	j	k	l	m
code	m	l	k	j	i	h	g	f	e	d	c	b	a
letter	n	o	p	q	r	s	t	u	v	w	x	y	z

1. plmrthyfit _____

2. xovzib _____

3. wzso _____

4. ildormt _____

5. nvbvih _____

6. hgrmv _____

Writing Practice: Write a fan letter to your favorite author.

       ©Teacher Created Resources, Inc.

Math Practice: Geometry

Find the measurement of the unknown angle. Then solve problem 5.

1. 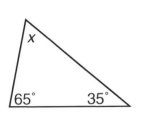 x = _____	2. 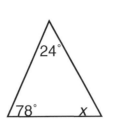 x = _____	3. 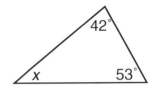 x = _____

4. 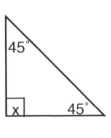 x = _____	5. Each table in the lunchroom can hold four people. How many tables are needed for 125 students? _____

Language Practice: Context Clues

Write the words that complete the paragraph.

Word Bank		
psychological	committed	mentor
psychiatrist	psychiatry	commencement

Dr. Lee, a young _____, works at a mental health clinic. She has

learned much from her _____, Dr. Harvey. They have practiced

_____ together since their _____ from Baylor

University. They help people with _____ problems. They are

_____ to helping others.

 Writing Practice: Imagine that you are a marine biologist. Write a descriptive paragraph about the different things you would see during your sea expeditions.

Math Practice: Ratios

Write the ratio for each problem. Then solve problem 5.

1. triangles to squares	2. nickels in a dollar to pennies in a dollar	3. seconds in an hour to minutes in an hour
△ △ △ ☐ ☐ ☐ ☐ _____	_____	_____

4. circles to rectangles	5. Milk, butter, yogurt, cheese, and juice are on a refrigerator shelf. If milk is between the yogurt and cheese, yogurt is between the milk and butter, and cheese is directly to the left of the juice, in what order will you find them?
○ ○ ○ ○ ○ ○ ☐ ☐ ☐ ☐ ☐ ☐ ☐ ☐ ☐ _____	_____ _____

Language Practice: Word Usage

Write a word that fits each group.

1. horsefly, wasp, bumblebee, _____

2. wolf, coyote, fox, _____

3. boa, anaconda, rattlesnake, _____

4. ear, nose, eye, _____

5. cafeteria, library, gymnasium, _____

6. cowboy, baseball, visor, _____

 Writing Practice: Imagine that you are an explorer (like Sir Francis Drake). Write a descriptive paragraph about the different people and civilizations you would encounter.

Math Practice: Variables

Solve for *n* for each pair of equivalent fractions. Then solve problem 5.

1. $\dfrac{5}{6} = \dfrac{n}{24}$ *n* = _____	2. $\dfrac{2}{3} = \dfrac{n}{18}$ *n* = _____	3. $\dfrac{6}{9} = \dfrac{n}{45}$ *n* = _____
4. $\dfrac{7}{12} = \dfrac{n}{48}$ *n* = _____	5. In Seattle, it rains about 22 days out of every 30. About how many days would it possibly rain in 90 days? _____	

Language Practice: Homographs

Using two different meanings for each word, write two sentences.

1. stable

_____

_____

2. ball

_____

_____

3. contract

_____

_____

4. yard

_____

_____

5. star

_____

_____

 Writing Practice: Imagine you are a spy. Write a short story describing your adventures.

Math Practice: Percents

Write each number as a percent. Then solve problem 5.

1. 6 out of 100 _____	2. $\frac{43}{100}$ _____	3. 58 to 100 _____
4. $\frac{79}{100}$ _____	5. Tami had $1.00. She spent 42¢. What percent of a dollar does she have left? _____	

Language Practice: Analogies

Complete each analogy.

1. animal is to herd as person is to _____

2. drought is to dry as rain is to _____

3. end is to begin as finish is to _____

4. clean is to neat as _____ is to grimy

5. adult is to thirty as _____ is to ten

6. small is to enormous as _____ is to difficult

✎ **Writing Practice:** Write the steps involved in baking a cake or cupcakes.

   ©Teacher Created Resources, Inc.

Math Practice: Mixed Computation

Write +, −, ÷, or x in each box to make each equation correct. Then solve problem 5.

1. $\dfrac{2}{3} \boxed{} \dfrac{2}{3} = \dfrac{4}{9}$	2. $\dfrac{2}{7} \boxed{} \dfrac{8}{14} = \dfrac{6}{7}$	3. $1\dfrac{4}{5} \boxed{} \dfrac{3}{4} = 1\dfrac{1}{20}$

4. $\dfrac{3}{4} \boxed{} \dfrac{7}{9} = \dfrac{7}{12}$

5. A 35 mm camera costs $72.00, but it's on sale for 20% off. How much does it cost now?

_____

Language Practice: Antonyms

Circle the antonym for the first word in each row.

1. abolish	destroy	restore
2. begin	start	terminate
3. correct	false	accurate
4. dingy	dull	bright
5. expect	surprise	anticipate
6. famous	celebrated	unknown

 Writing Practice: Write about similarities and differences between doctors and lawyers.

Name

Math Practice: Geometry

Find the circumference of each figure. (Remember C = dπ or 2rπ. Use 3.14 for π.) Then solve for problem 5.

1.

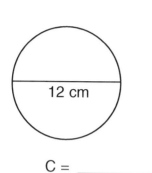

12 cm

C = _____

2.

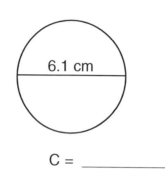

6.1 cm

C = _____

3.

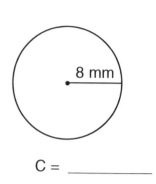

8 mm

C = _____

4.

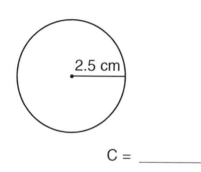

2.5 cm

C = _____

5. Mindy got 9 out of every 10 problems correct. If the test had 50 questions, how many problems did she answer correctly?

_____

Language Practice: Synonyms

Circle the synonym for the first word in each row.

1. zest	clean	enjoyment
2. yearn	crave	shudder
3. potent	value	demerit
4. valid	powerless	strong
5. unfit	like	unsuitable
6. tremble	shake	calm

 Writing Practice: What route do you take to get from your house to school every day? Write a set of directions.

Math Practice: Multiplication

Use multiplication to solve the problems below.

1.	2.	3.
$\frac{2}{3} \times 20 =$	$15 \times \frac{4}{5} =$	$6.48 \times .23 =$

4.	5. Sean is $\frac{1}{3}$ as old as his brother. His brother is 21. How old is Sean?
$3.729 \times 45 =$	_____

Language Practice: Direct Object

Underline the direct object in each sentence.

1. Robin hit a homerun during the ballgame.

2. He brought a friend to the game.

3. We liked the trip to the museum.

4. They played some music by Bach.

5. Pete wrote a story about caves.

6. Bats eat insects flying around at night.

Writing Practice: What type of music do you like to listen to? Why?

Math Practice: Geometry

Calculate the perimeter or area.

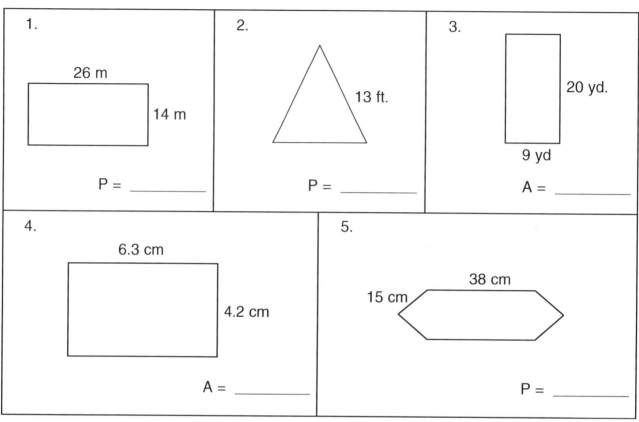

1.
26 m
14 m
P = _____

2.
13 ft.
P = _____

3.
20 yd.
9 yd
A = _____

4.
6.3 cm
4.2 cm
A = _____

5.
38 cm
15 cm
P = _____

Language Practice: Comprehension

Answer the questions about the story.

"I'm going to become a lawyer someday," said Matt. Kevin replied that he wanted to study astronomy. The two best friends were thinking about what college they wanted to attend. After looking at scholarships, Kevin decided to go to Penn State; however, Matt was leaning toward Indiana University, due to the law program offered. "It's for sure that no matter what college we choose, we'll have to study!" said Matt. Kevin agreed.

1. Who wanted to study astronomy? _____

2. Why did Kevin want to go to Penn State?

   _____

3. What did Matt want to do someday? _____

4. Why did Indiana University interest Matt?

   _____

5. What will both boys have to do when they get to college?

   _____

Writing Practice: Imagine you are up in a hot air balloon traveling around the world. Write about some of the things that you see from the hot air balloon.

Math Practice: Division/Decimals

Solve each problem below.

1. $2\overline{)3.15}$	2. $4\overline{)7.82}$	3. $9\overline{)34.56}$
4. $4\overline{)19.48}$	5. Darryl worked 23 hours last week at $6.25 an hour. How much did he earn the entire week? _____	

Language Practice: Sequencing

Put these steps in order.

Making a Mask

_____ Next, cut out eye holes.

_____ You need colored paper, scissors, an elastic band, and glue to make a mask.

_____ Then cut the mask to be the shape you want.

_____ First, cut a piece of paper to fit your head.

_____ Finally, punch holes on both sides and secure elastic bands.

_____ Now glue any decorations you want on your mask.

Writing Practice: If you could meet any person in history, who would it be? Why?

Name _____

Math Practice: Estimation

Using front-end digits, estimate the total of each set of dollar amounts. Then solve problem 5.

1.	2.	3.
$2.45 1.76 3.44 3.19 + 5.68 total _____	$6.77 3.98 1.20 4.43 + 2.04 total _____	$9.43 1.89 4.22 3.95 + 2.70 total _____

4.

$2.95
7.55
9.79
3.45
+ 3.05

total _____

5. You bought items at $5.79, $6.59, $5.13, and $8.43. You have $30. Will you have enough money? If so, how much change will you get back?

_____

Language Practice: Nouns/Plurals

Write S for singular or P for plural by each noun.

1. _____ path

2. _____ benches

3. _____ men

4. _____ geese

5. _____ experience

6. _____ spyglass

7. _____ cargo ships

8 _____ mice

9. _____ knights

10. _____ ship

11. _____ oxen

12. _____ dice

13. _____ nickel

14. _____ shoes

15. _____ lunch

16. _____ people

 Writing Practice: If you were a magician, describe a new magic trick that you have created to entertain your audience.

Name _____

Math Practice: Graph

Answer the questions using the provided pictograph.

1. How many students ate pizza? _____	2. How many students ate corn dogs? _____	3. How many students ate fries? _____

4. How many more students ate pizza than salad? _____	**Student's Lunch on Friday**

Student's Lunch on Friday

pizza   corn dog   fries   salad

= 10 students

Language Practice: Cause/Effect

Underline the effect in each sentence.

1. I go to bed when I am tired.

2. The hunter stopped and shot the bear.

3. Because he wanted to sing, Hans joined the choir.

4. I got soaked walking home in the thunderstorm.

5. When Andrew organized his folder, he found his assignment.

6. The swimming pool was crowded after we arrived.

Writing Practice: Write a personal narrative about going on a picnic. Underline any cause/effect statements.

Math Practice: Mean, Median, Mode

Use the information provided on the list to answer the following questions.

1. What is the mean?	2. What is the median?	Jeff received these amounts of money for his birthday.
_____	_____	grandparents $40 parents $30 aunt $15
3. What is the mode?	4. What is the total he received?	3 brothers $10 each sister $15 best friend $20
_____	_____	neighbor $5

Language Practice: Nouns

Write "noun" if the word names a person, place, thing, or idea. Write "verb" if it describes action, existence, or occurrence. (*Hint:* There are some words that are not nouns or verbs)

1. Rachel   _____
2. discover   _____
3. socks   _____
4. cheered   _____
5. yellow   _____
6. talked   _____
7. peace   _____
8. up   _____
9. gratitude   _____
10. her   _____

 Writing Practice: Write a paragraph using at least five of the nouns listed above. Then circle any other nouns in your paragraph.

Name _____

Math Practice: Measurement

Solve each equation and give each answer in centimeters. Then solve problem 5.

1.	2.	3.
2 m + 32 cm = _____	30 cm + 80 mm = _____	24 mm + 3.6 cm = _____

4.	5. How many squares are in this figure?
5 m + 16 cm = _____	 _____

Language Practice: Nouns/Word Usage

Fill in the blanks with a word to make each sentence complete.

1. Clark wrote his _____ and told about his trip to _____.

2. Mary Sue and _____ went to visit _____ in _____.

3. John, my _____, asked if he could give me a _____.

4. In _____, there is a special holiday called _____.

5. My sister lives on _____, right next door to _____.

6. My _____ gave me homework in _____.

✎ **Writing Practice:** What is the best way to travel—by bus, car, train, plane, etc.? Why?

Math Practice: Measurement

Select the best unit (mm, cm, m) for measuring each object. Then solve problem 5.

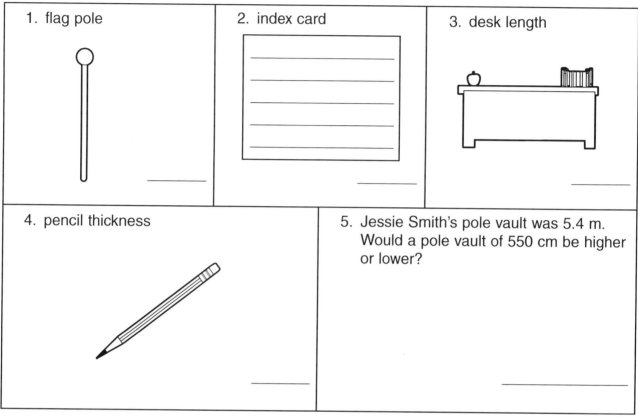

1. flag pole	2. index card	3. desk length

4. pencil thickness

5. Jessie Smith's pole vault was 5.4 m. Would a pole vault of 550 cm be higher or lower?

Language Practice: Writing Practice

Write the following rules in your best handwriting.

Tips for Being a Good Listener

1. Pay close attention to the speaker.

_____

2. Look at the speaker except when taking notes.

_____

3. Respond to the speaker with appropriate facial expressions.

_____

4. Compliment the speaker after the presentation.

_____

Writing Practice: You have to give a speech. Write some rules for being a good speaker.

 ©Teacher Created Resources, Inc.

Math Practice: Place Value

Circle the correct place value of the underlined and boldfaced number. Then solve problem 5.

1. 25,640	2. 2,117,470	3. 10,012
thousands	millions	ten thousands
tens	hundreds	tens
ones	tens	ones

4. 936,415	5. At the season's opening game, 34,523 people were present. The stadium held 45,000 people. How many empty seats were there?
hundred thousands ten thousands hundreds	_____

Language Practice: Main Idea

Write a category for each group.

1. lettuce   alien
   grass   emerald

   category _____

3. clock   telephone
   math book   keyboard

   category _____

2. carrot   scarf
   coal   sticks

   category _____

4. bowling ball button
   cherry   moon

   category _____

Writing Practice: Choose a list from above and write a paragraph.

Math Practice: Comparing Numbers

Add <, >, or = between each pair of numbers. Then solve problem 5.

1. 45,697 ◯ 46,597	**2.** 1,520,019 ◯ 1,519,020	**3.** 43 hundreds ◯ 430 tens

4. 710 hundreds ◯ 71 thousands

5. Victor can run 3 miles in 32 minutes. Maurice can run it in 1,950 seconds. Who runs it faster and by how much?

Who runs faster? _____

By how much? _____

Language Practice: Abbreviations

Write each abbreviation.

1. number _____
2. company _____
3. postscript _____
4. mountain _____
5. ounce _____
6. square _____
7. Junior _____
8. afternoon _____
9. minute _____
10. gallon _____

Writing Practice: Invent a new type of currency or form of money. Describe how it is to be used and what it looks like, and what it is made of.

Name _____

Math Practice: Comparing Numbers

For problems 1 and 2, write in order from least to greatest. For problems 3 and 4, write in order from greatest to least. Then solve problem 5.

1. 421, 468, 372, 327, 447	2. 9.54, 8.21, 6.87, 7.33, 4.78	3. 99,000,000 99,000 99,900,000 999,000
_____	_____	_____
_____	_____	_____
_____	_____	_____
_____	_____	_____

4. 405,000, 45,000, 455,000, 54,000	5. At 3:30 P.M. Joyce put a roast in the oven. It should cook 2 1/2 hours. When will it be done?
_____	
_____	
_____	
_____	_____

Language Practice: Verbs

Circle the correct verb.

1. Ritchie hadn't (did, done) his math homework.

2. I (seen, saw) that Mrs. Winters wasn't there.

3. I have (worn, wore) that dress before.

4. What time does your train (leave, left)?

5. They (don't, doesn't) know what you are talking about.

6. I have (broke, broken) my arm twice.

 Writing Practice: What is one of the most important things that you have learned from your parent(s)?

Name _____

Math Practice: Mixed Computation

Solve each problem below.

1.	2.	3.
1,382 9,217 + 463	11,846 − 7,271	3,240 x 81

4.	5. Gina had $1,000 in a savings account. In six months, she received $25 interest. How much would she have earned with $5,000 in her savings account?
17) 734	_____

Language Practice: Sentences/Conjunctions

Combine the sentences by using a conjunction *(and, but, or, nor, for, yet)*.

1. I like to watch television. I don't watch it too much.

   _____

2. I watch movies. I watch sports.

   _____

3. Don went to camp in Missouri. He really wants to go to Florida.

   _____

4. JoAnn came to help us move. We had lots of heavy boxes.

   _____

5. Bones are easily broken. They are not easily mended.

   _____

6. You can play. You can sit on the bleachers.

   _____

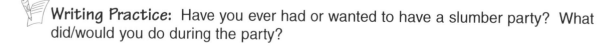 **Writing Practice:** Have you ever had or wanted to have a slumber party? What did/would you do during the party?

Math Practice: Multiplication

Solve each problem below.

1.	2.	3.
464 x 183	814 x 572	8,723 x 602

4.	5. There are five chairs in the front row. Each successive row has two more chairs. How many chairs are in the sixth row?
3,435 x 242	_____

Language Practice: Homographs

Write sentences showing the different meanings of each pair of words.

1. fine _____

2. fine _____

3. wound _____

4. wound _____

5. shed _____

6. shed _____

 Writing Practice: What was the happiest moment of your life?

Math Practice: Writing Numbers

Write out each number in words. Then solve problem 5.

1. 0.007 _____ _____ _____	2. 0.0019 _____ _____ _____	3. 25.103 _____ _____ _____

4. 0.050 _____ _____ _____	5. Mrs. Park needed 2 pencils for each of her students for their achievement tests. She has 27 students. Pencils come in boxes of 8 each. How many pencils will she need? How many boxes will she need to buy? pencils _____ boxes _____

Language Practice: Word Usage

Write either *its* or *it's* in the blanks below.

1. _____ too late to watch television.

2. The rabbit was eating _____ food.

3. The bird broke _____ wing.

4. No, _____ the only one I want.

5. _____ Clara's suitcase.

6. The dog lost _____ toy.

 Writing Practice: Write a descriptive paragraph about your most memorable summer camp experience.

Name _____

Math Practice: Decimals/Comparing Numbers

For problems 1 and 2, write < or > between each pair of numbers. For problems 3 and 4, write the numbers in order from least to greatest. Then solve problem 5.

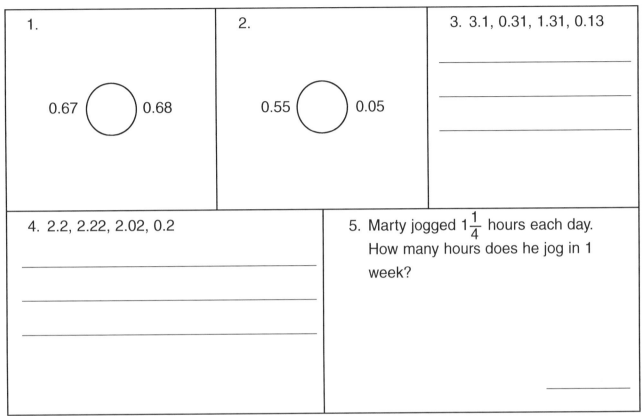

1.

0.67 ◯ 0.68

2.

0.55 ◯ 0.05

3. 3.1, 0.31, 1.31, 0.13

_____

_____

_____

4. 2.2, 2.22, 2.02, 0.2

_____

_____

_____

5. Marty jogged $1\frac{1}{4}$ hours each day. How many hours does he jog in 1 week?

_____

Language Practice: Adverbs

Circle each adverb. (There are two in each sentence.)

1. She watched eagerly as the storm grew near.

2. Down came the rain violently.

3. She fed her bird early today.

4. Softly and sweetly the children sang.

5. He arrived late at the party tonight.

6. Mr. Brown drove carefully and slowly.

Writing Practice: What do you like to do for fun, and who do you like to hang out with?

Name _____

Math Practice: Patterns/Decimals

Determine the pattern for each set of numbers and then solve problem 5.

1. 0.2, ___, ___, 0.8	2. 23,006, 23,016, _____ _____	3. 4,488, 4,491, _____ _____
4. 0.121, _____ 0.123, _____	5. Manny finished his race in 31.34 seconds. C. J. finished 1.50 seconds later. How long did it take C. J. to finish the race? _____	

Language Practice: Interjections

Circle all interjections.

Aha	Slowly	Gee
Oh, no	Of course	Below
Strong	Down	Yuck
Wow	Out	Hey

Writing Practice: Write five sentences using five of the interjections above.

Math Practice: Geometry

Calculate the perimeter for each problem. Then solve problem 5.

1.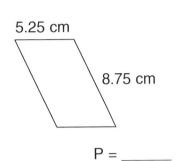

   4.25 cm

   4.1 cm

   P = _____

2. 5.25 cm

   8.75 cm

   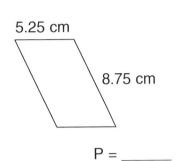

   P = _____

3.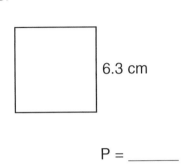

   6.3 cm

   P = _____

4.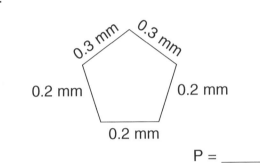

   0.3 mm   0.3 mm

   0.2 mm   0.2 mm

   0.2 mm

   P = _____

5. Kayla has to leave for school in two hours. If it takes her 45 minutes to eat breakfast and 30 minutes to get dressed, how many minutes will she have to pack her lunch and take a quick shower?

   _____

Language Practice: Adjectives

Underline the proper adjective(s) in each sentence.

1. I like to eat Italian food, don't you?

2. Spanish tortillas are delicious.

3. He bought a Swiss watch and gave it to his mom.

4. St. Croix is in the Caribbean Islands.

5. A French pastry is a crepe.

6. We ate at a Mexican restaurant last night.

 Writing Practice: Write a descriptive paragraph using as many proper nouns and adjectives as possible.

Math Practice: Division with Decimals

Solve each problem below.

1. $45.6 \div 100 =$ _____	2. $0.98 \div 10 =$ _____	3. $556 \div 100 =$ _____
4. $32.92 \div 100 =$ _____	5. The original price of a CD is $13.00. If it is on sale at $1.29 off, what is the price now? _____	

Language Practice: Punctuation and Capitalization

Choose the correctly punctuated words.

1. a. J. K. rowling
    b. J K Rowling
    c. J. K. Rowling

2. a. Dr. T C Trane
    b. Dr. T. C. Trane
    c. Dr. t c Trane

3. a. Mesa verde Park
    b. Mesa Verde Park
    c. Mesa Verde park

4. a. James Lee, Jr.
    b. James Lee, jr.
    c. James Lee jr.

5. a. Turner St
    b. turner st.
    c. Turner St.

6. a. Mrs. Bette L. Scott
    b. Mrs. Bette L Scott
    c. Mrs Bette L. Scott

 Writing Practice: Write the safety rules for leaving your classroom and the school during a fire drill or actual fire.

Name _____

Math Practice: Estimation

Add by rounding to the nearest one's place. Then solve problem 5.

1.	2.	3.
2.86 5.20 + 7.16	0.29 0.93 + 1.34	4.22 8.61 + 3.03

4.	5. On Saturday, 263 patients were at the local hospital. By Sunday, 43 patients were discharged, and 29 patients were admitted. How many patients are now in the hospital?
1.88 0.66 + 0.78	_____

Language Practice: Study Skills

Match the correct answer.

_____ 1. when book is published

_____ 2. topics and page numbers where information is found

_____ 3. chapter titles with page numbers

_____ 4. definitions of words

_____ 5. first page in a book

_____ 6. found on spine of book

a. glossary

b. copyright date

c. title page

d. index

e. table of contents

f. call number

 Writing Practice: Imagine life during Medieval times. Describe what your life would be like if you had lived during this time period.

©Teacher Created Resources, Inc.   157   #3303 Daily Skills Practice–Grades 5-6

Name _____

Math Practice: Place Value

Write the correct value for the underlined, boldfaced number. Then solve problem 5.

1. 23,851,049.7<u>6</u> _____	2. <u>2</u>3,851,049.76 _____	3. 23,851,<u>0</u>49.76 _____
4. 23,<u>8</u>51,049.76 _____	5. Kyle loves bubble gum. He chews about 3 pieces a week. Estimate how many pieces of gum he'd chew in one month. How about in one year? month _____ year _____	

Language Practice: Point of View

Write F for first person or T for third person.

_____ 1. We knew it was going to rain.

_____ 2. I said, "Go with me."

_____ 3. He replied, "Not today."

_____ 4. Their dog is a cocker spaniel.

_____ 5. Sue wondered if Cassie was sick.

_____ 6. My grandpa and I went fishing.

Writing Practice: What is your favorite cartoon on TV or in the comics section in your newspaper? Why?

Math Practice: Rounding

Choose the correctly rounded number. Then solve problem 5.

1.	2.	3.
2,631 to nearest 10 a. 2,630 b. 2,600	27,982,703 to nearest million a. 27,000,000 b. 28,000,000	$15.45 to nearest dollar a. $16.00 b. $15.00

4.	5. Andrew's mother bought groceries for a party. Estimate how much she spent if she bought the following: chips $1.69, soda $1.09, cookies $2.39, and cupcakes $3.89.
4,103,067 to nearest thousand a. 4,100,000 b. 4,103,000	_____

Language Practice: Author's Purpose

Using the choices from the box below, select the author's purpose.

_____ 1. The most common last name is Smith.

_____ 2. He ran the last part of his race crying with pain, yet he still finished.

_____ 3. There will be new rules for the cafeteria!

_____ 4. Buy "Super X Cereal" and start your day out right!

_____ 5. The blue whale is the largest of all whales.

_____ 6. But Wilbur said, "I don't want to die. Save me Charlotte!"

a. give information   b. persuade   c. entertain   d. arouse emotions

 Writing Practice: Who do you think was the most important person in history? Why?

Math Practice: Division

Circle the correct set of numbers that is divisible by the specific number given. Then solve problem 5.

1. What set of numbers is divisible by 2? a. 8, 15, 18, 23 b. 16, 24, 28, 32	2. What set of numbers is divisible by 3? a. 9, 18, 21, 39 b. 5, 15, 30, 36	3. What set of numbers is divisible by 5? a. 60, 75, 90, 100 b. 36, 40, 45, 55
4. What set of numbers is divisible by 12? a. 122, 130, 145, 152 b. 60, 84, 108, 144	5. A famous author was at the local bookstore signing copies of his book. Over 4,000 people showed up, but the author only signed 2,677 books. How many didn't get an autograph? _____	

Language Practice: Pronouns

Circle the word that the italicized pronoun replaces.

1. The house was dark, as though the family moved from *it*.

2. Peel the orange and separate *it* into sections.

3. Women used to stay at home and teach *their* children.

4. Mildred studied piano, and *she* became a great pianist.

5. Jasmine went home and wrote *her* friend a letter.

6. Sequoyah was a Cherokee Indian; *he* invented the Cherokee alphabet.

Writing Practice: Use this writing prompt to write a short paragraph:

One of my favorite memories when I was younger was...

         ©Teacher Created Resources, Inc.

Name _____

Math Practice: Prime Numbers

Circle all prime numbers. Then solve problem 5.

1. 23 46 21	2. 27 9 7	3. 11 20 15
4. 21 18 5	5. A car travels 65 mph. How far will it go in 8 hours? _____	

Language Practice: Homonyms/Homophones

Write the correct pairs of words under the correct headings.

		Homophone	Homonym
vein	vane	_____	_____
rumor	roomer	_____	_____
strain	strain	_____	_____
beat	beat	_____	_____
left	left	_____	_____
be	bee	_____	_____

Writing Practice: Use as many homonyms and homophones as you can in a short story.

Name _____

Math Practice: Factors

Circle all factors of each number. Then solve problem 5.

1. 24	2. 45	3. 36
1, 2, 3, 4, 5, 6, 7, 8, 9, 10, 11, 12	1, 2, 3, 4, 5, 6, 7, 8, 9, 10, 11, 12	1, 2, 3, 4, 5, 6, 7, 8, 9, 10, 11, 12

4. 50	5. If an average household receives four pieces of mail a day, how many pieces of mail would the postal clerk sort daily for a neighborhood with 283 houses?
1, 2, 3, 4, 5, 6, 7, 8, 9, 10, 11, 12	_____

Language Practice: Homophones

Circle the correct homophone for each sentence.

1. (Their, They're) dog had 3 puppies.

2. The shelf was (to, too) high for her to reach.

3. He made the (right, write) decision.

4. Shari had to buy a (knew, new) pencil.

5. The (isle, aisle) wasn't wide enough for the cart.

6. Alan picked the (pear, pair) off the tree.

Writing Practice: Write a short mystery using as many homophones as possible.

Name _____

Math Practice: Multiplication

Solve each problem below.

1. 6,728 x 123	2. 59 x 38	3. 3,604 x 49
4. 234 x 153	5. The local middle school sponsored a skating party for its students in 5th and 6th grades. The cost per child was $6.00. How much did the school pay if 213 students went? _____	

Language Practice: Real/Unreal

Write R if real or U if unreal.

_____ 1. book about Harry Potter

_____ 2. Dorothy in the *Wizard of Oz*

_____ 3. Martin Luther King, Jr.

_____ 4. novel read in English class

_____ 5. Wilbur said, "Charlotte, you have to save me."

_____ 6. book about kinds of animals

Writing Practice: Use this writing prompt to write a short paragraph:

Something important I learned this year was...

Name _____

Math Practice: Fractions

Change each numeral to a mixed number or an improper fraction. Reduce to lowest terms. Then solve problem 5.

1. $8 \frac{2}{3} =$ ____	2. $3 \frac{8}{7} =$ ____	3. $15 \frac{7}{10} =$ ____

4.

$7 \frac{4}{8} =$ ____

5. This past year the library bought 1,675 new books at the average cost of $9.00 per book. What was the total cost of books?

_____

Language Practice: Dictionary Skills

Answer these questions about the dictionary entries.

cus´-tard	n. sweet milk and egg mixture; like pudding	
cus´-to-dy	n. 1. guardianship; care	2. legal restraint
cut´	v. 1. divide with sharp tool	2. wounding remark
cute´	adj. 1. attractive	2. clever

1. How many syllables does custody have? _____

2. What part of speech is cute? _____

3. Which syllable is accented in custard? _____

4. Which definition of cut means "her words cut me like a knife"? _____

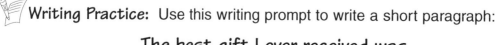 **Writing Practice:** Use this writing prompt to write a short paragraph:

The best gift I ever received was...

Math Practice: Fractions

Simplify all fractions to their lowest terms. Then solve problem 5.

1. $$\frac{10}{12} =$$	2. $$\frac{7}{42} =$$	3. $$\frac{9}{15} =$$
4. $$\frac{14}{20} =$$		5. A can of vegetable soup contains 13 ounces. How many ounces are there in 57 cans? _____

Language Practice: Spelling

Circle the word with the correct spelling.

1. receive   recieve

2. pade   paid

3. rember   remember

4. efficient   eficcient

5. baloon   balloon

6. vacuum   vaccuum

7. ancient   anceint

8. myriad   miriad

Writing Practice: What is your favorite school subject? Why?

Name _____

Math Practice: Geometry

Solve the problems below.

1. YZ is _____ a. 7" c. diameter b. radius d. 10"	2. 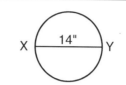 XY is _____ a. 7" c. diameter b. radius d. 10"	3. diameter of #1 is _____ a. 7" c. diameter b. radius d. 10"
4. radius of #2 is _____ a. 7" c. diameter b. radius d. 10"	5. The five members of the wrestling team weigh 102 lbs., 110 lbs., 113 lbs., 114 lbs., and 126 lbs. What is their average weight? _____	

Language Practice: Punctuation

Circle the words that need hyphens. Add the hyphens.

picnic table   class president   merry go round   mortal like

best known   one half   father in law   twenty one

nose dive   mountain range   parking lot   open house

 Writing Practice: Write a story about a dog doing tricks.

Math Practice: Multiplication/Decimals

Solve each problem below.

1.	2.	3.
4.2 x 0.6	0.73 x 4	1.6 x 3.7

4.	5. What is the mode of Sarah's history grades if she had the following grades? Sarah's history grades: 77, 58, 82, 95, 65, 100, 96, 95
1.06 x 5	_____

Language Practice: Punctuation

Add commas where needed.

1. My sister brother and cousin went to camp with me.

2. Jim my uncle took us last week.

3. Emily said "Let's go back next year."

4. I want this book but I will have to read it later.

5. We went to the library to the grocery store and then back home.

6. The poodle which is noted for its small size can be a great pet.

Writing Practice: Use this writing prompt to write a short paragraph:

My favorite belonging is...

Math Practice: Division/Decimals

Solve the problems below.

1. $3\overline{)5.52}$	2. $4\overline{)8.24}$	3. $5\overline{)6.35}$

4. $6\overline{)7.68}$	5. What is the median of the scores in Mr. Field's German class if they were the following scores: 100, 65, 60, 95, 80, 85, 65, 80, 90, 95, 75? _____

Language Practice: Possessives

Write C if a possessive is used correctly. Write I if it is used incorrectly.

_____ 1. a few of Anna's friends

_____ 2. the science teachers' meetings

_____ 3. the books' author

_____ 4. the childrens' rooms

_____ 5. the cat's litter box

_____ 6. a box of women's clothes

Writing Practice: Use this writing prompt to write a short paragraph:

The thing I like best about myself is...

Math Practice: Multiplication

Find the LCM (lowest common multiple) of each pair of numbers. Then solve problem 5.

1. 4 and 6: _____	2. 3 and 5: _____	3. 4 and 8: _____
4. 5 and 6: _____	5. What is the range in these numbers? 45, 82, 63, 51, 78 _____	

Language Practice: Prepositions

Circle the underlined word that is a preposition.

1. <u>Do</u> not put <u>your</u> books <u>on</u> the <u>floor</u>.

2. He <u>was</u> <u>looking</u> <u>at</u> the <u>picture</u> on the <u>wall</u>.

3. We could <u>see</u> the <u>smoke</u> <u>from</u> the <u>building</u>.

4. The <u>children</u> <u>hid</u> <u>behind</u> the <u>trees</u>.

5. <u>This</u> <u>present</u> is <u>for</u> <u>my</u> mother.

6. I <u>went</u> to the zoo <u>after</u> <u>school</u> <u>yesterday</u>.

Writing Practice: What would life on Earth be like if dinosaurs had never become extinct?

Math Practice: Fractions

Find the LCD (lowest common denominator) of each pair of fractions. Then solve problem 5.

1. $\dfrac{1}{2}$ and $\dfrac{2}{3}$: _____	2. $\dfrac{3}{9}$ and $\dfrac{1}{3}$: _____	3. $\dfrac{6}{10}$ and $\dfrac{3}{4}$: _____

4. $\dfrac{1}{4}$ and $\dfrac{3}{7}$: _____

5. Jean, Jane, June, Joy, and Jill are in line at the bookstore. Joy is beside Jean. Jill is in front of Jane, but behind Jean. And June is between Jill and Jane. What order are they lined up?

_____

_____

Language Practice: Sentences

Determine if each sentence is complex or compound.

_____ 1. After the ballgame was over, I went home.

_____ 2. Angie went to church, and she saw her friend.

_____ 3. Before they left for the circus, they had lunch.

_____ 4. The movie was long, but we stayed till it was over.

_____ 5. The hot dog looked good, so I ate it.

_____ 6. When Bill was in his room, he could hear his sister on the phone.

 Writing Practice: Use this writing prompt to write a short paragraph:

Once when I was at my grandparents' house, I saw...

Math Practice: Measurement

Circle the reasonable measurement for each of the listed items. Then solve problem 5.

1. width of a bulletin board	2. trip from Cleveland to Columbus	3. length of your finger
a. kilometer	a. kilometer	a. kilometer
b. meter	b. meter	b. meter
c. millimeter	c. millimeter	c. millimeter
d. centimeter	d. centimeter	d. centimeter

4. width of your desk	5. Camille has a portfolio of her drawings. It has 32 pages and each page has four drawings. How many drawings are in her portfolio?
a. kilometer	
b. meter	
c. millimeter	
d. centimeter	_____

Language Practice: Analogies

Write the word to complete each analogy.

1. pen : draw as boat : _____   hot

2. give : take as cold : _____   remote

3. rain : umbrella as leaves : _____   tools

4. computer : keys as television: _____   neigh

5. book : pages as tool box : _____   sailing

6. kitten : meow as horse : _____   rake

Writing Practice: Use this writing prompt to write a short paragraph:

My friend called me on the phone to tell me that...

Name

Math Practice: Ratios

Write the ratio for each problem. Then solve problem 5.

1. shaded to nonshaded	2. X's to O's	3. numbers in a telephone number to numbers in a zip code

1. shaded to nonshaded

_____

2. X's to O's

OOOXXXOOO

XXOOXXOOX

_____

3. numbers in a telephone number to numbers in a zip code

_____

4. girls to boys in your class

_____

5. The neighborhood grocery store donated 110 cartons of eggs to the school's annual egg hunt. If there are 12 eggs in a carton, how many total eggs are there?

_____

Language Practice: Prefix/Suffix

Underline the base word in each word.

1. unwelcomed

2. unlovely

3. misquoted

4. misunderstood

5. renewed

6. disliked

7. misinterpreted

8. nonmetallic

Writing Practice: What are good leadership traits?

Math Practice: Fractions

Circle the correct answer for each unknown. Then solve problem 5.

1. $\dfrac{4}{5} = \dfrac{?}{10}$ 5 6 7 8	**2.** $\dfrac{?}{8} = \dfrac{28}{32}$ 5 6 7 8	**3.** $\dfrac{2}{3} = \dfrac{14}{?}$ 20 21 22 23

4. $\dfrac{11}{?} = \dfrac{22}{40}$ 20 21 22 23	**5.** Mr. Roberts bought T-shirts for his classroom of 27 students. If the total amount was $357.75, how much did each shirt cost? _____

Language Practice: Spelling

Circle the correctly spelled form of each word.

1.	greedly	greedily	greedlly
2.	chillily	chillie	chilly
3.	batty	battey	battie
4.	riding	ridding	rideing
5.	fortunatly	fortunately	fortunatelly
6.	hideing	hidding	hiding

 Writing Practice: Write a descriptive paragraph about your neighborhood and community.

Name _____

Math Practice: Variables

Solve each problem below.

1. $y + 19 = 42$	**2.** $26 - b = 14$	**3.** $23 + x = 50$
$y = $ _____	$b = $ _____	$x = $ _____

4.
$$\frac{24}{n} = 6$$
$n = $ _____

5. The decorating committee bought crepe paper for the school party. If the total cost was $15.87, how many rolls did they buy at 69¢ each?

_____

Language Practice: Spelling

Choose the correctly spelled word.

1. laid — layed — layied
2. hankerchief — handkerchief — handerchief
3. forty — fourty — fourtty
4. daugter — dauther — daughter
5. farer — farther — farthor
6. running — runing — runnying

Writing Practice: Use this writing prompt to write a short paragraph:

Things I like in a friend...

Name _____

Math Practice: Exponents

For problems 1 and 2, rewrite each problem in exponent form. For problems 3 and 4, rewrite each problem in factored form.

1.	2.	3.
3 x 3 x 3 x 3 x 3 = _____	16 cubed = _____	5^4 = _____

4.	5. Meg ran 3 ½ miles on Tuesday and 4 ⅖ miles on Thursday. How many miles did she run in all?
24^2 = _____	_____

Language Practice: Writing Practice

Write a tongue twister poem.

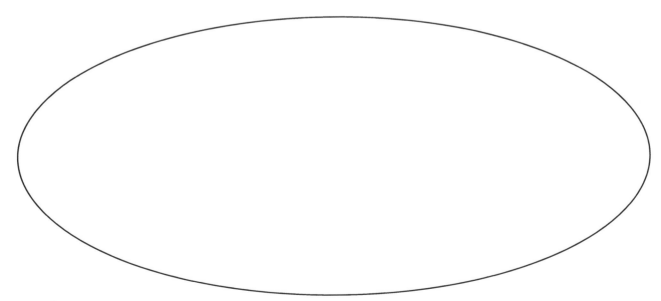

Writing Practice: Write a name poem using a classmate's first name.

Name

Math Practice: Comparing Numbers

For problems 1 and 2, arrange fractions from least to greatest. For problems 3 and 4, arrange fractions from greatest to least. Then solve problem 5.

1. $\dfrac{1}{5}$ $\dfrac{1}{2}$ $\dfrac{1}{3}$ $\dfrac{1}{6}$	2. $\dfrac{2}{3}$ $\dfrac{1}{4}$ $\dfrac{3}{4}$ $\dfrac{1}{3}$	3. $\dfrac{3}{9}$ $\dfrac{5}{35}$ $\dfrac{4}{16}$ $\dfrac{6}{30}$

4. $\dfrac{3}{5}$ $\dfrac{1}{2}$ $\dfrac{2}{6}$ $\dfrac{1}{5}$	5. If Bob has 4⅔ boxes of party favors left over from a party and gives Cindy ½ of them, how much do each get?

Language Practice: Adverbs

Circle the underlined word which is an adverb.

1. Buddy <u>said</u> that <u>math</u> <u>class</u> would start <u>soon</u>.

2. The <u>pizza</u> <u>was</u> delivered <u>promptly</u> at <u>our</u> house.

3. <u>Our</u> <u>team</u> played <u>well</u> <u>at</u> the tournament.

4. The turtle <u>walked</u> <u>slowly</u> <u>across</u> the <u>street</u>.

5. The <u>child</u> <u>ran</u> <u>away</u> <u>from</u> his mother.

6. He <u>searched</u> <u>longer</u> <u>than</u> <u>his</u> friends.

Writing Practice: Why is it important to eat balanced, nutritional meals during the day?

Math Practice: Number Properties

Match the correct multiplication property for each equation.

1. $9 \times 3 = 3 \times 9$ _____	**2.** $(7 \times 5) \times 6 = 7 \times (5 \times 6)$ _____	**3.** $16 \times 0 = 0$ _____

4. $4 \times 23 = 4 \times 20 + 4 \times 3$ _____	a. commutative c. distributive b. zero property d. associative

Language Practice: Kinds of Sentences

Match sentences to their descriptions.

_____ 1. Have you been to Disney World?

_____ 2. Last summer we went to Kentucky.   a. declarative

_____ 3. Wow, the scenery was beautiful!   b. interrogative

_____ 4. We drove our new car on the trip.   c. imperative

_____ 5. "Fasten your seatbelt," Mom told us.   d. exclamatory

_____ 6. What a great vacation we had!

Writing Practice: Use this writing prompt to write a short paragraph:

If I could star in a television show, it would be ...

Name _____

Math Practice: Geometry

Match the correct term for each pair of shapes.

1.	2.	3.

1. _____

2. _____

3. _____

4.

_____

a. similar

b. congruent

c. similar and congruent

d. neither similar nor congruent

Language Practice: Punctuation

Add the correct punctuation for each sentence.

1. That movie was interesting ___

2. Who are the main characters ___

3. The movie last week was great ___

4. I like movies about real people ___

5. Did you see *Titanic* ___

6. It was so sad at times ___

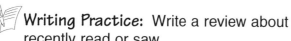 **Writing Practice:** Write a review about a movie, TV program, or book that you recently read or saw.

Math Practice: Geometry

Determine if each figure has a line of symmetry. Write symmetrical or not symmetrical for each problem. Then solve problem 5.

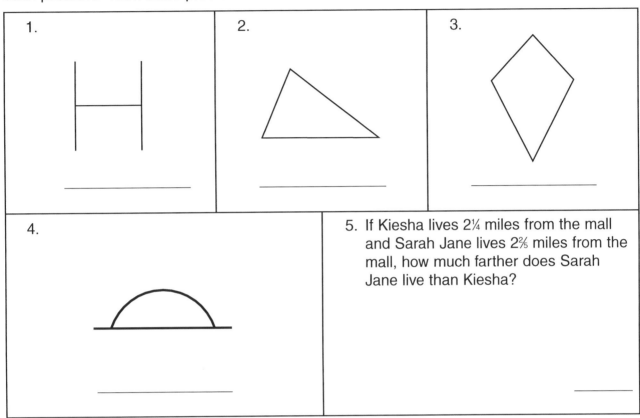

5. If Kiesha lives 2¼ miles from the mall and Sarah Jane lives 2⅖ miles from the mall, how much farther does Sarah Jane live than Kiesha?

Language Practice: Plurals

Circle the correctly spelled plural form of each word.

1. toy   toyies   toyes   toys

2. boss   boss's   bosses   boss

3. deer   deers   deer   deeres

4. fox   foxes   foxs   foxen

5. knife   knives   knifes   knife's

6. lunch   lunchs   lunch's   lunches

Writing Practice: What do you do when it rains and you can't go outside?

Name

Math Practice: Geometry

Find the area of each right triangle. (Remember, A = 1/2 bh.) Then solve problem 5.

1.

4 cm

8 cm

A = _____

2.

15 yd

12 yd

A = _____

3.

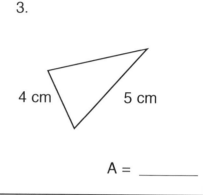

4 cm   5 cm

A = _____

4.

3.6 in.

2.5 in.

A = _____

5. On Saturday, Brad got up at 9:00 A. M. If he spent 3½ hours doing yard work, ¾ hours eating lunch, and 2¼ hours playing baseball, what time is it?

_____

Language Practice: Possessives

Underline the possessive noun in each sentence.

1. She is coming over for Jenna's party.

2. The Egyptians' pyramids are so enormous.

3. Those five girls' dolls are made of china.

4. The bird's nest is on the top branch of the tree.

5. The students' desks were rearranged differently today.

6. The teacher's desk was all the way in the back.

 Writing Practice: What board game do you like to play? Write a paragraph about playing the game.

Math Practice: Mean, Median, Mode

If Tamara's math test scores are 96, 92, 83, 71, 83, and 91, calculate the answer for each problem. Then solve problem 5.

1. mean	2. median	3. mode
_____	_____	_____

4. range	5. Mr. Garcia bought a new car. His payments for 48 months are $185.00 per month. What is the price of the car?
_____	_____

Language Practice: Pronouns

Circle the underlined pronoun in each sentence.

1. The <u>coach</u> <u>was</u> <u>talking</u> to <u>him</u>.

2. He said <u>for</u> the <u>team</u> to put on <u>their</u> uniforms.

3. <u>They</u> would <u>be</u> practicing <u>after</u> school <u>tomorrow</u>.

4. <u>We</u> <u>had</u> an assembly in <u>school</u> <u>today</u>.

5. <u>It</u> was <u>about</u> <u>Black</u> History <u>month</u>.

6. My friend <u>said</u>, "<u>I</u> have <u>seen</u> the program <u>before</u>."

Writing Practice: Can you cook? Do you like to cook? Write about something you can cook or something you'd like to learn to cook.

Math Practice: Roman Numerals

Solve each problem and write each answer in Roman numerals. Then solve problem 5.

1. LXIII – XXXV = _____	2. XLI – XXIX = _____	3. CD – XCIX = _____

4. MCMLV – MCCXI = _____	5. Kelly and Scott planted 10 tomato plants the first year. If they add 2 every year, how many will they plant in 6 years? _____

Language Practice: Verbs

Select the correct verb to complete each sentence.

1. We (eaten, ate) at Burger King yesterday.

2. The dogs (is running, are running) down the street.

3. Our class (will attend, are attend) the assembly on Monday.

4. We have (come, came) to see it.

5. Jon (tied, tyed) the rope to the tree.

6. He (was, were) making a swing with a tire.

 Writing Practice: If you were allowed to be a judge for a day, what kind of changes would you make? What kind of laws would you create?

Name _____

Math Practice: Variables

Solve each problem below.

1.	2.	3.
If $a = 3$ and $b = \dfrac{1}{2}$, then $3a + b = ?$ ___	If $a = 2.3$ and $b = 4$, then $2a + 2b = ?$ ___	$x - 1\dfrac{1}{2} = 6\dfrac{3}{4}$ $x = ?$ ___

4.	5. Leo and Larry work at 2 different theaters. Leo's theater employs 12 people, and Larry's theater employs 2/3 as many as Leo's. How many people does Larry's theater employ?
$6m = 24$ $m =$ ___	___

Language Practice: Subjects

Write simple or compound once you identify the type of subject used in each sentence.

_____ 1. Pauline went to the mall and bought a sweater.

_____ 2. Sandy and Jason found a stray dog.

_____ 3. They nursed the dog back to health.

_____ 4. Mom and Dad played Scrabble® with us.

_____ 5. The children ran and played on the playground.

_____ 6. We all like to eat pizza.

✍ **Writing Practice:** Describe a fun day at the beach.

Name _____

Math Practice: Comparing Numbers

Compare each pair of numbers and write < or >. Then solve problem 5.

1. 18 ◯ – 5	**2.** – 12 ◯ – 3	**3.** – 4 ◯ 0

4. 23 ◯ – 23

5. Joey has 24 CDs. Kyle has 3/4 as many CDs as Joey. How many does Kyle have?

_____

Language Practice: Adjectives

Choose the correct adjective to complete each sentence.

1. This is the (slower, slowest) turtle I've ever seen.

2. Her dog is (playfuller, more playful) than mine.

3. Andy is the (good, best) football player in the past two years.

4. It was the (larger, largest) monster I had ever seen.

5. The bathroom is (darker, darkest) than the kitchen.

6. She lived (closer, closest) to me than Tara did.

 Writing Practice: Write 10 adjectives that describe you. Then write 5 sentences with 5 of these adjectives.

Name _____

Math Practice: Square Roots

Solve for the square root of each number. Then solve problem 5.

1. $\sqrt{16} =$	2. $\sqrt{100} =$	3. $\sqrt{225} =$
4. $\sqrt{529} =$	5. The school cafeteria baked 420 rolls. Each package had 8 rolls. How many packages did they use? _____	

Language Practice: Adverbs

Choose the correct adverb to make the sentence complete.

1. The moon shone (more brilliant, brilliantly) last night.

2. The rabbit ran (quickly, quicklier) through the meadow.

3. She needs to talk (louder, more loud) so we can hear her.

4. We jogged (farther, farthest) than ever before.

5. Of the 25 science fair projects, Jodi received the (less, least) number of awards and ribbons.

6. Mom said we could have a snack as (soon, sooner) as we did our chores.

Writing Practice: Write a paragraph about your favorite season and your least favorite season.

Math Practice: Geometry

Use the graph to find the matching point to each coordinate given.

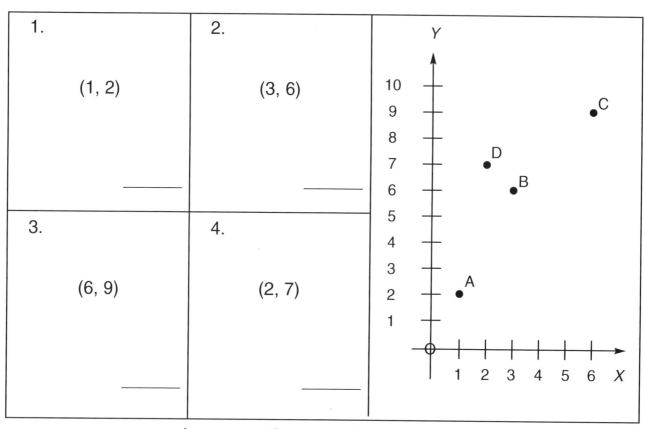

1. (1, 2) _____

2. (3, 6) _____

3. (6, 9) _____

4. (2, 7) _____

Language Practice: Contractions

Circle the correct contraction.

1. you will youw'll you'll

2. she would shew'd she'd

3. will not won't willn't

4. let us let's lets'

5. they have they'ave they've

6. I am I'am I'm

 Writing Practice: You have been asked to design a new national monument to be displayed at a state park. Describe what your monument looks like and what it represents.

Name _____

Math Practice: Mental Math

Solve each problem below.

1. 20% of 40 _____	2. 25% of 100 _____	3. 50% of 30 _____
4. $33\frac{1}{3}$ % of 99 _____	5. If your eyes blink about 20 times per minute, how many times will you blink in an hour? _____	

Language Practice: Cause/Effect

Underline the word that signals a cause or effect relationship.

1. The teacher gave a retest because so many students were absent.

2. Since we had a mild winter, we will have a hot summer.

3. I didn't feel safe when the news said a tornado was coming.

4. If you work hard, you should do well on the test.

5. As the day went on, the rain turned to snow.

6. The bicycle wouldn't go since the tires were flat.

 Writing Practice: How do you feel when you accomplish a goal that you worked hard to achieve? Give a recent example of a goal that you have set and met.

Name _____

Math Practice: Geometry

Use the graph to answer the questions.

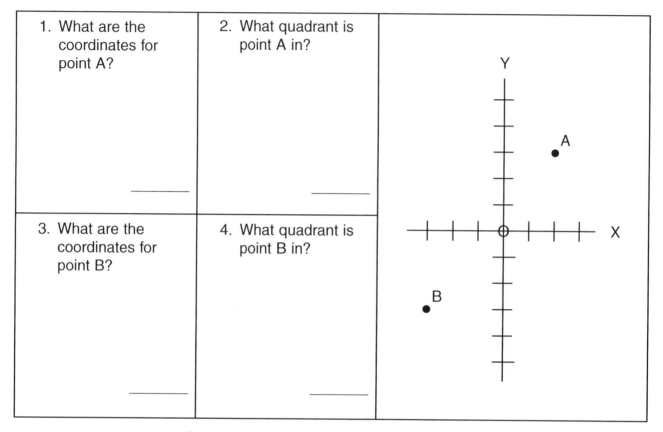

1. What are the coordinates for point A? _____	2. What quadrant is point A in? _____
3. What are the coordinates for point B? _____	4. What quadrant is point B in? _____

Language Practice: Context Clues

Circle the best definition for each underlined word.

1. The dog wouldn't listen; it was <u>mulish</u>.
   a. obedient   b. stubborn

2. We moved <u>gingerly</u> across the swinging bridge.
   a. afraid   b. cautiously

3. Stephanie was <u>exhilarated</u> when everyone yelled, "Surprise!"
   a. happy   b. upset

4. The <u>drought</u> was a concern of farmers for their crops.
   a. lack of weather   b. lack of water

5. The violence was so <u>horrid</u>, we left before the movie was over.
   a. strange   b. terrible

6. Mrs. Nations was able to <u>visualize</u> her students when they won the contest.
   a. see   b. hear

 Writing Practice: Write a paragraph about winning a contest. What was the contest, and why did you win?

Name _____

Math Practice: Percents

Calculate the percent. Then solve problem 5.

1. 8% of 20 _____	2. 6% of 16 _____	3. 100% of 239 _____
4. 12% of 65 _____		5. Mrs. Coleman begins her first class at 8:45 A.M. If her next class starts 52 minutes later, what time does it start? _____

Language Practice: Dictionary Skills

Read the entry and definitions. Identify the best meaning for each underlined word.

> hold *v.* 1. have in the hand.   2. keep from moving or changing.   3. embrace.
> 4. contain.   5. remain firm or fixed.   6. cargo space (also, holding or held).

_____ a. We had to hold our luggage for 1 hour.

_____ b. It couldn't be put in the holding area.

_____ c. We held our niece before boarding the plane.

_____ d. Our eyes held each other anxiously.

_____ e. Finally, we held our breath as the plane took off.

_____ f. Our carry-on bag held pictures of our visit.

Writing Practice: If you could create a new language and alphabet, what would it be like? How would it be useful for people?

Math Practice: Probability

Refer to the spinner to answer the following questions. What is the probability the spinner will land on the choices?

1. math _____	**2.** reading or spelling _____
3. anything but band _____	**4.** subject that begins with the letter "s" _____

Spinner with sections: band, math, science, reading, social studies, spelling

Language Practice: Study Skills

Where would you find the following information?

_____ 1. map of Antarctica

_____ 2. meaning of diligent   a. atlas

_____ 3. states that border Tennessee   b. encyclopedia

_____ 4. information about the Middle Ages   c. dictionary

_____ 5. another word for "rotate"   d. thesaurus

_____ 6. who invented the pencil

 Writing Practice: Would you or wouldn't you like to have lived on the prairie during the early colonial years?

Math Practice: Probability

For problem 1, what is the probability of tossing a coin and getting the result listed? For problems 2, 3, and 4, what is the probability that the spinner will land on the results listed?

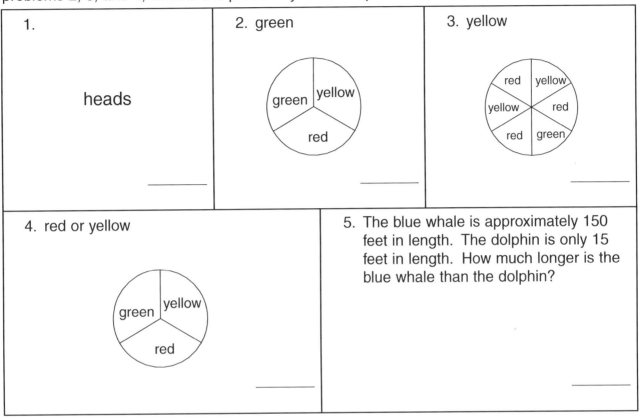

1.

heads

_____

2. green

_____

3. yellow

_____

4. red or yellow

_____

5. The blue whale is approximately 150 feet in length. The dolphin is only 15 feet in length. How much longer is the blue whale than the dolphin?

_____

Language Practice: Main Idea

Find the main idea in the paragraph.

A cat is an interesting animal. It spends its day either sleeping or snooping. It takes as many as 20 catnaps a day. When it is awake, it walks around searching for something to do. What an unusual animal!

1. The main idea is _____.

   a. cats eat

   b. cats sleep

   c. cats are interesting

2. One detail is _____.

   a. cats like to eat

   b. cats like to sleep

   c. cats are different colors

Write 2 more sentences that would be a detail of the main idea.

3. _____

4. _____

 **Writing Practice:** Write a paragraph describing another unusual animal.

Name _____

Math Practice: Mixed Computation

Solve each problem below.

1. (35 ÷ 5) + 6 = _____	2. (12 − 8) x 4 = _____	3. 15 − (21 ÷ 3) = _____

4. 8 x (4 x 2) = _____	5. What is the perimeter of a soccer field 110 yds. by 80 yds.? What is the area? perimeter = _____ area = _____

Language Practice: Conjunctions

Circle the conjunction in each sentence.

1. Jose and Maria are exchange students from Mexico.

2. They enjoy American food, but they like Mexican food the best.

3. Maria's mom used to make tortillas or tacos everyday for lunch.

4. Now she cooks hamburgers or hot dogs some days.

5. They like school but have difficulty with the English language.

6. Math and science are most interesting to them.

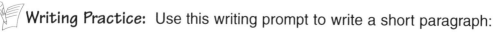 Writing Practice: Use this writing prompt to write a short paragraph:

The sky was a clear blue, and the clouds above looked like...

Math Practice: Estimation

Estimate by rounding to the nearest thousand. Then solve problem 5.

1.	2.	3.
12,378 − 9,629 est. _____	4,862 − 2,153 est. _____	34,692 − 18,023 est. _____

5.	5. In 1840, 458 patents were given to inventors, but 4 years earlier only 103 were given. How many more were given in 1840 than in 1836?
6,823 + 8,346 est. _____	_____

Language Practice: Clauses

Underline the dependent clause in each sentence.

1. When he was a young boy, he moved to Wyoming.

2. Until baseball season is here, Joshua plays basketball.

3. He watched quietly as the paramedic helped his brother.

4. Because their car broke down, he had to walk to school.

5. I waited for an hour before the bus came.

6. I jumped back when the door slowly opened.

Writing Practice: Imagine that you are an astronomer and discover a new planet. Describe what the physical features of the planet are and what life on it is like.

Name _____

Math Practice: Division

Calculate the quotients. Then solve problem 5.

1. $60\overline{)417}$	2. $23\overline{)281}$	3. $51\overline{)673}$

4. $40\overline{)837}$	5. Andie is making a quilt that is 1.5 meters long and 1.25 meters wide. What is the area? _____

Language Practice: Forms of Literature

Match the form with its description.

_____ 1. an informational story about real things   a. legend

_____ 2. a made-up story   b. fiction

_____ 3. a story of a person's life written by someone else   c. poetry

_____ 4. a story that has come down from the past   d. biography

_____ 5. a story of a person's life written by the person   e. nonfiction

_____ 6. a composition written in verse   f. autobiography

 Writing Practice: Imagine that you are a zoologist and have recently discovered a new species of animal. Describe the physical features of this new species and how and where you discovered it.

Math Practice: Factors

Find the GCF (greatest common factor) for each pair of numbers. Then solve problem 5.

1. 30 and 35 _____	2. 35 and 28 _____	3. 52 and 78 _____

4. 18 and 90 _____	5. Jefferson Middle School has 760 students and 45% are girls. How many girls are there? boys? girls _____ boys _____

Language Practice: Fact or Opinion

Decide whether the statement is fact or opinion.

_____ 1. Columbus discovered America in 1492.

_____ 2. Florida is the best place to go on vacation.

_____ 3. Evergreen trees stay green year round.

_____ 4. Mars is the best candy bar.

_____ 5. The elm tree is the best tree for birds to live in.

_____ 6. Large animals should not be kept in zoos.

Writing Practice: Rewrite "Jack in the Beanstalk" from the giant's point of view.

Name _____

Math Practice: Division/Fractions

Solve each problem below.

1. $\dfrac{2}{3} \div \dfrac{12}{18} =$	**2.** $\dfrac{4}{5} \div \dfrac{6}{8} =$	**3.** $\dfrac{7}{12} \div \dfrac{3}{4} =$
4. $\dfrac{2}{5} \div \dfrac{9}{12} =$	**5.** The temperature in Minnesota was -5° F. If it dropped 4°, what would be the new temperature? _____	

Language Practice: Main Idea

Write a category for each group of words.

1. tree
   children
   grass
   mold
   category _____

3. peanuts
   potatoes
   treasure
   fossil
   category _____

2. rose
   carnation
   marigold
   daffodil
   category _____

4. hairbrush
   comb
   headband
   barrette
   category _____

 Writing Practice: Why is it important to protect endangered animals and rain forests?

Math Practice: Patterns

Find the missing integers. Then solve problem 5.

1.	2.	3.
-29, ____, ____, -26	-307, ____, -303,____	-10, -5, ____, ____

4.	5. Marla had a bank balance of $462. She wrote checks for $82, $61, $17, and $43. What is her new balance?
-1,000, ____, -980, ____	_____

Language Practice: Figurative Language

Match each term with its description.

_____ 1. repetition of beginning sounds

_____ 2. exaggeration

_____ 3. using "like" and "as" to compare two things

_____ 4. nonhumans given human characteristics

_____ 5. comparing two things without using "like" or "as"

_____ 6. a word that imitates an actual sound

a. hyperbole

b. simile

c. alliteration

d. personification

e. onomatopoeia

f. metaphor

 Writing Practice: Write a descriptive paragraph of what a role model is and who is one in your life.

Math Practice: Addition

Solve each problem below.

1. 15 + -10 + -5 = _____	2. -17 + 6 + -3 = _____	3. 24 + -27 + -6 = _____
4. 32 + -6 + -5 = _____	5. At midnight, the temperature was 4°F below zero. By 7:00 A. M. it was then 15°F above zero. What was the change in temperature? _____	

Language Practice: Compound Words

Match two words that make a compound word. Then write the new word.

day	space
class	head
up	week
mates	dream
right	ship
end	ache

1. _____

2. _____

3. _____

4. _____

5. _____

6. _____

 Writing Practice: Write a story using these compound words: moonlight, someone, and footprints.

Math Practice: Geometry

Use the graph and write the matching point to each set of coordinates for each problem.

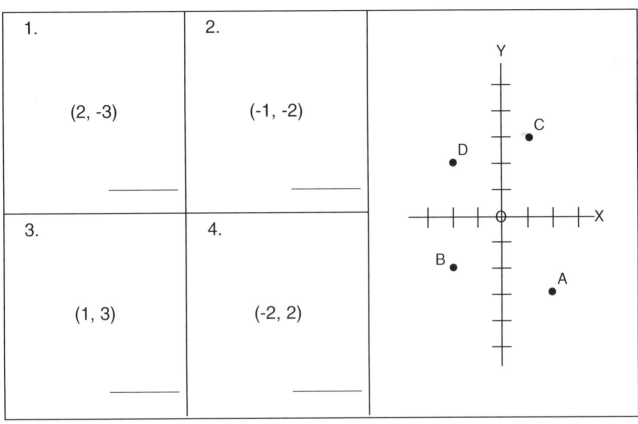

1. (2, -3) _____	2. (-1, -2) _____
3. (1, 3) _____	4. (-2, 2) _____

Language Practice: Nouns

Write a noun for each letter in "nouns." Then write a sentence with each word.

1. N: _____

2. O: _____

3. U: _____

4. N: _____

5. S: _____

 Writing Practice: Write a review of a restaurant that you have recently been to. Be sure to describe what sort of food is served there and where it is located.

Name _____

Math Practice: Geometry

Calculate the volume for each problem. (Remember, V = l x w x h)

1.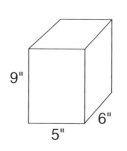

9"
6"
5"

V = _____

2.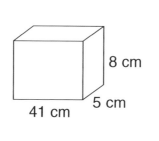

8 cm
5 cm
41 cm

V = _____

3. S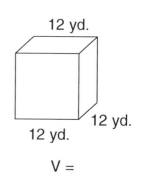

12 yd.
12 yd.
12 yd.

V = _____

4.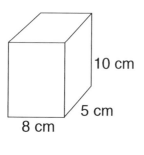

10 cm
5 cm
8 cm

V = _____

5. A cereal box is 6" by 3" by 9". What is the volume?

_____

Language Practice: Syllables

Divide these words into syllables. Be sure to include the accent marks.

1. danger _____

2. eagle _____

3. mystery _____

4. transparent _____

5. receiver _____

6. overpass _____

 Writing Practice: Have you ever felt like you were in danger? Write a paragraph about what happened and how you felt.

Math Practice: Ratios

Draw pictures to represent each ratio. Then solve problem 5.

1. $\frac{2}{3}$	2. $\frac{4}{5}$	3. $\frac{1}{4}$
4. $\frac{3}{8}$		5. Tracey earns $90 in 12 hours. How much does she earn each hour? _____

Language Practice: Main Idea

Read the story and answer the questions.

Morris's parents gave him a surprise birthday party. All of his friends from school were there. They ate pizza and had ice cream and cake afterward. He received many presents, but his ball cap signed by his favorite baseball player was his favorite gift.

1. The main idea is _____

    a. they all ate cake and ice cream.

    b. his parents gave him a party.

    c. his friends came to his party.

2. One detail is _____

    a. he received presents.

    b. his friends yelled, "Surprise."

    c. he celebrated his eleventh birthday.

Write two more sentences that would be a detail of the main idea.

3. _____

4. _____

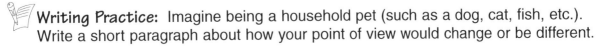 **Writing Practice:** Imagine being a household pet (such as a dog, cat, fish, etc.). Write a short paragraph about how your point of view would change or be different.

Math Practice: Time

Solve the problems below.

1.	2.	3.
$2\frac{1}{2}$ hours after 6 A.M. _____	3 hours 45 minutes before 7 P.M. _____	420 seconds = _____ minutes

4.	5. Find the batting average of Ty Cobb. He hit 4,191 times out of 11,429 times at bat.
35 days = _____ weeks	_____

Language Practice: Synonyms/Antonyms

Determine whether each pair of words is a synonym (S) or an antonym (A).

_____ 1. grief – mourning

_____ 2. flood – drought

_____ 3. establish – settle

_____ 4. oval – oblong

_____ 5. wander – halt

_____ 6. ugly – hideous

_____ 7. special – extraordinary

_____ 8. thick – sparse

Writing Practice: If you could design your own school, describe how it would be different from or similar to the one you currently attend.

Math Practice: Measurement

Solve the problems below.

1.	2.	3.
___ pecks = 24 quarts	20 pecks = ___ bushels	18 pints = ___ quarts

4.	5. Sheila's mom bought 4 candy bars for 69¢. How much would it cost if she bought enough for Sheila's class of 24 students?
80 pints = ___ pecks	_____

Language Practice: Proofreading

Rewrite the sentences correctly.

1. one of jeffs favorite movies is a bug's life

   _____

2. what is you favoritte movie

   _____

3. mom and I go for a walk threw yellowstone national park

   _____

4. we seen too deers on the path

   _____

5. would you lik to here my cousin terrys poem

   _____

6. the road less traveled are it's name

   _____

 Writing Practice: What would life be like if you were two inches tall?

Math Practice: Rounding

Round to the nearest underlined and boldfaced digit. Then solve problem 5.

1.	2.	3.
13.4<u>7</u>3	<u>0</u>.6075	5.<u>2</u>08
___	___	___

4.	5. Out of 120 students, 30 said they drank milk at lunch. What percent of the students drank milk?
92<u>3</u>.63	
___	___

Language Practice: Comprehension

Answer the questions about the following paragraph:

The Loch Ness monster is said to live in Scotland. It got its name from living in a lake, or loch. The lake is very deep and is dark and cold. Many people have claimed to have seen the monster; however, no one is really sure if it really exists.

1. What country is the Loch Ness monster from? _____

2. How did the monster get its name? _____

3. What three adjectives are used to describe the lake? _____

_____

4. Does the monster really exist? _____

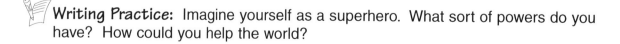 **Writing Practice:** Imagine yourself as a superhero. What sort of powers do you have? How could you help the world?

Math Practice: Comparing Numbers

For problems 1 and 2, order the numbers from least to greatest. For problems 3 and 4, order the numbers from greatest to least. Then solve problem 5.

1. -7, 0, 17, -17, 7 _____ _____	**2.** 15, 0, -13, 3, -5 _____ _____	**3.** 15,000.01, 15,001.01, 15,001.10, 15,010.01 _____ _____ _____ _____

4. 1,234.3, 12.343, 1.2343, 123.43 _____ _____ _____ _____	**5.** Hilda takes 20 minutes to type her three-page report. If she begins at 3:00 P.M., when will she be finished? _____

Language Practice: Sentences

Circle *yes* if the words make a sentence or *no* if they do not.

yes   no   1. Barry is a cute baby.

yes   no   2. The blue and white car in the garage.

yes   no   3. Candy is sweet.

yes   no   4. A big bus in an accident.

yes   no   5. Like a pizza.

yes   no   6. See my pencil?

Writing Practice: Some people say that all children need to eat a good breakfast before they come to school. Write a persuasive paragraph about this topic.

Math Practice:

Language Practice:

Writing Practice:

©Teacher Created Resources, Inc.

Page 4

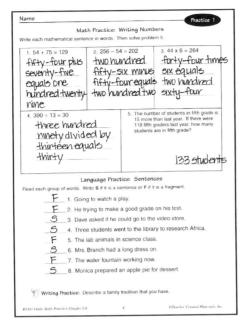

Name _____ Practice 1

Math Practice: Writing Numbers

Write each mathematical sentence in words. Then solve problem 5.

1. 54 + 75 = 129	2. 256 − 54 = 202	3. 44 x 6 = 264
fifty-four plus seventy-five equals one hundred twenty-nine	two hundred fifty-six minus fifty-four equals two hundred two	forty-four times six equals two hundred sixty-four

4. 390 ÷ 13 = 30	5. The number of students in fifth grade is 15 more than last year. If there were 118 fifth graders last year, how many students are in fifth grade?
three hundred ninety divided by thirteen equals thirty	133 students

Language Practice: Sentences

Read each group of words. Write S if it is a sentence or F if it is a fragment.

F 1. Going to watch a play.
F 2. He trying to make a good grade on his test.
S 3. Dave asked if he could go to the video store.
S 4. Three students went to the library to research Africa.
F 5. The lab animals in science class.
S 6. Mrs. Branch had a long dress on.
F 7. The water fountain working now.
S 8. Monica prepared an apple pie for dessert.

Writing Practice: Describe a family tradition that you have.

#3303 Daily Skills Practice–Grades 5-6   4   ©Teacher Created Materials, Inc.

Page 5

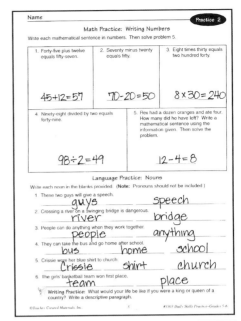

Name _____ Practice 2

Math Practice: Writing Numbers

Write each mathematical sentence in numbers. Then solve problem 5.

1. Forty-five plus twelve equals fifty-seven.	2. Seventy minus twenty equals fifty.	3. Eight times thirty equals two hundred forty.
45 + 12 = 57	70 − 20 = 50	8 x 30 = 240

4. Ninety-eight divided by two equals forty-nine.	5. Rex had a dozen oranges and ate four. How many did he have left? Write a mathematical sentence using the information given. Then solve the problem.
98 ÷ 2 = 49	12 − 4 = 8

Language Practice: Nouns

Write each noun in the blanks provided. (Note: Pronouns should not be included.)

1. These two guys will give a speech.
guys   speech
2. Crossing a river on a swinging bridge is dangerous.
river   bridge
3. People can do anything when they work together.
people   anything
4. They can take the bus and go home after school.
bus   home   school
5. Crissie wore her blue shirt to church.
Crissie   shirt   church
6. The girls' basketball team won first place.
team   place

Writing Practice: What would your life be like if you were a king or queen of a country? Write a descriptive paragraph.

©Teacher Created Materials, Inc.   5   #3303 Daily Skills Practice–Grades 5-6

Page 6

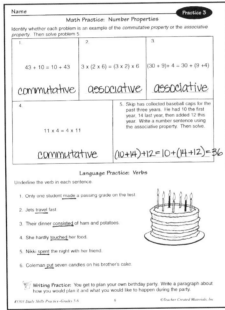

Name _____ Practice 3

Math Practice: Number Properties

Identify whether each problem is an example of the *commutative property* or the *associative property*. Then solve problem 5.

1.	2.	3.
43 + 10 = 10 + 43	3 x (2 x 6) = (3 x 2) x 6	(30 + 9) + 4 = 30 + (9 + 4)
commutative	associative	associative

4.	5. Skip has collected baseball caps for the past three years. He had 10 the first year, 14 last year, then added 12 this year. Write a number sentence using the associative property. Then solve.
11 x 4 = 4 x 11 commutative	(10 + 14) + 12 = 10 + (14 + 12) = 36

Language Practice: Verbs

Underline the verb in each sentence.

1. Only one student made a passing grade on the test.
2. Jets travel fast.
3. Their dinner consisted of ham and potatoes.
4. She hardly touched her food.
5. Nikki spent the night with her friend.
6. Coleman put seven candles on his brother's cake.

Writing Practice: You get to plan your own birthday party. Write a paragraph about how you would plan it and what you would like to happen during the party.

#3303 Daily Skills Practice–Grades 5-6   6   ©Teacher Created Materials, Inc.

Page 7

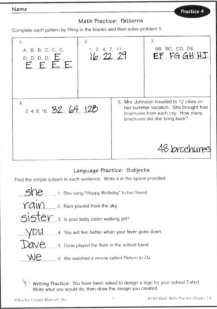

Name _____ Practice 4

Math Practice: Patterns

Complete each pattern by filling in the blanks and then solve problem 5.

1.	2.	3.
A, B, B, C, C, C, D, D, D, D, E. E, E, E	1, 2, 4, 7, 11 16, 22, 29	AB, BC, CD, DE, EF, FG GH HI

4. 2, 4, 8, 16, 32, 64, 128	5. Mrs. Johnston traveled to 12 cities on her summer vacation. She brought four brochures from each city. How many brochures did she bring back?
	48 brochures

Language Practice: Subjects

Find the simple subject in each sentence. Write it in the space provided.

she 1. She sang "Happy Birthday" to her friend.
rain 2. Rain poured from the sky.
sister 3. Is your baby sister walking yet?
you 4. You will feel better when your fever goes down.
Dave 5. Dave played the flute in the school band.
we 6. We watched a movie called *Return to Oz*.

Writing Practice: You have been asked to design a logo for your school T-shirt. Write what you would do, then draw the design you created.

©Teacher Created Materials, Inc.   7   #3303 Daily Skills Practice–Grades 5-6

Page 8

Name _____ Practice 5

Math Practice: Chart

Using the information in the chart, answer the following questions below.

1. How many more dogs were owned in 2000 than 1990?	2. What was the total number of cats and dogs owned in 2000?	3. Which pet had the smallest increase?
340	1,680	bird

4. How many pets were owned in 1990? In 2000?	Pet Population		
1990: 1,296 2000: 1,869	Pet	1990	2000
	Cat	540	718
	Dog	622	962
	Bird	83	110
	Fish	51	79

Language Practice: Sentences

Rewrite each sentence to make more sense.

1. Under the table were her shoes.
Her shoes were under the table.
2. For the party I had to pick her up.
I had to pick her up for the party.
3. Across the room sat Miss Michaels.
Miss Michaels sat across the room.
4. Near the couch was the baby's toy.
The baby's toy was near the couch.
5. For quietly just a moment she sat.
She sat quietly for just a moment.
6. Faster and faster came the runners.
The runners came faster and faster.

Writing Practice: Write a paragraph about a pet you have or a pet you've always wanted.

#3303 Daily Skills Practice–Grades 5-6   8   ©Teacher Created Materials, Inc.

Page 9

Name _____ Practice 6

Math Practice: Estimation

Estimate each answer.

1. About how much more money would you need to buy a sweater that cost $29.95 if you have $15.00?	2. You want to buy paper and 2 pencils for $1.89 and you have $5.00. About how much would your change be?	3. What is the estimated total of students in your class if there are 18 girls and 13 boys?
$15.00	$3.00	30 students

4. How many movie tickets could you buy with a ten dollar bill if each ticket cost $4.00?	5. Sue bought 10 stamps that cost 32¢ each. Estimate how much she paid for her stamps.
2 tickets	$3.00

Language Practice: Punctuation

Add punctuation marks where needed in the following paragraph.

My mother took me to a picnic on Memorial Day. There were so many people there so we had to park far away. We ate the following foods: hot dogs, hamburgers, potato salad, and baked beans. Then it started to rain, so we had to go home.

Writing Practice: What do you think life would be like if people were invisible?

©Teacher Created Materials, Inc.   9   #3303 Daily Skills Practice–Grades 5-6

Page 10

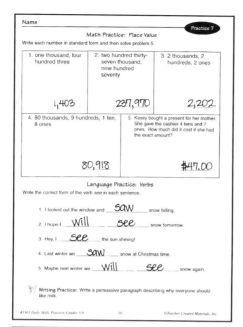

Page 11

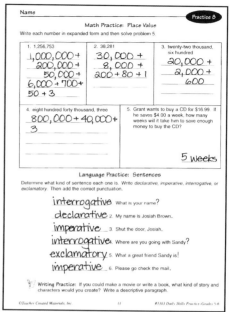

Page 12

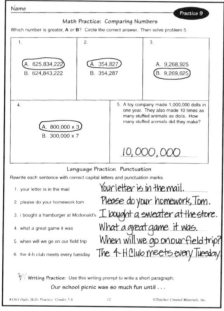

Page 13

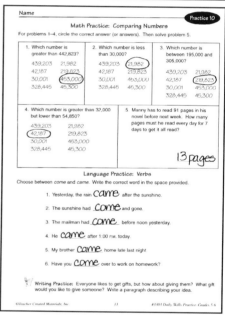

Page 14

Page 15

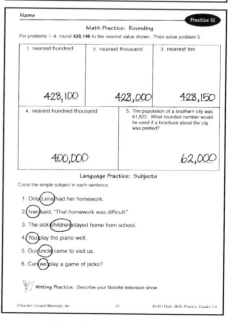

Page 16

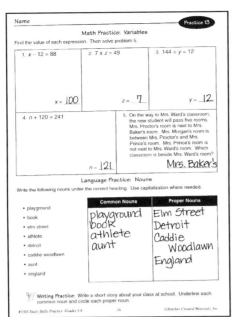

Name _____ Practice 13

Math Practice: Variables

Find the value of each expression. Then solve problem 5.

1. $x - 12 = 88$	2. $7 \times z = 49$	3. $144 \div y = 12$
$x = 100$	$z = 7$	$y = 12$

4. $n + 120 = 241$	5. On the way to Mrs. Ward's classroom, the new student will pass five rooms. Mrs. Proctor's room is next to Mrs. Baker's room. Mrs. Morgan's room is between Mrs. Proctor's and Mrs. Prince's rooms. Mrs. Prince's room is not next to Mrs. Ward's room. Which classroom is beside Mrs. Ward's room?
$n = 121$	Mrs. Baker's

Language Practice: Nouns

Write the following nouns under the correct heading. Use capitalization where needed.

- playground
- book
- elm street
- athlete
- detroit
- caddie woodlawn
- aunt
- ongland

Common Nouns	Proper Nouns
playground book athlete aunt	Elm Street Detroit Caddie Woodlawn England

Writing Practice: Write a short story about your class at school. Underline each common noun and circle each proper noun.

#3303 Daily Skills Practice–Grades 5-6   16   ©Teacher Created Materials, Inc.

Page 17

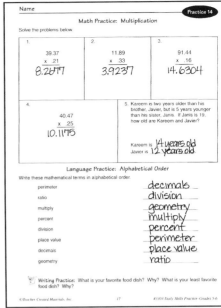

Name _____ Practice 14

Math Practice: Multiplication

Solve the problems below.

1.	2.	3.
39.37 x .21 8.2677	11.89 x .33 3.9237	91.44 x .16 14.6304

4.	5. Kareem is two years older than his brother, Javier, but is 5 years younger than his sister, Janis. If Janis is 19, how old are Kareem and Javier?
40.47 x .25 10.1175	Kareem is 14 years old Javier is 12 years old

Language Practice: Alphabetical Order

Write these mathematical terms in alphabetical order.

perimeter	decimals
ratio	division
multiply	geometry
percent	multiply
division	percent
place value	perimeter
decimals	place value
geometry	ratio

Writing Practice: What is your favorite food dish? Why? What is your least favorite food dish? Why?

©Teacher Created Materials, Inc.   17   #3303 Daily Skills Practice–Grades 5-6

Page 18

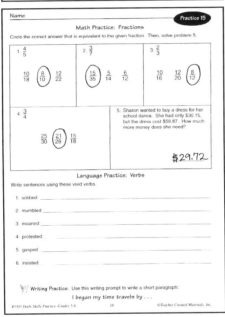

Name _____ Practice 15

Math Practice: Fractions

Circle the correct answer that is equivalent to the given fraction. Then, solve problem 5.

1. $\frac{4}{5}$	2. $\frac{3}{7}$	3. $\frac{2}{3}$
$\frac{10}{18}$ ⊙$\frac{8}{10}$ $\frac{12}{22}$	$\frac{15}{35}$ $\frac{5}{14}$ $\frac{6}{12}$	$\frac{10}{16}$ $\frac{12}{20}$ ⊙$\frac{8}{12}$

4. $\frac{3}{4}$	5. Sharon wanted to buy a dress for her school dance. She had only $30.15, but the dress cost $59.87. How much more money does she need?
$\frac{25}{30}$ ⊙$\frac{21}{28}$ $\frac{15}{18}$	$29.72

Language Practice: Verbs

Write sentences using these vivid verbs.

1. sobbed: _____
2. mumbled: _____
3. moaned: _____
4. protested: _____
5. gasped: _____
6. insisted: _____

Writing Practice: Use this writing prompt to write a short paragraph:
I began my time travels by . . .

#3303 Daily Skills Practice–Grades 5-6   18   ©Teacher Created Materials, Inc.

Page 19

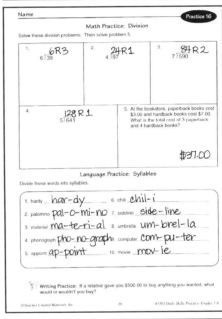

Name _____ Practice 16

Math Practice: Division

Solve these division problems. Then solve problem 5.

1. $6)\overline{39}$ 6R3	2. $4)\overline{97}$ 24R1	3. $7)\overline{590}$ 84R2

4. $5)\overline{641}$ 128 R1	5. At the bookstore, paperback books cost $3.00 and hardback books cost $7.00. What is the total cost of 3 paperback and 4 hardback books?
	$37.00

Language Practice: Syllables

Divide these words into syllables.

1. hardy har-dy	6. chili chil-i
2. palomino pal-o-mi-no	7. sideline side-line
3. material ma-te-ri-al	8. umbrella um-brel-la
4. phonograph pho-no-graph	9. computer com-pu-ter
5. appoint ap-point	10. movie mov-ie

Writing Practice: If a relative gave you $500.00 to buy anything you wanted, what would or wouldn't you buy?

©Teacher Created Materials, Inc.   19   #3303 Daily Skills Practice–Grades 5-6

Page 20

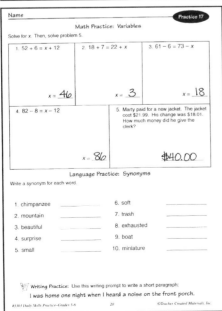

Name _____ Practice 17

Math Practice: Variables

Solve for x. Then, solve problem 5.

1. $52 + 6 = x + 12$	2. $18 + 7 = 22 + x$	3. $61 - 6 = 73 - x$
$x = 46$	$x = 3$	$x = 18$

4. $82 - 8 = x - 12$	5. Marty paid for a new jacket. The jacket cost $21.99. His change was $18.01. How much money did he give the clerk?
$x = 86$	$40.00

Language Practice: Synonyms

Write a synonym for each word.

1. chimpanzee _____   6. soft _____
2. mountain _____   7. trash _____
3. beautiful _____   8. exhausted _____
4. surprise _____   9. boat _____
5. small _____   10. miniature _____

Writing Practice: Use this writing prompt to write a short paragraph:
I was home one night when I heard a noise on the front porch.

#3303 Daily Skills Practice–Grades 5-6   20   ©Teacher Created Materials, Inc.

Page 21

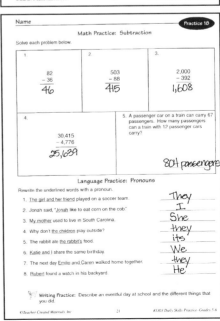

Name _____ Practice 18

Math Practice: Subtraction

Solve each problem below.

1.	2.	3.
82 − 36 46	503 − 88 415	2,000 − 392 1,608

4.	5. A passenger car on a train can carry 67 passengers. How many passengers can a train with 12 passenger cars carry?
30,415 − 4,776 25,639	804 passengers

Language Practice: Pronouns

Rewrite the underlined words with a pronoun.

1. The girl and her friend played on a soccer team.   They
2. Jonah said, "Jonah like to eat corn on the cob."   I
3. My mother used to live in South Carolina.   She
4. Why do the children play outside?   they
5. The rabbit ate the rabbit's food.   its
6. Katie and I share the same birthday.   We
7. The next day Emilio and Caren walked home together.   they
8. Rubert found a watch in his backyard.   He

Writing Practice: Describe an eventful day at school and the different things that you did.

©Teacher Created Materials, Inc.   21   #3303 Daily Skills Practice–Grades 5-6

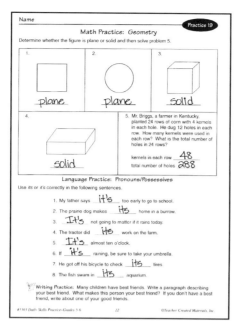

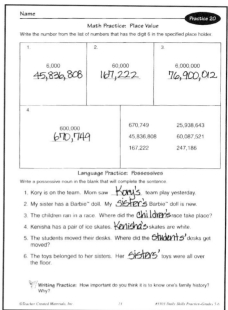

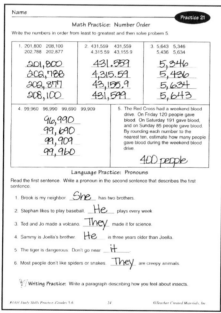

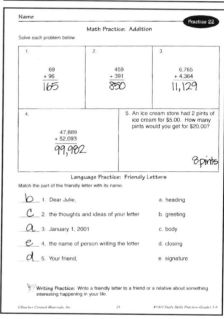

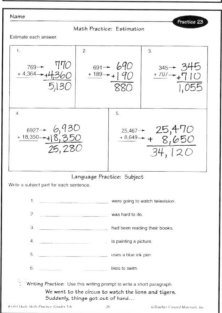

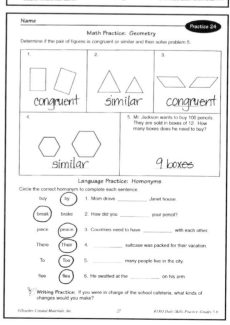

Page 28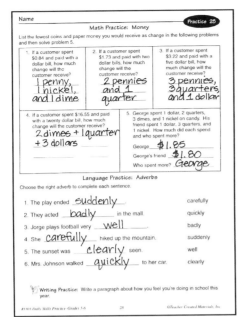

Name

Math Practice: Money — Practice 25

List the fewest coins and paper money you will receive as change in the following problems and then solve problem 5.

1. If a customer spent $0.84 and paid with a dollar bill, how much change will the customer receive?
1 penny, 1 nickel, and 1 dime

2. If a customer spent $1.73 and paid with two dollar bills, how much change will the customer receive?
2 pennies and 1 quarter

3. If a customer spent $3.22 and paid with a five dollar bill, how much change will the customer receive?
3 pennies, 3 quarters, and 1 dollar

4. If a customer spent $16.55 and paid with a twenty dollar bill, how much change will the customer receive?
2 dimes + 1 quarter + 3 dollars

5. George spent 1 dollar, 2 quarters, 3 dimes, and 1 nickel on candy. His friend spent 1 dollar, 3 quarters, and 1 nickel. How much did each spend and who spent more?

George **$1.85**

George's friend **$1.80**

Who spent more? **George**

Language Practice: Adverbs

Choose the right adverb to complete each sentence.

1. The play ended **suddenly** .
2. They acted **badly** in the mall.
3. Jorge plays football very **well** .
4. She **carefully** hiked up the mountain.
5. The sunset was **clearly** seen.
6. Mrs. Johnson walked **quickly** to her car.

carefully
quickly
badly
suddenly
well
clearly

Writing Practice: Write a paragraph about how you feel you're doing in school this year.

#3303 Daily Skills Practice-Grades 5-6   28   ©Teacher Created Materials, Inc.

Page 29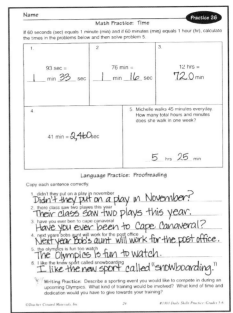

Name

Math Practice: Time — Practice 26

If 60 seconds (sec) equals 1 minute (min) and if 60 minutes (min) equals 1 hour (hr), calculate the times in the problems below and then solve problem 5.

1. 93 sec = **1** min **33** sec

2. 76 min = **1** min **16** sec

3. 12 hrs = **720** min

4. 41 min = **2,460** sec

5. Michelle walks 45 minutes everyday. How many total hours and minutes does she walk in one week?
5 hrs **25** min

Language Practice: Proofreading

Copy each sentence correctly.

1. didn't they put on a play in november?
Didn't they put on a play in November?

2. there class saw two plays this year
Their class saw two plays this year.

3. have you ever ben to cape canaveral
Have you ever been to Cape Canaveral?

4. next ygare bobs aunt will work for the post office
Next year Bob's aunt will work for the post office.

5. the olympics is fun too watch
The Olympics is fun to watch.

6. I like the knew sport called snowboarding
I like the new sport called "snowboarding."

Writing Practice: Describe a sporting event you would like to compete in during an upcoming Olympics. What kind of training would be involved? What kind of time and dedication would you have to give towards your training?

©Teacher Created Materials, Inc.   29   #3303 Daily Skills Practice-Grades 5-6

Page 30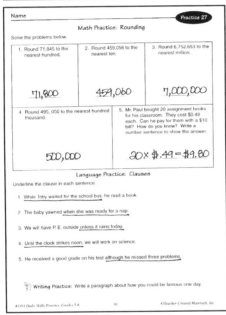

Name

Math Practice: Rounding — Practice 27

Solve the problems below.

1. Round 71,845 to the nearest hundred.
71,800

2. Round 459,056 to the nearest ten.
459,060

3. Round 6,752,653 to the nearest million.
7,000,000

4. Round 495,056 to the nearest hundred thousand.
500,000

5. Mr. Paul bought 20 assignment books for his classroom. They cost $0.49 each. Can he pay for them with a $10 bill? How do you know? Write a number sentence to show the answer.
20 × $.49 = $9.80

Language Practice: Clauses

Underline the clause in each sentence.

1. While Toby waited for the school bus, he read a book.

2. The baby yawned when she was ready for a nap.

3. We will have P. E. outside unless it rains today.

4. Until the clock strikes noon, we will work on science.

5. He received a good grade on his test although he missed three problems.

Writing Practice: Write a paragraph about how you could be famous one day.

#3303 Daily Skills Practice-Grades 5-6   30   ©Teacher Created Materials, Inc.

Page 31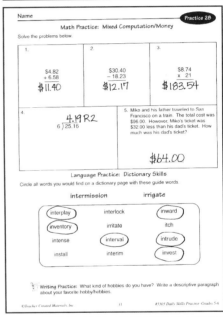

Name

Math Practice: Mixed Computation/Money — Practice 28

Solve the problems below.

1. $4.82 + 6.58 = **$11.40**

2. $30.40 − 18.23 = **$12.17**

3. $8.74 × 21 = **$183.54**

4. 6)25.16 = **4.19 R2**

5. Miko and his father traveled to San Francisco on a train. The total cost was $96.00. However, Miko's ticket was $32.00 less than his dad's ticket. How much was his dad's ticket?
$64.00

Language Practice: Dictionary Skills

Circle all words you would find on a dictionary page with these guide words.

intermission   irrigate

(interplay)   interlock   (inward)
(inventory)   irrigate   itch
intense   (interval) (intrude)
install   interim   (invest)

Writing Practice: What kind of hobbies do you have? Write a descriptive paragraph about your favorite hobby/hobbies.

©Teacher Created Materials, Inc.   31   #3303 Daily Skills Practice-Grades 5-6

Page 32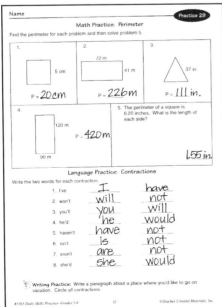

Name

Math Practice: Perimeter — Practice 29

Find the perimeter for each problem and then solve problem 5.

1. 5 cm   P = **20 cm**

2. 72 m, 41 m   P = **226 m**

3. 37 in.   P = **111 in.**

4. 120 m, 90 m   P = **420 m**

5. The perimeter of a square is 6.20 inches. What is the length of each side?
1.55 in.

Language Practice: Contractions

Write the two words for each contraction.

1. I've — **I have**
2. won't — **will not**
3. you'll — **you will**
4. he'd — **he would**
5. haven't — **have not**
6. isn't — **is not**
7. aren't — **are not**
8. she'd — **she would**

Writing Practice: Write a paragraph about a place where you'd like to go on vacation. Circle all contractions.

#3303 Daily Skills Practice-Grades 5-6   32   ©Teacher Created Materials, Inc.

Page 33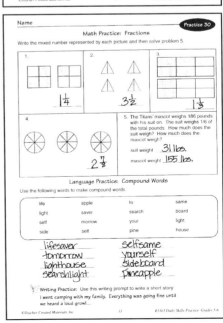

Name

Math Practice: Fractions — Practice 30

Write the mixed number represented by each picture and then solve problem 5.

1. **1¼**

2. **3½**

3. **1⅓**

4. **2⅞**

5. The Titans' mascot weighs 186 pounds with his suit on. The suit weighs 1/6 of the total pounds. How much does the suit weigh? How much does the mascot weigh?
suit weight **31 lbs.**
mascot weight **155 lbs.**

Language Practice: Compound Words

Use the following words to make compound words.

life	apple	to	same
light	saver	search	board
self	morrow	your	light
side	self	pine	house

lifesaver   **selfsame**
tomorrow   **yourself**
lighthouse **sideboard**
searchlight **pineapple**

Writing Practice: Use this writing prompt to write a short story. I went camping with my family. Everything was going fine until we heard a loud growl...

©Teacher Created Materials, Inc.   33   #3303 Daily Skills Practice-Grades 5-6

Name _____
Practice 31

Math Practice: Decimals/Writing Numbers
Write out each number in words and then create your own problem 5.

1. 3.379	2. 0.92	3. 1,201.6
three and three hundred seventy-nine thousandths	ninety-two hundredths	one thousand two hundred one and six tenths

4. 5.002	5. Make up your own story problem using the numbers 4, 6, and 24.
five and two thousandths	

Language Practice: Verbs
Complete each sentence with a verb or verb phrase.

1. The girls in the classroom _____
2. The clerk in the store _____
3. The dog at the vet's office _____
4. The woods around the corner _____
5. Children playing on a playground _____
6. Soldiers fighting in a war _____

Writing Practice: While watching television one evening, the show you were watching was interrupted with a "Special Report." Describe the breaking news.

#3303 Daily Skills Practice–Grades 5-6   34   ©Teacher Created Materials, Inc.

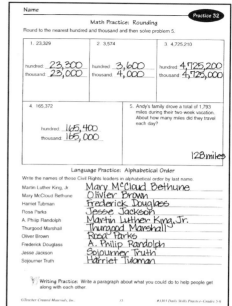

Name _____
Practice 32

Math Practice: Rounding
Round to the nearest hundred and thousand and then solve problem 5.

1. 23,329	2. 3,574	3. 4,725,210
hundred: 23,300 thousand: 23,000	hundred: 3,600 thousand: 4,000	hundred: 4,725,200 thousand: 4,725,000

4. 165,372	5. Andy's family drove a total of 1,793 miles during their two-week vacation. About how many miles did they travel each day?
hundred: 165,400 thousand: 165,000	128 miles

Language Practice: Alphabetical Order
Write the names of these Civil Rights leaders in alphabetical order by last name.

Martin Luther King, Jr. — Mary McCloud Bethune
Mary McCloud Bethune — Oliver Brown
Harriet Tubman — Frederick Douglass
Rosa Parks — Jesse Jackson
A. Philip Randolph — Martin Luther King, Jr.
Thurgood Marshall — Thurgood Marshall
Oliver Brown — Rosa Parks
Frederick Douglass — A. Philip Randolph
Jesse Jackson — Sojourner Truth
Sojourner Truth — Harriet Tubman

Writing Practice: Write a paragraph about what you could do to help people get along with each other.

©Teacher Created Materials, Inc.   35   #3303 Daily Skills Practice–Grades 5-6

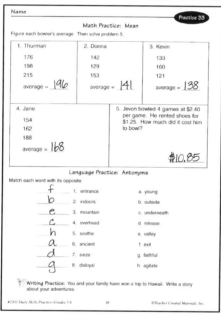

Name _____
Practice 33

Math Practice: Mean
Figure each bowler's average. Then solve problem 5.

1. Thurman	2. Donna	3. Kevin
176 198 215 average = 196	142 129 153 average = 141	133 160 121 average = 138

4. Jane	5. Jevon bowled 4 games at $2.40 per game. He rented shoes for $1.25. How much did it cost him to bowl?
154 162 188 average = 168	$10.85

Language Practice: Antonyms
Match each word with its opposite.

f 1. entrance   a. young
b 2. indoors   b. outside
e 3. mountain   c. underneath
c 4. overhead   d. release
h 5. soothe   e. valley
a 6. ancient   f. exit
d 7. sieze   g. faithful
g 8. disloyal   h. agitate

Writing Practice: You and your family have won a trip to Hawaii. Write a story about your adventures.

#3303 Daily Skills Practice–Grades 5-6   36   ©Teacher Created Materials, Inc.

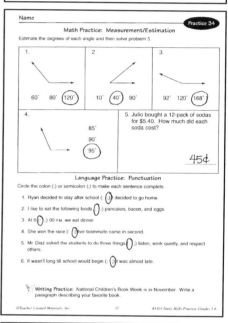

Name _____
Practice 34

Math Practice: Measurement/Estimation
Estimate the degrees of each angle and then solve problem 5.

1.	2.	3.
60° 80° (120°)	10° (40°) 90°	92° 120° (168°)

4.	5. Julio bought a 12-pack of sodas for $5.40. How much did each soda cost?
85° 90° (95°)	45¢

Language Practice: Punctuation
Circle the colon (:) or semicolon (;) to make each sentence complete.

1. Ryan decided to stay after school (;) decided to go home.
2. I like to eat the following foods (:) pancakes, bacon, and eggs.
3. At 6(:)00 P.M. we eat dinner.
4. She won the race (;) her teammate came in second.
5. Mr. Diaz asked the students to do three things (:) listen, work quietly, and respect others.
6. It wasn't long till school would begin (;) I was almost late.

Writing Practice: National Children's Book Week is in November. Write a paragraph describing your favorite book.

©Teacher Created Materials, Inc.   37   #3303 Daily Skills Practice–Grades 5-6

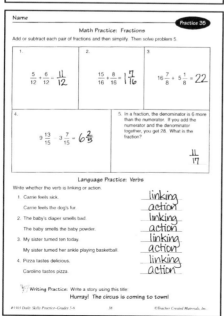

Name _____
Practice 35

Math Practice: Fractions
Add or subtract each pair of fractions and then simplify. Then solve problem 5.

1.	2.	3.
$\frac{5}{12} + \frac{6}{12} = \frac{11}{12}$	$\frac{15}{16} + \frac{8}{16} = 1\frac{7}{16}$	$16\frac{7}{8} + 5\frac{1}{8} = 22$

4.	5. In a fraction, the denominator is 6 more than the numerator. If you add the numerator and the denominator together, you get 28. What is the fraction?
$9\frac{13}{15} - 3\frac{7}{15} = 6\frac{2}{5}$	$\frac{11}{17}$

Language Practice: Verbs
Write whether the verb is linking or action.

1. Carrie feels sick. — linking
   Carrie feels the dog's fur. — action
2. The baby's diaper smells bad. — linking
   The baby smells the baby powder. — action
3. My sister turned ten today. — linking
   My sister turned her ankle playing basketball. — action
4. Pizza tastes delicious. — linking
   Caroline tastes pizza. — action

Writing Practice: Write a story using this title:
Hurray! The circus is coming to town!

#3303 Daily Skills Practice–Grades 5-6   38   ©Teacher Created Materials, Inc.

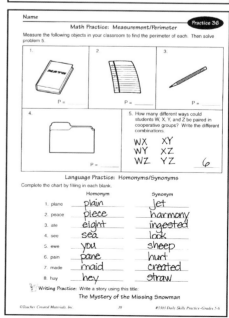

Name _____
Practice 36

Math Practice: Measurement/Perimeter
Measure the following objects in your classroom to find the perimeter of each. Then solve problem 5.

1.	2.	3.
P =	P =	P =

4.	5. How many different ways could students W, X, Y, and Z be paired in cooperative groups? Write the different combinations.
P =	WX XY WY XZ WZ YZ 6

Language Practice: Homonyms/Synonyms
Complete the chart by filling in each blank.

	Homonym	Synonym
1. plane	plain	jet
2. peace	piece	harmony
3. ate	eight	ingested
4. see	sea	look
5. ewe	you	sheep
6. pain	pane	hurt
7. made	maid	created
8. hay	hey	straw

Writing Practice: Write a story using this title:
The Mystery of the Missing Snowman

©Teacher Created Materials, Inc.   39   #3303 Daily Skills Practice–Grades 5-6

Page 40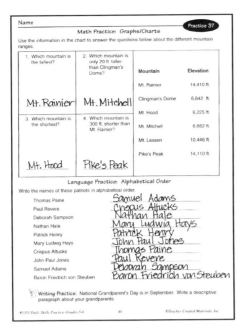

Page 41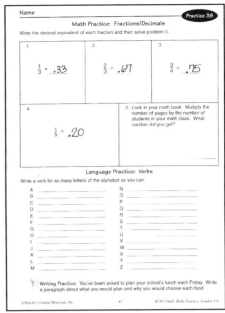

Page 42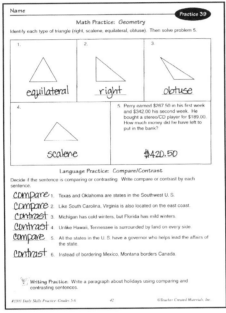

Page 43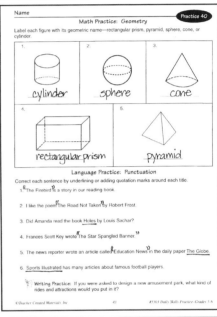

Page 44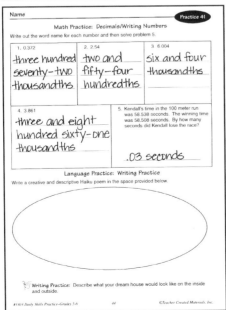

Page 45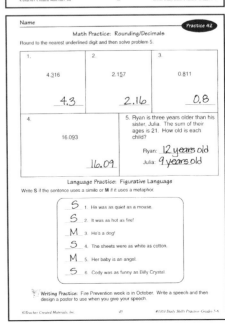

© Teacher Created Resources, Inc.

#3303 Daily Skills Practice–Grades 5-6

Page 46

Math Practice: Table/Money

Use the information in the chart to answer the questions below.

		Item	Price
1. You have $50.00 to spend. Which two items would you buy if your change was $10.00?	2. You have $50.00 to spend. Which two items would you buy if your change was $3.00?	shirt	$15.00
		shoes	$36.00
2 watches or shirt and jeans	*blouse and skirt*	blouse	$17.00
		necklace	$9.00
3. You have $50.00 to spend. Which two items would you buy if your change was $11.00?	4. You have $50.00 to spend. Which two items would you buy if your change was $21.00?	jeans	$25.00
		watch	$20.00
necklace and skirt or shoes and socks	*necklace and watch*	skirt	$30.00
		socks	$3.00

Language Practice: Figurative Language

Rewrite each sentence using literal language.

1. I'm dead!
I'm exhausted!
2. It's raining cats and dogs.
It's pouring rain.
3. We're like two ships that pass in the night.
We never see each other.
4. She cried a bucket of tears.
She cried and cried.
5. He's blind as a bat.
He cannot see.
6. Stanley has a chip on his shoulder.
Stanley felt he was wronged.

Writing Practice: The 19th Amendment to the Constitution of the United States gave women the right to vote. If you could add an amendment for children, what would it be and why?

Page 47

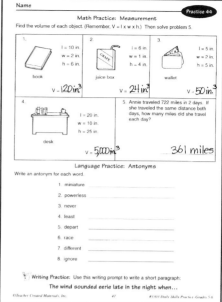

Math Practice: Measurement

Find the volume of each object. (Remember, $V = l \times w \times h$.) Then solve problem 5.

1. book
$l = 10$ in.
$w = 2$ in.
$h = 6$ in.
$v = 120$ in^3

2. juice box
$l = 6$ in.
$w = 1$ in.
$h = 4$ in.
$v = 24$ in^3

3. wallet
$l = 5$ in.
$w = 2$ in.
$h = 5$ in.
$v = 50$ in^3

4. desk
$l = 20$ in.
$w = 10$ in.
$h = 25$ in.
$v = 5000$ in^3

5. Annie traveled 722 miles in 2 days. If she traveled the same distance both days, how many miles did she travel each day?
361 miles

Language Practice: Antonyms

Write an antonym for each word.

1. miniature
2. powerless
3. never
4. least
5. depart
6. race
7. different
8. ignore

Writing Practice: Use this writing prompt to write a short paragraph:

The wind sounded eerie late in the night when...

Page 48

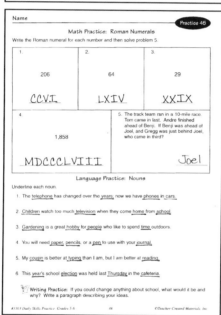

Math Practice: Roman Numerals

Write the Roman numeral for each number and then solve problem 5.

1. 206	2. 64	3. 29
CCVI	*LXIV*	*XXIX*

4. 1,858	5. The track team ran in a 10-mile race. Tom came in last. Andre finished ahead of Benji. If Benji was ahead of Joel, and Gregg was just behind Joel, who came in third?
MDCCCLVIII	*Joel*

Language Practice: Nouns

Underline each noun.

1. The telephone has changed over the years; now we have phones in cars.
2. Children watch too much television when they come home from school.
3. Gardening is a great hobby for people who like to spend time outdoors.
4. You will need paper, pencils, or a pen to use with your journal.
5. My cousin is better at typing than I am, but I am better at reading.
6. This year's school election was held last Thursday in the cafeteria.

Writing Practice: If you could change anything about school, what would it be and why? Write a paragraph describing your ideas.

Page 49

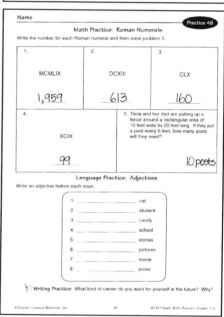

Math Practice: Roman Numerals

Write the number for each Roman numeral and then solve problem 5.

1. MCMLIX	2. DCXIII	3. CLX
1,959	*613*	*160*

4. XCIX	5. Tricia and her dad are putting up a fence around a rectangular area of 10 feet wide by 20 feet long. If they put a post every 6 feet, how many posts will they need?
99	*10 posts*

Language Practice: Adjectives

Write an adjective before each noun.

1. _____ cat
2. _____ student
3. _____ candy
4. _____ school
5. _____ stories
6. _____ pictures
7. _____ movie
8. _____ picnic

Writing Practice: What kind of career do you want for yourself in the future? Why?

Page 50

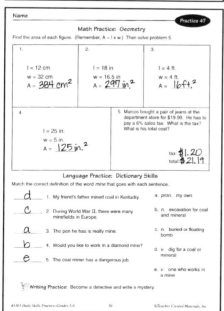

Math Practice: Geometry

Find the area of each figure. (Remember, $A = l \times w$.) Then solve problem 5.

1. $l = 12$ cm $w = 32$ cm $A = 384$ cm^2	2. $l = 18$ in $w = 16.5$ in $A = 297$ in^2	3. $l = 4$ ft. $w = 4$ ft. $A = 16$ ft^2

4. $l = 25$ in. $w = 5$ in. $A = 125$ in^2	5. Marcos bought a pair of jeans at the department store for $19.99. He has to pay a 6% sales tax. What is the tax? What is his total cost? tax: *$1.20* total: *$21.19*

Language Practice: Dictionary Skills

Match the correct definition of the word *mine* that goes with each sentence.

d 1. My friend's father mined coal in Kentucky.
c 2. During World War II, there were many minefields in Europe.
a 3. The pen he has is really mine.
b 4. Would you like to work in a diamond mine?
e 5. The coal miner has a dangerous job.

a. *pron.* my own

b. *n.* excavation for coal and mineral

c. *n.* buried or floating bomb

d. *v.* dig for coal or mineral

e. *v.* one who works in a mine

Writing Practice: Become a detective and write a mystery.

Page 51

Math Practice: Multiplication

Use the information about the different symbols provided on the chart to solve each problem.

1. ✿ 45
$\times$ ☐ 15
675

2. ◗ 30
$\times$ ✾ 40
1,200

3. △ 20
◆ 35
$\times$ ◯ 25
17,500

4. ☆ 5
✧ 50
$\times$ ♡ 10
2,500

☆ = 5   ◗ = 30
♡ = 10   ◆ = 35
☐ = 15   ✾ = 40
△ = 20   ✿ = 45
◯ = 25   ✧ = 50

Language Practice: Adverbs

Cross out every third letter to find the names of adverbs. Write the adverb in the space provided, then write a sentence with it.

1. somftaly *softly*
2. menrreilay *merrily*
3. fuyrmouksbpy *furiously*
4. bepaudthifulscy *beautifully*
5. thderae *there*

Writing Practice: If you combined two fruits or vegetables into a new product, how would you advertise this new product?

Page 52

Math Practice: Multiplication

Write the answer to each multiplication problem below.

1. 9 x 20 x 5	2. 12 x 9 x 7	3. 3 x 8 x 2 x 11
900	756	528

4. 8 x 15 x 3	5. 3 x 4 x 6 x 10
360	720

Language Practice: Word Order

Rearrange the words in each group to make a complete sentence. Write each sentence.

1. Sweep The the class Toning wanted story to the hear
   The class wanted to hear the story Toning the Sweep.

2. grades good get classwork do have You to your to
   You have to do your classwork to get good grades.

3. Marcia best and friends Barbie in were grade sixth
   Marcia and Barbie were best friends in sixth grade.

4. anything try be can you You if want you
   You can be anything you want if you try.

5. Yesterday school to player CD a brought Alex
   Yesterday, Alex brought a CD player to school.

Writing Practice: Write about a family vacation that you are going to take or have already taken.

Page 53

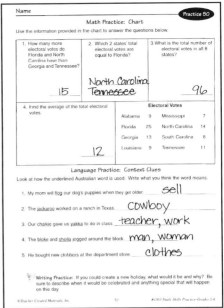

Math Practice: Chart

Use the information provided in the chart to answer the questions below.

1. How many more electoral votes do Florida and North Carolina have than Georgia and Tennessee?	2. Which 2 states' total electoral votes are equal to Florida?	3. What is the total number of electoral votes in all 8 states?
15	North Carolina Tennessee	96

4. Find the average of the total electoral votes.

12

Electoral Votes			
Alabama	9	Mississippi	7
Florida	25	North Carolina	14
Georgia	13	South Carolina	8
Louisiana	9	Tennessee	11

Language Practice: Context Clues

Look at how the underlined Australian word is used. Write what you think the word means.

1. My mom will flog our dog's puppies when they get older. ___ sell
2. The jackaroo worked on a ranch in Texas. ___ cowboy
3. Our chalkie gave us yakka to do in class. ___ teacher, work
4. The bloke and sheila jogged around the block. ___ man, woman
5. He bought new clobbers at the department store. ___ clothes

Writing Practice: If you could create a new holiday, what would it be and why? Be sure to describe when it would be celebrated and anything special that will happen on this day.

Page 54

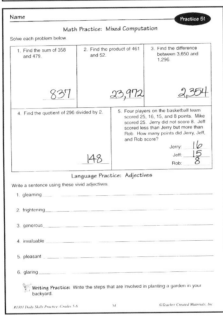

Math Practice: Mixed Computation

Solve each problem below.

1. Find the sum of 358 and 479.	2. Find the product of 461 and 52.	3. Find the difference between 3,650 and 1,296.
837	23,972	2,354

4. Find the quotient of 296 divided by 2.	5. Four players on the basketball team scored 25, 16, 15, and 8 points. Mike scored 25. Jerry did not score 8. Jeff scored less than Jerry but more than Rob. How many points did Jerry, Jeff, and Rob score?
148	Jerry: 16 Jeff: 15 Rob: 8

Language Practice: Adjectives

Write a sentence using these vivid adjectives.

1. gleaming _____
2. frightening _____
3. generous _____
4. invaluable _____
5. pleasant _____
6. glaring _____

Writing Practice: Write the steps that are involved in planting a garden in your backyard.

Page 55

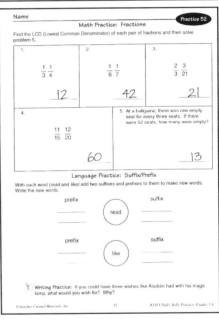

Math Practice: Fractions

Find the LCD (Lowest Common Denominator) of each pair of fractions and then solve problem 5.

1. $\frac{1}{3}$ $\frac{1}{4}$	2. $\frac{1}{6}$ $\frac{1}{7}$	3. $\frac{2}{3}$ $\frac{3}{21}$
12	42	21

4. $\frac{11}{15}$ $\frac{12}{20}$	5. At a ballgame, there was one empty seat for every three seats. If there were 52 seats, how many were empty?
60	13

Language Practice: Suffix/Prefix

With each word (read and like) add two suffixes and prefixes to them to make new words. Write the new words.

prefix ___ read ___ suffix

prefix ___ like ___ suffix

Writing Practice: If you could have three wishes like Aladdin had with his magic lamp, what would you wish for? Why?

Page 56

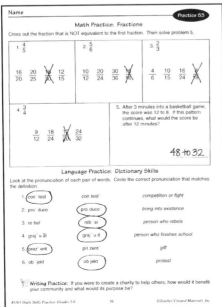

Math Practice: Fractions

Cross out the fraction that is NOT equivalent to the first fraction. Then solve problem 5.

1. $\frac{4}{5}$	2. $\frac{5}{6}$	3. $\frac{2}{3}$
$\frac{16}{20}$ $\frac{20}{25}$ $\frac{18}{15}$ $\frac{12}{15}$	$\frac{10}{12}$ $\frac{20}{24}$ $\frac{30}{36}$ $\frac{25}{40}$	$\frac{4}{6}$ $\frac{10}{15}$ $\frac{16}{24}$ $\frac{12}{18}$

4. $\frac{3}{4}$	5. After 3 minutes into a basketball game, the score was 12 to 8. If this pattern continues, what would the score be after 12 minutes?
$\frac{9}{12}$ $\frac{18}{24}$ $\frac{20}{24}$ $\frac{24}{32}$	48 to 32

Language Practice: Dictionary Skills

Look at the pronunciation of each pair of words. Circle the correct pronunciation that matches the definition.

1. (con´test)   con test´   competition or fight
2. pro´duce   (pro duce´)   bring into existence
3. re bel   (reb´el)   person who rebels
4. graj´u āt   (graj´u it)   person who finishes school
5. (prez´ent)   pri zent´   gift
6. ob ject   (ob jekt´)   protest

Writing Practice: If you were to create a charity to help others, how would it benefit your community and what would its purpose be?

Page 57

Math Practice: Geometry

Use the diagram to solve the problems.

1. △ ABC is congruent to △ ACD	2. ED is equal to BE or EB	3. ∠BEC is equal to ∠ AED

4. AB is parallel to CD or DC

Language Practice: Adjectives

Fill in the acrostic with adjectives describing parents.

P _____
A _____
R _____
E _____
N _____
T _____
S _____

Writing Practice: Write a story using this title:

The Birthday I'll Never Forget

Page 58

Page 59

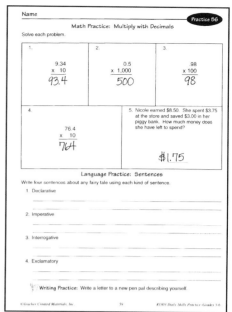

Page 60

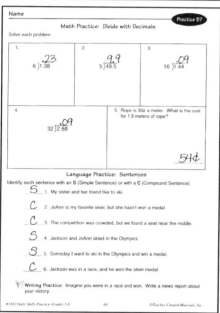

Page 61

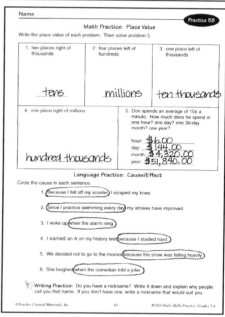

Page 62

Page 63

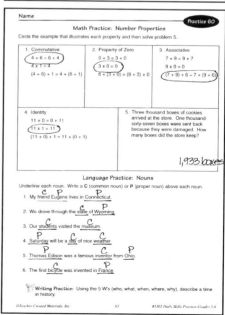

Page 64

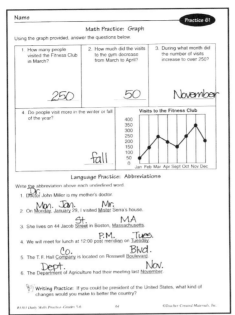

Page 65

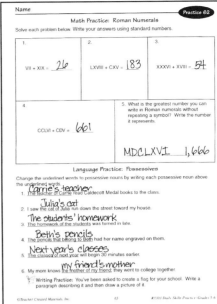

Page 66

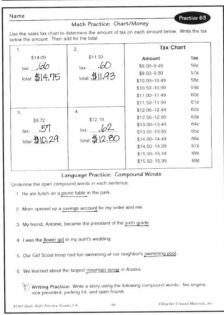

Page 67

Page 68

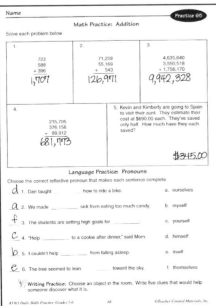

Page 69

Page 70

Practice 67

Math Practice: Multiplication

Multiply the number in the center by each point. Write the answer by the point. Then solve problem 5.

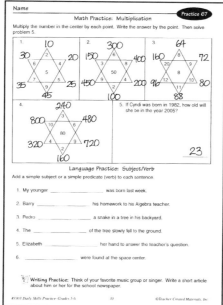

5. If Cyndi was born in 1982, how old will she be in the year 2005?

23

Language Practice: Subject/Verb

Add a simple subject or a simple predicate (verb) to each sentence.

1. My younger _____ was born last week.

2. Barry _____ his homework to his Algebra teacher.

3. Pedro _____ a snake in a tree in his backyard.

4. The _____ of the tree slowly fell to the ground.

5. Elizabeth _____ her hand to answer the teacher's question.

6. _____ were found at the space center.

✏️ Writing Practice: Think of your favorite music group or singer. Write a short article about him or her for the school newspaper.

#3303 Daily Skills Practice–Grades 5-6   70   ©Teacher Created Materials, Inc.

Page 71

Practice 68

Math Practice: Mental Math/Multiplication

Solve each problem.

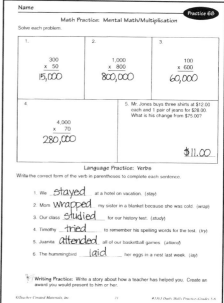

1.	2.	3.
300 × 50 = **15,000**	1,000 × 800 = **800,000**	100 × 600 = **60,000**

4. 4,000 × 70 = **280,000**

5. Mr. Jones buys three shirts at $12.00 each and 1 pair of jeans for $28.00. What is his change from $75.00?

$11.00

Language Practice: Verbs

Write the correct form of the verb in parentheses to complete each sentence.

1. We **stayed** at a hotel on vacation. (stay)

2. Mom **wrapped** my sister in a blanket because she was cold. (wrap)

3. Our class **studied** for our history test. (study)

4. Timothy **tried** to remember his spelling words for the test. (try)

5. Juanita **attended** all of our basketball games. (attend)

6. The hummingbird **laid** her eggs in a nest last week. (lay)

✏️ Writing Practice: Write a story about how a teacher has helped you. Create an award you would present to him or her.

©Teacher Created Materials, Inc.   71   #3303 Daily Skills Practice–Grades 5-6

Page 72

Practice 69

Math Practice: Mean

Find the average monthly earning for cutting grass for each student last summer and then solve problem 5.

1. Joe	2. Luke	3. Hans
$768 $541 + $582 **$1,891**	$808 $712 + $500 **$2,020**	$692 $377 + $640 **$1,709**
average: **$630.33**	average: **$673.33**	average: **$569.67**

4. Kobe
$724
$700
+ $483
$1,907
average: **$635.67**

5. If you burn 520 calories an hour playing basketball, how many calories would you burn in a three-hour game?

1,560 calories

Language Practice: Nouns

Fill in the chart with five nouns in each category.

Sight	Sound	Smell	Taste	Touch

✏️ Writing Practice: Imagine you are a reporter for the school newspaper. Interview one of your classmates and write a student spotlight.

#3303 Daily Skills Practice–Grades 5-6   72   ©Teacher Created Materials, Inc.

Page 73

Practice 70

Math Practice: Division with Exponents

Solve each problem below.

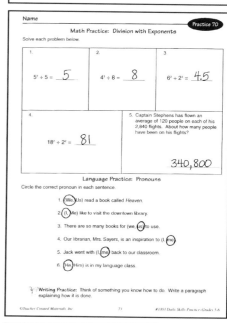

1.	2.	3.
$5^2 \div 5 = $ **5**	$4^3 \div 8 = $ **8**	$6^2 \div 2^3 = $ **4.5**

4. $18^2 \div 2^2 = $ **81**

5. Captain Stephens has flown an average of 120 people on each of his 2,840 flights. About how many people have been on his flights?

340,800

Language Practice: Pronouns

Circle the correct pronoun in each sentence.

1. (We, Us) read a book called *Heaven*.

2. (I, Me) like to visit the downtown library.

3. There are so many books for (we, us) to use.

4. Our librarian, Mrs. Sayers, is an inspiration to (I, me).

5. Jack went with (I, me) back to our classroom.

6. (He, Him) is in my language class.

✏️ Writing Practice: Think of something you know how to do. Write a paragraph explaining how it is done.

©Teacher Created Materials, Inc.   73   #3303 Daily Skills Practice–Grades 5-6

Page 74

Practice 71

Math Practice: Mixed Computation

Columbus discovered the West Indies in 1492. Calculate the following from the current year. Then solve problem 5.

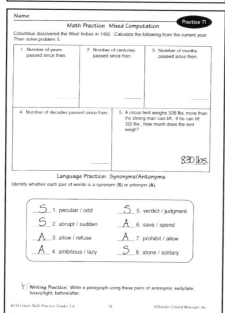

1. Number of years passed since then.	2. Number of centuries passed since then.	3. Number of months passed since then.

4. Number of decades passed since then.

5. A circus tent weighs 508 lbs. more than the strong man can lift. If he can lift 322 lbs, how much does the tent weigh?

830 lbs.

Language Practice: Synonyms/Antonyms

Identify whether each pair of words is a synonym (S) or antonym (A).

S 1. peculiar / odd
S 2. abrupt / sudden
A 3. allow / refuse
A 4. ambitious / lazy
S 5. verdict / judgment
A 6. save / spend
A 7. prohibit / allow
S 8. alone / solitary

✏️ Writing Practice: Write a paragraph using these pairs of antonyms: early/late, heavy/light, before/after.

#3303 Daily Skills Practice–Grades 5-6   74   ©Teacher Created Materials, Inc.

Page 75

Practice 72

Math Practice: Multiplication

Circle each correct problem. Then solve problem 5.

1.	2.	3.
49 × 9 = 421	(338 × 7 = 2,366)	742 × 36 = 25,712

4. (482 × 65 = 31,330)

5. A dog fell in a 12-foot well. Everyday, he climbed up 3 feet and slipped back 2 feet. How many days did it take him to reach the top?

10 days

Language Practice: Adjective

Write two adjectives to describe the noun. Be sure they begin with the same letter as the noun.

1. children _____

2. pie _____

3. book _____

4. leaf _____

5. sister _____

6. dog _____

✏️ Writing Practice: If you were a fashion designer, what kind of clothing and shoes would you design? Write a short descriptive paragraph about your fashion collection.

©Teacher Created Materials, Inc.   75   #3303 Daily Skills Practice–Grades 5-6

Page 76

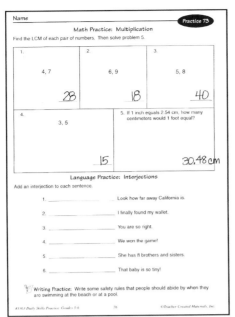

Math Practice: Multiplication

Find the LCM of each pair of numbers. Then solve problem 5.

1. 4, 7 28	2. 6, 9 18	3. 5, 8 40
4. 3, 5 15	5. If 1 inch equals 2.54 cm, how many centimeters would 1 foot equal? 30.48 cm	

Language Practice: Interjections

Add an interjection to each sentence.

1. _____ Look how far away California is.
2. _____ I finally found my wallet.
3. _____ You are so right.
4. _____ We won the game!
5. _____ She has 8 brothers and sisters.
6. _____ That baby is so tiny!

Writing Practice: Write some safety rules that people should abide by when they are swimming at the beach or at a pool.

#3303 Daily Skills Practice–Grades 5-6   76   ©Teacher Created Materials, Inc.

Page 77

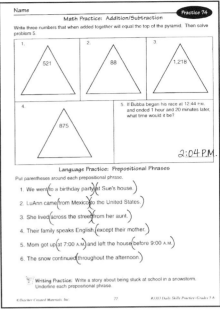

Math Practice: Addition/Subtraction

Write three numbers that when added together will equal the top of the pyramid. Then solve problem 5.

1. 521	2. 88	3. 1,218
4. 875	5. If Bubba began his race at 12:44 P.M. and ended 1 hour and 20 minutes later, what time would it be? 2:04 P.M.	

Language Practice: Prepositional Phrases

Put parentheses around each prepositional phrase.

1. We went (to a birthday party) (at Sue's house).
2. LuAnn came (from Mexico) (to the United States).
3. She lived (across the street) (from her aunt).
4. Their family speaks English (except their mother).
5. Mom got up (at 7:00 A.M.) and left the house (before 9:00 A.M.)
6. The snow continued (throughout the afternoon).

Writing Practice: Write a story about being stuck at school in a snowstorm. Underline each prepositional phrase.

©Teacher Created Materials, Inc.   77   #3303 Daily Skills Practice–Grades 5-6

Page 78

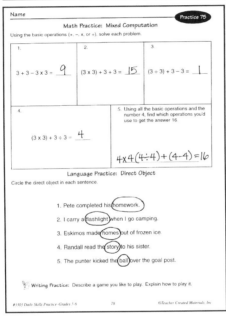

Math Practice: Mixed Computation

Using the basic operations (+, −, ×, or ÷), solve each problem.

1. $3 + 3 − 3 \times 3 = 9$	2. $(3 \times 3) + 3 + 3 = 15$	3. $(3 \div 3) + 3 − 3 = 1$
4. $(3 \times 3) + 3 \div 3 = 4$	5. Using all the basic operations and the number 4, find which operations you'd use to get the answer 16. $4 \times 4 (4 \div 4) + (4 − 4) = 16$	

Language Practice: Direct Object

Circle the direct object in each sentence.

1. Pete completed his (homework).
2. I carry a (flashlight) when I go camping.
3. Eskimos made (homes) out of frozen ice.
4. Randall read the (story) to his sister.
5. The punter kicked the (ball) over the goal post.

Writing Practice: Describe a game you like to play. Explain how to play it.

#3303 Daily Skills Practice–Grades 5-6   78   ©Teacher Created Materials, Inc.

Page 79

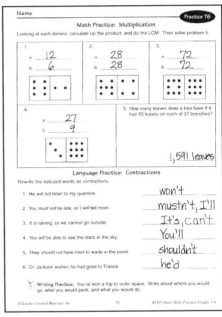

Math Practice: Multiplication

Looking at each domino, calculate (a) the product, and (b) the LCM. Then solve problem 5.

1. a. 12 b. 6	2. a. 28 b. 28	3. a. 72 b. 72
4. a. 27 b. 9	5. How many leaves does a tree have if it has 43 leaves on each of 37 branches? 1,591 leaves	

Language Practice: Contractions

Rewrite the italicized words as contractions.

1. He *will not* listen to my question.   won't
2. You *must not* be late, or *I will* tell mom.   mustn't, I'll
3. *It is* raining, so we *cannot* go outside.   It's, can't
4. *You will* be able to see the stars in the sky.   You'll
5. They *should not* have tried to wade in the pond.   shouldn't
6. Dr. Jackson wishes *he had* gone to France.   he'd

Writing Practice: You've won a trip to outer space. Write about where you would go, what you would pack, and what you would do.

©Teacher Created Materials, Inc.   79   #3303 Daily Skills Practice–Grades 5-6

Page 80

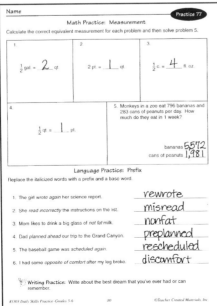

Math Practice: Measurement

Calculate the correct equivalent measurement for each problem and then solve problem 5.

1. $\frac{1}{2}$ gal = 2 qt	2. 2 pt = 1 qt	3. $\frac{1}{2}$ c. = 4 fl. oz.
4. $\frac{1}{2}$ qt = 1 pt.	5. Monkeys in a zoo eat 796 bananas and 283 cans of peanuts per day. How much do they eat in 1 week? bananas 5,572 cans of peanuts 1,981	

Language Practice: Prefix

Replace the italicized words with a prefix and a base word.

1. The girl *wrote again* her science report.   rewrote
2. She *read incorrectly* the instructions on the list.   misread
3. Mom likes to drink a big glass of *not fat* milk.   nonfat
4. Dad *planned ahead* our trip to the Grand Canyon.   preplanned
5. The baseball game was *scheduled again*.   rescheduled
6. I had some *opposite of comfort* after my leg broke.   discomfort

Writing Practice: Write about the best dream that you've ever had or can remember.

#3303 Daily Skills Practice–Grades 5-6   80   ©Teacher Created Materials, Inc.

Page 81

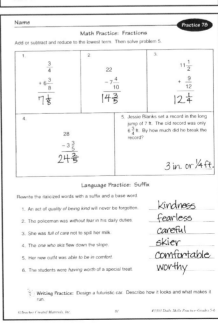

Math Practice: Fractions

Add or subtract and reduce to the lowest term. Then solve problem 5.

1. $\frac{3}{4} + 6\frac{3}{8} = 7\frac{1}{8}$	2. $22 − 7\frac{4}{10} = 14\frac{3}{5}$	3. $11\frac{1}{2} + \frac{9}{12} = 12\frac{1}{4}$
4. $28 − 3\frac{3}{5} = 24\frac{2}{5}$	5. Jessie Blanks set a record in the long jump of 7 ft. The old record was only $6\frac{3}{4}$ ft. By how much did he break the record? 3 in. or $\frac{1}{4}$ ft.	

Language Practice: Suffix

Rewrite the italicized words with a suffix and a base word.

1. An act of *quality of being kind* will never be forgotten.   kindness
2. The policeman was *without fear* in his daily duties.   fearless
3. She was *full of care* not to spill her milk.   careful
4. The one who *skis* flew down the slope.   skier
5. Her new outfit was *able to be in comfort*.   comfortable
6. The students were *having worth* of a special treat.   worthy

Writing Practice: Design a futuristic car. Describe how it looks and what makes it run.

©Teacher Created Materials, Inc.   81   #3303 Daily Skills Practice–Grades 5-6

Page 82

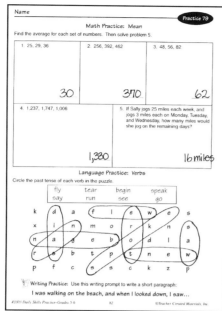

Name _____

Math Practice: Mean

Find the average for each set of numbers. Then solve problem 5.

1. 25, 29, 36	2. 256, 392, 462	3. 48, 56, 82
30	370	62

4. 1,237, 1,747, 1,006	5. If Sally jogs 25 miles each week, and jogs 3 miles each on Monday, Tuesday, and Wednesday, how many miles would she jog on the remaining days?
1,330	16 miles

Language Practice: Verbs

Circle the past tense of each verb in the puzzle.

fly	tear	begin	speak
say	run	see	go

Writing Practice: Use this writing prompt to write a short paragraph:
I was walking on the beach, and when I looked down, I saw...

#3303 Daily Skills Practice–Grades 5-6   82   ©Teacher Created Materials, Inc.

Page 83

Name _____

Math Practice: Median

Find the median for each set of numbers and then solve problem 5.

1. 17, 24, 34, 28, 16	2. 215, 219, 225, 200, 231	3. 48, 68, 51, 65, 55
24	219	55

4. $3.63, $4.74, $3.59, $4.62, $3.48	5. Mrs. Forrest gave a questionnaire to her math class of 12 boys and 13 girls. 7 boys and 7 girls returned their questionnaires. How many will she still need to get back from the boys? from the girls?
$3.63	boys 5 girls 6

Language Practice: Proofreading

Rewrite each sentence correctly.

1. the temperature in the woods were below freezing and i got two cold
The temperature in the woods was below freezing and I got too cold.

2. the story about dr. terry were interesting
The story about Dr. Terry was interesting.

3. last tuesday i go to see the movie the patriot
Last Tuesday, I went to see the movie, "The Patriot."

4. canada be on the border of the united states
Canada is on the border of the United States.

5. do you like to ate shrimp
Do you like to eat shrimp?

Writing Practice: Write a story for a newspaper with the title "Whale Survives Oil Spill."

©Teacher Created Materials, Inc.   83   #3303 Daily Skills Practice–Grades 5-6

Page 84

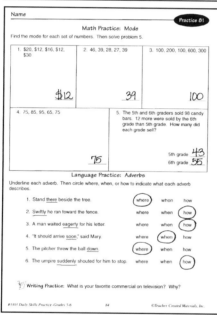

Name _____

Math Practice: Mode

Find the mode for each set of numbers. Then solve problem 5.

1. $20, $12, $16, $12, $30	2. 46, 39, 28, 27, 39	3. 100, 200, 100, 600, 300
$12	39	100

4. 75, 85, 95, 65, 75	5. The 5th and 6th graders sold 98 candy bars. 12 more were sold by the 6th grade than 5th grade. How many did each grade sell?
75	5th grade 43 6th grade 55

Language Practice: Adverbs

Underline each adverb. Then circle where, when, or how to indicate what each adverb describes.

1. Stand there beside the tree. — where
2. Swiftly he ran toward the fence. — how
3. A man waited eagerly for his letter. — how
4. "It should arrive soon," said Mary. — when
5. The pitcher threw the ball down. — where
6. The umpire suddenly shouted for him to stop. — how

Writing Practice: What is your favorite commercial on television? Why?

#3303 Daily Skills Practice–Grades 5-6   84   ©Teacher Created Materials, Inc.

Page 85

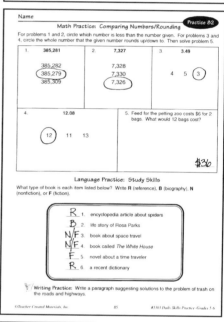

Name _____

Math Practice: Comparing Numbers/Rounding

For problems 1 and 2, circle which number is less than the number given. For problems 3 and 4, circle the whole number that the given number rounds up/down to. Then solve problem 5.

1. 385,281	2. 7,327	3. 3.49
385,282 385,279 385,309	7,328 7,330 7,326	4 5 3

4. 12.08	5. Feed for the petting zoo costs $6 for 2 bags. What would 12 bags cost?
12 11 13	$36

Language Practice: Study Skills

What type of book is each item listed below? Write R (reference), B (biography), N (nonfiction), or F (fiction).

R 1. encyclopedia article about spiders
B 2. life story of Rosa Parks
N/F 3. book about space travel
N/F 4. book called The White House
F 5. novel about a time traveler
R 6. a recent dictionary

Writing Practice: Write a paragraph suggesting solutions to the problem of trash on the roads and highways.

©Teacher Created Materials, Inc.   85   #3303 Daily Skills Practice–Grades 5-6

Page 86

Name _____

Math Practice: Addition with Decimals

Solve each problem below.

1. 46.8 + 9.6	2. 8.982 + 24.83	3. 0.84 + 0.67
56.4	33.812	1.51

4. 36.341 + 22.8	5. The cost of 2 books is $10.50. One cost $2.50 more than the other. What is the cost of each book?
59.141	Book 1 $4.00 Book 2 $6.50

Language Practice: Nouns

Underline 11 common nouns in the paragraph about whales.

Whales are one of the most intelligent animals. They are mammals, which mean they give birth to live young and use lungs to breathe. They migrate thousands of miles each year. When there isn't much food, they can live off their blubber.

Writing Practice: October is National Clock Month. Write about a time you lost track of time and were late for an important event/appointment.

#3303 Daily Skills Practice–Grades 5-6   86   ©Teacher Created Materials, Inc.

Page 87

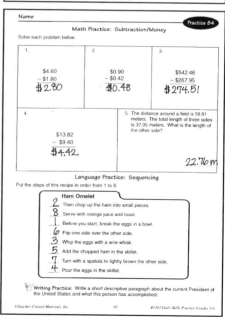

Name _____

Math Practice: Subtraction/Money

Solve each problem below.

1. $4.60 − $1.80	2. $0.90 − $0.42	3. $542.46 − $267.95
$2.80	$0.48	$274.51

4. $13.82 − $9.40	5. The distance around a field is 59.81 meters. The total length of three sides is 37.05 meters. What is the length of the other side?
$4.42	22.76 m

Language Practice: Sequencing

Put the steps of this recipe in order from 1 to 8.

Ham Omelet

2 Then chop up the ham into small pieces.
8 Serve with orange juice and toast.
1 Before you start, break the eggs in a bowl.
6 Flip one side over the other side.
3 Whip the eggs with a wire whisk.
5 Add the chopped ham in the skillet.
7 Turn with a spatula to lightly brown the other side.
4 Pour the eggs in the skillet.

Writing Practice: Write a short descriptive paragraph about the current President of the United States and what this person has accomplished.

©Teacher Created Materials, Inc.   87   #3303 Daily Skills Practice–Grades 5-6

Page 88

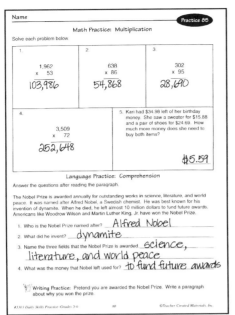

Name _____   Practice 85

Math Practice: Multiplication

Solve each problem below.

1.	2.	3.
1,962 x 53 **103,986**	638 x 86 **54,868**	302 x 95 **28,690**

4.	5. Kari had $34.98 left of her birthday money. She saw a sweater for $15.88 and a pair of shoes for $24.69. How much more money does she need to buy both items?
3,509 x 72 **252,648**	**$5.59**

Language Practice: Comprehension

Answer the questions after reading the paragraph.

The Nobel Prize is awarded annually for outstanding works in science, literature, and world peace. It was named after Alfred Nobel, a Swedish chemist. He was best known for his invention of dynamite. When he died, he left almost 10 million dollars to fund future awards. Americans like Woodrow Wilson and Martin Luther King, Jr. have won the Nobel Prize.

1. Who is the Nobel Prize named after? **Alfred Nobel**
2. What did he invent? **dynamite**
3. Name the three fields that the Nobel Prize is awarded **science, literature, and world peace**
4. What was the money that Nobel left used for? **to fund future awards**

Writing Practice: Pretend you are awarded the Nobel Prize. Write a paragraph about why you won the prize.

#3303 Daily Skills Practice–Grades 5-6   88   ©Teacher Created Materials, Inc.

Page 89

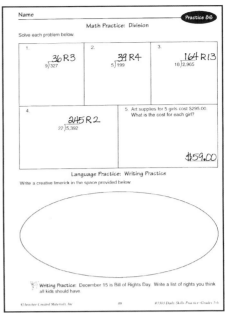

Name _____   Practice 86

Math Practice: Division

Solve each problem below.

1.	2.	3.
36 R3 9)327	**39 R4** 5)199	**164 R13** 18)2,965

4.	5. Art supplies for 5 girls cost $295.00. What is the cost for each girl?
245 R2 22)5,392	**$59.00**

Language Practice: Writing Practice

Write a creative limerick in the space provided below.

Writing Practice: December 15 is Bill of Rights Day. Write a list of rights you think all kids should have.

©Teacher Created Materials, Inc.   89   #3303 Daily Skills Practice-Grades 5-6

Page 90

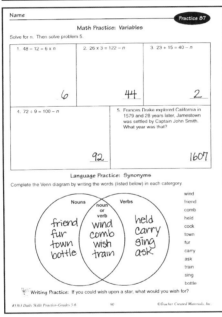

Name _____   Practice 87

Math Practice: Variables

Solve for n. Then solve problem 5.

1. 48 – 12 = 6 x n	2. 26 x 3 = 122 – n	3. 23 + 15 = 40 – n
6	**44**	**2**

4. 72 ÷ 9 = 100 – n	5. Frances Drake explored California in 1579 and 28 years later, Jamestown was settled by Captain John Smith. What year was that?
92	**1607**

Language Practice: Synonyms

Complete the Venn diagram by writing the words (listed below) in each category.

Nouns: **friend, fur, town, bottle**
noun or verb: **wind, comb, wish, train**
Verbs: **held, carry, sing, ask**

wind
friend
comb
held
cook
town
fur
carry
ask
train
sing
bottle

Writing Practice: If you could wish upon a star, what would you wish for?

#3303 Daily Skills Practice–Grades 5-6   90   ©Teacher Created Materials, Inc.

Page 91

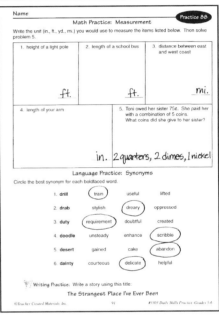

Name _____   Practice 88

Math Practice: Measurement

Write the unit (in., ft., yd., mi.) you would use to measure the items listed below. Then solve problem 5.

1. height of a light pole	2. length of a school bus	3. distance between east and west coast
ft.	**ft.**	**mi.**

4. length of your arm	5. Toni owed her sister 75¢. She paid her with a combination of 5 coins. What coins did she give to her sister?
in.	**2 quarters, 2 dimes, 1 nickel**

Language Practice: Synonyms

Circle the best synonym for each boldfaced word.

1. **drill**   (train)   useful   lifted
2. **drab**   stylish   (dreary)   oppressed
3. **duty**   (requirement)   doubtful   created
4. **doodle**   unsteady   enhance   (scribble)
5. **desert**   gained   cake   (abandon)
6. **dainty**   courteous   (delicate)   helpful

Writing Practice: Write a story using this title:
The Strangest Place I've Ever Been

©Teacher Created Materials, Inc.   91   #3303 Daily Skills Practice-Grades 5-6

Page 92

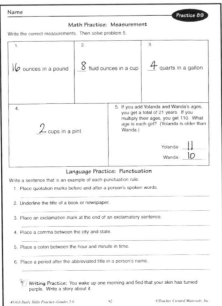

Name _____   Practice 89

Math Practice: Measurement

Write the correct measurements. Then solve problem 5.

1.	2.	3.
16 ounces in a pound	**8** fluid ounces in a cup	**4** quarts in a gallon

4.	5. If you add Yolanda and Wanda's ages, you get a total of 21 years. If you multiply their ages, you get 110. What age is each girl? (Yolanda is older than Wanda.)
2 cups in a pint	Yolanda: **11** Wanda: **10**

Language Practice: Punctuation

Write a sentence that is an example of each punctuation rule.

1. Place quotation marks before and after a person's spoken words.
2. Underline the title of a book or newspaper.
3. Place an exclamation mark at the end of an exclamatory sentence.
4. Place a comma between the city and state.
5. Place a colon between the hour and minute in time.
6. Place a period after the abbreviated title in a person's name.

Writing Practice: You wake up one morning and find that your skin has turned purple. Write a story about it.

#3303 Daily Skills Practice–Grades 5-6   92   ©Teacher Created Materials, Inc.

Page 93

Name _____   Practice 90

Math Practice: Multiplication/Fractions

Use multiplication to solve the problems below.

1.	2.	3.
$\frac{1}{5}$ x 40 = **8**	$\frac{2}{3}$ x 12 = **8**	8 x $\frac{3}{4}$ = **6**

4.	5. Of 60 5th grade students, 2/3 of them are in choir. How many are in choir?
45 x $\frac{2}{9}$ = **10**	**40**

Language Practice: Alphabetical Order

Write the names of these famous American women in alphabetical order by last name.

Amelia Earhart
Sally Ride
Dorothea Dix
Sandra Day O'Conner
Coretta Scott King
Annie Oakley
Sacagawea
Emily Dickinson
Wilma Rudolph
Elizabeth Cady Stanton

Emily Dickinson
Dorothea Dix
Amelia Earhart
Coretta Scott King
Annie Oakley
Sandra Day O'Conner
Sally Ride
Wilma Rudolph
Sacagawea
Elizabeth Cady Stanton

Writing Practice: Rewrite a classic fairy tale with a different ending and from a different point of view.

©Teacher Created Materials, Inc.   93   #3303 Daily Skills Practice-Grades 5-6

Page 94

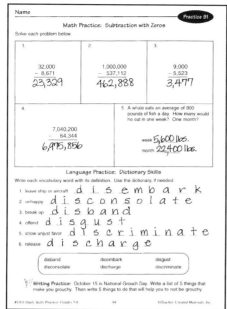

Math Practice: Subtraction with Zeros
Solve each problem below.

1.	2.	3.
32,000 − 8,671 = 23,329	1,000,000 − 537,112 = 462,888	9,000 − 5,523 = 3,477

4.	5. A whale eats an average of 800 pounds of fish a day. How many would he eat in one week? One month?
7,040,200 − 64,344 = 6,975,856	week 5,600 lbs. month 24,000 lbs.

Language Practice: Dictionary Skills
Write each vocabulary word with its definition. Use the dictionary, if needed.

1. leave ship or aircraft — disembark
2. unhappy — disconsolate
3. break up — disband
4. offend — disgust
5. show unjust favor — discriminate
6. release — discharge

| disband | disembark | disgust |
| disconsolate | discharge | discriminate |

Writing Practice: October 15 is National Grouch Day. Write a list of 5 things that make you grouchy. Then write 5 things to do that will help you to not be grouchy.

#3303 Daily Skills Practice–Grades 5-6   94   ©Teacher Created Materials, Inc.

Page 95

Math Practice: Money
Use the information in the chart to answer the questions.

| 1. How much would it cost for 2 small ornaments and 1 large ornament? $5.50 | 2. Would it cost more for 1 regular set of lights or 2 boxes of cards? lights |
| 3. Will $5.00 be enough to purchase 1 roll of wrapping paper, 3 bags of bows, and 1 small ornament? no | 4. What would the total cost be if you purchased 1 of each item? $19.61 |

Christmas Sale	
ornaments	
small	2/$3.00
large	2/$5.00
lights	
regular	$4.89
icicle	$5.89
cards	$2.25 box
wrapping paper	$1.99/roll
bows in bag	$0.59/bag 2 bags/$1.00

Language Practice: Verbs
Underline any verb and helping verb in each sentence.

1. It seemed colder yesterday.
2. We were walking down the street.
3. Bob was going to play football.
4. It began to snow heavily.
5. It was so cold, so I went inside.
6. Maybe tomorrow it will be warmer.

Writing Practice: Write a persuasive paragraph explaining your position on students going to school for nine months versus year-round school.

©Teacher Created Materials, Inc.   95   #3303 Daily Skills Practice–Grades 5-6

Page 96

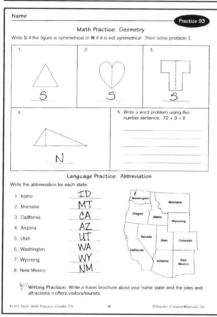

Math Practice: Geometry
Write S if the figure is symmetrical or N if it is not symmetrical. Then solve problem 5.

1. S
2. S
3. S
4. N
5. Write a word problem using this number sentence: 72 ÷ 9 = 8

Language Practice: Abbreviation
Write the abbreviation for each state.

1. Idaho — ID
2. Montana — MT
3. California — CA
4. Arizona — AZ
5. Utah — UT
6. Washington — WA
7. Wyoming — WY
8. New Mexico — NM

Writing Practice: Write a travel brochure about your home state and the sites and attractions it offers visitors/tourists.

#3303 Daily Skills Practice–Grades 5-6   96   ©Teacher Created Materials, Inc.

Page 97

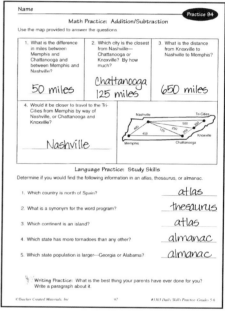

Math Practice: Addition/Subtraction
Use the map provided to answer the questions.

| 1. What is the difference in miles between Memphis and Chattanooga and between Memphis and Nashville? 50 miles | 2. Which city is the closest from Nashville to Chattanooga or Knoxville? By how much? Chattanooga 125 miles | 3. What is the distance from Knoxville to Nashville to Memphis? 650 miles |
| 4. Would it be closer to travel to the Tri-Cities from Memphis by way of Nashville, or Chattanooga and Knoxville? Nashville | |

Language Practice: Study Skills
Determine if you would find the following information in an atlas, thesaurus, or almanac.

1. Which country is north of Spain? — atlas
2. What is a synonym for the word program? — thesaurus
3. Which continent is an island? — atlas
4. Which state has more tornadoes than any other? — almanac
5. Which state population is larger—Georgia or Alabama? — almanac

Writing Practice: What is the best thing your parents have ever done for you? Write a paragraph about it.

©Teacher Created Materials, Inc.   97   #3303 Daily Skills Practice–Grades 5-6

Page 98

Math Practice: Addition/Subtraction
Find the dates of these events in African American history. Then solve problem 5.

| 1. Beginning of slavery in America (25 years before 1644) 1619 | 2. Slavery is abolished. (246 years after #1) 1865 | 3. African Americans are granted the right to vote. (5 years after #2) 1870 |
| 4. Civil Rights Act was signed in Washington (99 years after #2) 1964 | 5. Marcus bought a super burger for $1.59, fries for $0.89 and a soda for $0.69. What is his change from $5.00? $1.83 | |

Language Practice: Adjective/Adverbs
Fill in the chart with an adjective and adverb that begins with the same letter.

	adjective	adverb
1. a		
2. d		
3. g		
4. l		
5. n		
6. r		

Writing Practice: What happened after "happily ever after"? Write a continuation story of a fairy tale. (For example, after Cinderella and Prince Charming got married, what happened afterwards?)

#3303 Daily Skills Practice–Grades 5-6   98   ©Teacher Created Materials, Inc.

Page 99

Math Practice: Division/Money
Circle the price which is the best bargain for each product. Then solve problem 5.

| 1. 2/69¢ or 4/$1.09 | 2. 3/$1.00 or 2/59¢ | 3. 6/$1.59 or 8/$2.39 |
| 4. 8 oz./89¢ or 16 oz./$1.69 | 5. The video that Jane bought was 1/3 off. If it originally cost $27.99, what would the sale price be? $18.66 | |

Language Practice: Compare and Contrast
Describe how each is the same and different.

	same	different
1. rectangle and square		
2. acute angle and obtuse angle		
3. notebook paper and computer paper		
4. math book and language book		
5. your math teacher and your P. E. teacher		
6. you and your best friend		

Writing Practice: How useful are computers and the Internet? Describe several ways how they help you today.

©Teacher Created Materials, Inc.   99   #3303 Daily Skills Practice–Grades 5-6

Page 100

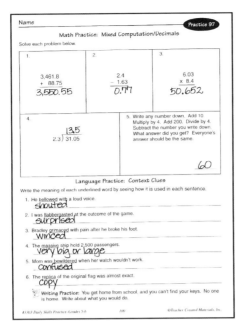

Name _____ *Practice 97*

Math Practice: Mixed Computation/Decimals

Solve each problem below.

1.	2.	3.
3,461.8 + 88.75 **3,550.55**	2.4 − 1.63 **0.77**	6.03 × 8.4 **50.652**

4.	5. Write any number down. Add 10. Multiply by 4. Add 200. Divide by 4. Subtract the number you write down. What answer did you get? Everyone's answer should be the same.
135 2.3) 31.05	**60**

Language Practice: Context Clues

Write the meaning of each underlined word by seeing how it is used in each sentence.

1. He bellowed with a loud voice. **shouted**
2. I was flabbergasted at the outcome of the game. **surprised**
3. Bradley grimaced with pain after he broke his foot. **winced**
4. The massive ship hold 2,500 passengers. **very big or large**
5. Mom was bewildered when her watch wouldn't work. **confused**
6. The replica of the original flag was almost exact. **copy**

Writing Practice: You get home from school, and you can't find your keys. No one is home. Write about what you would do.

#3303 Daily Skills Practice–Grades 5-6   100   ©Teacher Created Materials, Inc.

Page 101

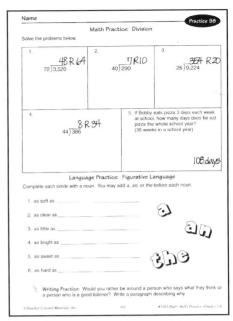

Name _____ *Practice 98*

Math Practice: Division

Solve the problems below.

1.	2.	3.
48 R 64 72)3,520	**7 R10** 40)290	**354 R 20** 26)9,224

4.	5. If Bobby eats pizza 3 days each week at school, how many days does he eat pizza the whole school year? (36 weeks in a school year)
8 R 34 44)386	**108 days**

Language Practice: Figurative Language

Complete each simile with a noun. You may add *a, an,* or *the* before each noun.

1. as soft as _____
2. as clear as _____
3. as little as _____
4. as bright as _____
5. as sweet as _____
6. as hard as _____

a an the

Writing Practice: Would you rather be around a person who says what they think or a person who is a good listener? Write a paragraph describing why.

©Teacher Created Materials, Inc.   101   #3303 Daily Skills Practice–Grades 5-6

Page 102

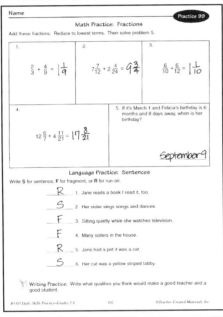

Name _____ *Practice 99*

Math Practice: Fractions

Add these fractions. Reduce to lowest terms. Then solve problem 5.

1.	2.	3.
$\frac{2}{3} + \frac{4}{9} = 1\frac{1}{9}$	$7\frac{7}{12} + 2\frac{4}{24} = 9\frac{3}{4}$	$\frac{6}{10} + \frac{6}{12} = 1\frac{1}{10}$

4.	5. If it's March 1 and Felicia's birthday is 6 months and 8 days away, when is her birthday?
$12\frac{6}{7} + 4\frac{11}{21} = 17\frac{8}{21}$	**September 9**

Language Practice: Sentences

Write **S** for sentence, **F** for fragment, or **R** for run-on.

R 1. Jane reads a book I read it, too.
S 2. Her sister sings songs and dances.
F 3. Sitting quietly while she watches television.
F 4. Many sisters in the house.
R 5. Jane had a pet it was a cat.
S 6. Her cat was a yellow striped tabby.

Writing Practice: Write what qualities you think would make a good teacher and a good student.

#3303 Daily Skills Practice–Grades 5-6   102   ©Teacher Created Materials, Inc.

Page 103

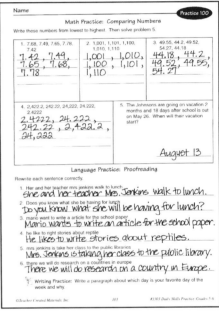

Name _____ *Practice 100*

Math Practice: Comparing Numbers

Write these numbers from lowest to highest. Then solve problem 5.

1. 7.68, 7.49, 7.65, 7.78, 7.42	2. 1,001, 1,101, 1,100, 1,010, 1,110	3. 49.55, 44.2, 49.52, 54.27, 44.18
7.42, 7.49, 7.65, 7.68, 7.78	**1,001, 1,010, 1,100, 1,101, 1,110**	**44.18, 44.2, 49.52, 49.55, 54.27**

4. 2,422.2, 242.22, 24,222, 2.4222	5. The Johnsons are going on vacation 2 months and 18 days after school is out on May 26. When will their vacation start?
2.4222, 24.222, 242.22, 2,422.2, 24,222	**August 13**

Language Practice: Proofreading

Rewrite each sentence correctly.

1. Her and her teacher mrs jenkins walk to lunch. **She and her teacher Mrs. Jenkins walk to lunch.**
2. Does you know what she be having for lunch **Do you know what she will be having for lunch?**
3. mario want to write an article for the school paper **Mario wants to write an article for the school paper.**
4. he like to right stories about reptile **He likes to write stories about reptiles.**
5. mrs jenkins is take her class to the public libraries **Mrs. Jenkins is taking her class to the public library.**
6. there we will do research on a countries in europe **There we will do research on a country in Europe.**

Writing Practice: Write a paragraph about which day is your favorite day of the week and why.

©Teacher Created Materials, Inc.   103   #3303 Daily Skills Practice–Grades 5-6

Page 104

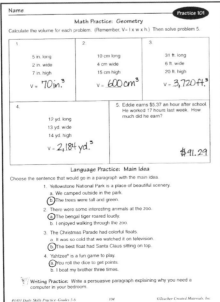

Name _____ *Practice 101*

Math Practice: Geometry

Calculate the volume for each problem. (Remember, V = l x w x h.) Then solve problem 5.

1.	2.	3.
5 in. long 2 in. wide 7 in. high V = **70 in.³**	10 cm long 4 cm wide 15 cm high V = **600 cm³**	31 ft. long 6 ft. wide 20 ft. high V = **3,720 ft.³**

4.	5. Eddie earns $5.37 an hour after school. He worked 17 hours last week. How much did he earn?
12 yd. long 13 yd. wide 14 yd. high V = **2,184 yd.³**	**$91.29**

Language Practice: Main Idea

Choose the sentence that would go in a paragraph with the main idea.

1. Yellowstone National Park is a place of beautiful scenery.
   a. We camped outside in the park.
   b. The trees were tall and green.
2. There were some interesting animals at the zoo.
   a. The bengal tiger roared loudly.
   b. I enjoyed walking through the zoo.
3. The Christmas Parade had colorful floats.
   a. It was so cold that we watched it on television.
   b. The best float had Santa Claus sitting on top.
4. Yahtzee® is a fun game to play.
   a. You roll the dice to get points.
   b. I beat my brother three times.

Writing Practice: Write a persuasive paragraph explaining why you need a computer in your bedroom.

#3303 Daily Skills Practice–Grades 5-6   104   ©Teacher Created Materials, Inc.

Page 105

Name _____ *Practice 102*

Math Practice: Time

Calculate how much time has passed in each problem. Then solve problem 5.

1. 8:10 A.M. to 3:40 P.M.	2. 12:46 P.M. to 9:06 P.M.	3. 5:28 A.M. to 12:00 P.M.
7 hrs. 30 min.	**8 hrs. 20 min.**	**6 hrs. 32 min.**

4. 10:37 P.M. to 9:00 A.M.	5. It's 38° at 7:00 A.M. By 3:00 P.M. it is 52°. How much did the temperature rise?
10 hrs. 23 min.	**14°**

Language Practice: Possessives

Fill in the chart with the correct possessive nouns.

Noun	Singular Possessive	Plural Possessive
class	class's	classes'
town	town's	towns'
child	child's	children's
beach	beach's	beaches'
whale	whale's	whales'

Writing Practice: Write a letter to your local newspaper expressing your concerns and views about an issue (examples: pollution, driving safety, pet adoption, etc.) that you feel needs some attention.

©Teacher Created Materials, Inc.   105   #3303 Daily Skills Practice–Grades 5-6

Page 106

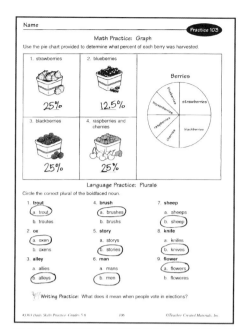

Practice 103

Math Practice: Graph

Use the pie chart provided to determine what percent of each berry was harvested.

1. strawberries	2. blueberries
25%	12.5%

Berries

3. blackberries	4. raspberries and cherries
25%	25%

Language Practice: Plurals

Circle the correct plural of the boldfaced noun.

1. **trout** — (a. trout) / b. troutes
2. **ox** — (a. oxen) / b. oxens
3. **alley** — a. allies / (b. alleys)
4. **brush** — (a. brushes) / b. brushs
5. **story** — a. storys / (b. stories)
6. **man** — a. mans / (b. men)
7. **sheep** — a. sheeps / (b. sheep)
8. **knife** — a. knifes / (b. knives)
9. **flower** — (a. flowers) / b. floweres

✎ **Writing Practice:** What does it mean when people vote in elections?

Page 107

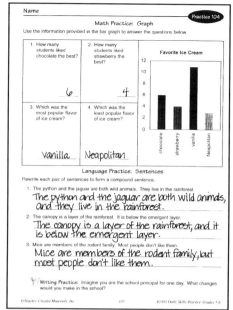

Practice 104

Math Practice: Graph

Use the information provided in the bar graph to answer the questions below.

1. How many students liked chocolate the best? **6**
2. How many students liked strawberry the best? **4**
3. Which was the most popular flavor of ice cream? **vanilla**
4. Which was the least popular flavor of ice cream? **Neapolitan**

Favorite Ice Cream

Language Practice: Sentences

Rewrite each pair of sentences to form a compound sentence.

1. The python and the jaguar are both wild animals. They live in the rainforest.
   The python and the jaguar are both wild animals, and they live in the rainforest.
2. The canopy is a layer of the rainforest. It is below the emergent layer.
   The canopy is a layer of the rainforest, and it is below the emergent layer.
3. Mice are members of the rodent family. Most people don't like them.
   Mice are members of the rodent family, but most people don't like them.

✎ **Writing Practice:** Imagine you are the school principal for one day. What changes would you make in the school?

Page 108

Practice 105

Math Practice: Addition

Find the minuend of each subtraction problem by using the numbers already given. Then solve problem 5.

1. 189,046 − 73,281 = 115,765
2. 26,202 − 48 = 26,154
3. 118,225 − 45,439 = 72,786
4. 7,547 − 1,764 = 5,783
5. After spending $342.80 for a television, D. J. had $186.20 left. How much did she have before she bought the television? **$529.00**

Language Practice: Nouns

Fill in each blank with a common (C) or proper (P) noun.

1. _____ (P) was born in the _____ (C) of May.
2. The _____ (C) visited the _____ (P) Zoo.
3. On _____ (P) we will take a spelling _____ (C).
4. _____ (P) sold magazines to his _____ (C).
5. Our _____ (C) is named _____ (P) School.
6. We drove through the _____ (C) in the beautiful state of _____ (P).

✎ **Writing Practice:** Describe what your life would be like if you lived underwater.

Page 109

Practice 106

Math Practice: Addition

Solve each problem below.

1. 26,407 + 389 + 1,683 + 42 = 28,521
2. 705 + 3,060 + 129 + 5,783 = 9,677
3. 5,863 + 19,700 + 85,708 + 635 = 111,906
4. 595 + 1,460 + 3,790 + 295 = 6,140
5. During the month of November, Shawn spent $42.00 for lunches, $14.00 for movies, and $67.23 for clothes. How much did he spend in all? **$123.23**

Language Practice: Figurative Language

Tell what you think each figurative statement really means.

1. He's all ears! **He is listening intently.**
2. Get off my back! **Leave me alone!**
3. Lend me your ear. **Listen to me.**
4. Give me a hand. **Help me.**
5. Who let the cat out of the bag? **Who told the secret?**
6. I've got my eye on you. **I'm watching you.**

✎ **Writing Practice:** Write a "how-to" paragraph on how to make a ham sandwich.

Page 110

Practice 107

Math Practice: Rounding

Round each number to the nearest thousand. Then solve problem 5.

1. 703 → **1,000**
2. 28,619 → **29,000**
3. 14,005,221 → **14,005,000**
4. 340,530 → **341,000**
5. Irene made a 97, 73, 82, and 91 on her tests in biology. How much higher was her best score than her lowest? **24 points**

Language Practice: Sentences

Rewrite these fragments as complete sentences.

1. burning leaves
2. ran to the door
3. caught in the escalator
4. the famous man
5. a noise outside
6. with his homework

✎ **Writing Practice:** April 1 is April Fool's Day. Describe a time when someone really fooled you.

Page 111

Practice 108

Math Practice: Roman Numerals

Circle the number that stands for each Roman Numeral. Then solve problem 5.

1. LXI — a. 56 / b. 66 / (c. 61)
2. CLIV — a. 155 / (b. 154) / c. 164
3. XCIX — a. 91 / (b. 99) / c. 109
4. MCMXLV — (a. 1,945) / b. 1,055 / c. 1,155
5. If 2,982,123,000 pounds of chocolate were made into candy bars in 1985 and 2,306,582,000 pounds of chocolate were made into candy bars in 1995, how many more pounds of chocolate were used in 1985 than in 1995? **675,541,000 pounds**

Language Practice: Verbs

Finish each sentence with a compound verb.

1. At the store, Mom _____.
2. During the basketball game, Marty _____.
3. On our vacation, my family _____.
4. The animals in the zoo _____.
5. The children _____.
6. The visitors at school _____.

✎ **Writing Practice:** President's Day is in February. What would you do if you were president of your class?

Page 112

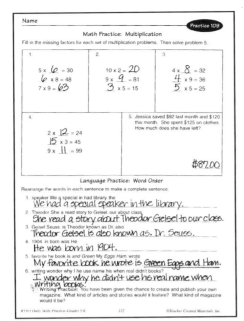

Practice 109

Math Practice: Multiplication

Fill in the missing factors for each set of multiplication problems. Then solve problem 5.

1.	2.	3.
$5 \times 6 = 30$	$10 \times 2 = 20$	$4 \times 8 = 32$
$6 \times 8 = 48$	$9 \times 9 = 81$	$4 \times 9 = 36$
$7 \times 9 = 63$	$3 \times 5 = 15$	$5 \times 5 = 25$

4.	5. Jessica saved $92 last month and $120 this month. She spent $125 on clothes. How much does she have left?
$2 \times 12 = 24$	
$15 \times 3 = 45$	
$9 \times 11 = 99$	$87.00

Language Practice: Word Order

Rearrange the words in each sentence to make a complete sentence.

1. speaker We a special in had library. the
   We had a special speaker in the library.

2. Theodor She a read story to Geisel. our about class
   She read a story about Theodor Geisel to our class.

3. Geisel Seuss. is Theodor known as Dr. also
   Theodor Geisel is also known as. Dr. Seuss.

4. 1904. in born was He
   He was born in 1904.

5. favorite he book is and Green My Eggs Ham. wrote
   My favorite book he wrote is Green Eggs and Ham.

6. writing wonder why I use name his when real didn't books?
   I wonder why he didn't use his real name when writing books!

Writing Practice: You have been given the chance to create and publish your own magazine. What kind of articles and stories would it feature? What kind of magazine would it be?

#3303 Daily Skills Practice–Grades 5-6   112   ©Teacher Created Materials, Inc.

Page 113

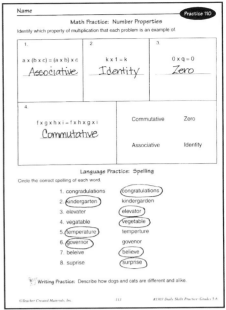

Practice 110

Math Practice: Number Properties

Identify which property of multiplication that each problem is an example of.

1. $a \times (b \times c) = (a \times b) \times c$	2. $k \times 1 = k$	3. $0 \times q = 0$
Associative	Identity	Zero

4. $f \times g \times h \times i = f \times h \times g \times i$	Commutative Zero
Commutative	Associative Identity

Language Practice: Spelling

Circle the correct spelling of each word.

1. congradulations — (congratulations)
2. (kindergarten) — kindergarden
3. elevator — (elevator)
4. vegatable — (vegetable)
5. (temperature) — temperture
6. (governor) — govenor
7. believe — (believe)
8. suprise — (surprise)

Writing Practice: Describe how dogs and cats are different and alike.

©Teacher Created Materials, Inc.   113   *#3303 Daily Skills Practice–Grades 5-6*

Page 114

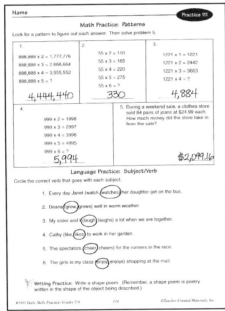

Practice 111

Math Practice: Patterns

Look for a pattern to figure out each answer. Then solve problem 5.

1.	2.	3.
$888,888 \times 2 = 1,777,776$	$55 \times 2 = 110$	$1221 \times 1 = 1221$
$888,888 \times 3 = 2,666,664$	$55 \times 3 = 165$	$1221 \times 2 = 2442$
$888,888 \times 4 = 3,555,552$	$55 \times 4 = 220$	$1221 \times 3 = 3663$
$888,888 \times 5 = ?$	$55 \times 5 = 275$	$1221 \times 4 = ?$
	$55 \times 6 = ?$	
4,444,440	330	4,884

4.	5. During a weekend sale, a clothes store sold 84 pairs of jeans at $24.99 each. How much money did the store take in from the sale?
$999 \times 2 = 1998$	
$999 \times 3 = 2997$	
$999 \times 4 = 3996$	
$999 \times 5 = 4995$	
$999 \times 6 = ?$	
5,994	$2,099.16

Language Practice: Subject/Verb

Circle the correct verb that goes with each subject.

1. Every day Janet (watch, (watches)) her daughter get on the bus.
2. Beans ((grow), grows) well in warm weather.
3. My sister and I ((laugh), laughs) a lot when we are together.
4. Cathy ((likes), likes) to work in her garden.
5. The spectators ((cheer), cheers) for the runners in the race.
6. The girls in my class ((enjoy), enjoys) shopping at the mall.

Writing Practice: Write a shape poem. (Remember, a shape poem is poetry written in the shape of the object being described.)

#3303 Daily Skills Practice–Grades 5-6   114   ©Teacher Created Materials, Inc.

Page 115

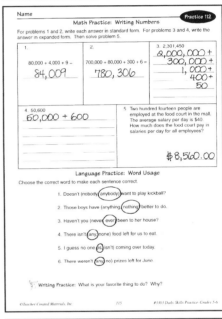

Practice 112

Math Practice: Writing Numbers

For problems 1 and 2, write each answer in standard form. For problems 3 and 4, write the answer in expanded form. Then solve problem 5.

1. $80,000 + 4,000 + 9 =$	2. $700,000 + 80,000 + 300 + 6 =$	3. 2,301,450
84,009	780,306	2,000,000 + 300,000 + 1,000 + 400 + 50

4. 50,600	5. Two hundred fourteen people are employed at the food court in the mall. The average salary per day is $40. How much does the food court pay in salaries per day for all employees?
50,000 + 600	$8,560.00

Language Practice: Word Usage

Choose the correct word to make each sentence correct.

1. Doesn't (nobody, (anybody)) want to play kickball?
2. Those boys have (anything, (nothing)) better to do.
3. Haven't you (never, (ever)) been to her house?
4. There isn't ((any), none) food left for us to eat.
5. I guess no one ((is), isn't) coming over today.
6. There weren't ((any), no) prizes left for June.

Writing Practice: What is your favorite thing to do? Why?

©Teacher Created Materials, Inc.   115   *#3303 Daily Skills Practice–Grades 5-6*

Page 116

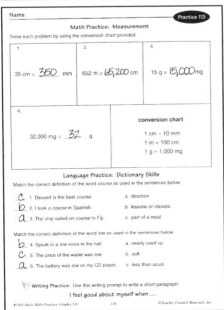

Practice 113

Math Practice: Measurement

Solve each problem by using the conversion chart provided.

1.	2.	3.
35 cm = 350 mm	652 m = 65,200 cm	15 g = 15,000 mg

4.	conversion chart
32,000 mg = 32 g	1 cm = 10 mm
	1 m = 100 cm
	1 g = 1,000 mg

Language Practice: Dictionary Skills

Match the correct definition of the word *course* as used in the sentences below.

c 1. Dessert is the best *course*.   a. direction
b 2. I took a *course* in Spanish.   b. lessons or classes
a 3. The ship sailed on course to Fiji.   c. part of a meal

Match the correct definition of the word *low* as used in the sentences below.

b 4. Speak in a *low* voice in the hall.   a. nearly used up
c 5. The price of the wallet was *low*.   b. soft
a 6. The battery is *low* on my CD player.   c. less than usual

Writing Practice: Use this writing prompt to write a short paragraph:
I feel good about myself when …

#3303 Daily Skills Practice–Grades 5-6   116   ©Teacher Created Materials, Inc.

Page 117

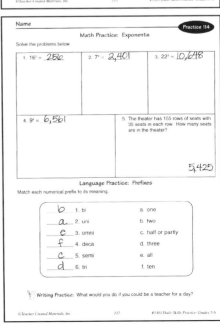

Practice 114

Math Practice: Exponents

Solve the problems below.

1. $16^2 = 256$	2. $7^4 = 2,401$	3. $22^3 = 10,648$

4. $9^4 = 6,561$	5. The theater has 155 rows of seats with 35 seats in each row. How many seats are in the theater?
	5,425

Language Practice: Prefixes

Match each numerical prefix to its meaning.

b 1. bi   a. one
a 2. uni   b. two
e 3. omni   c. half or partly
f 4. deca   d. three
c 5. semi   e. all
d 6. tri   f. ten

Writing Practice: What would you do if you could be a teacher for a day?

©Teacher Created Materials, Inc.   117   *#3303 Daily Skills Practice–Grades 5-6*

Page 118

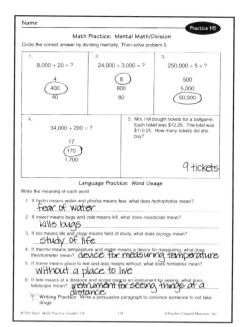

Name _____ Practice 115

Math Practice: Mental Math/Division
Circle the correct answer by dividing mentally. Then solve problem 5.

1. 8,000 ÷ 20 = ?	2. 24,000 ÷ 3,000 = ?	3. 250,000 ÷ 5 = ?
4 / (400) / 40	(8) / 800 / 80	500 / 5,000 / (50,000)

4. 34,000 ÷ 200 = ?	5. Mrs. Hill bought tickets for a ballgame. Each ticket was $12.25. The total was $110.25. How many tickets did she buy?
17 / (170) / 1,700	9 tickets

Language Practice: Word Usage
Write the meaning of each word.

1. If *hydro* means water and *phobia* means fear, what does *hydrophobia* mean?
   fear of water
2. If *insect* means bugs and *cide* means kill, what does *insecticide* mean?
   kills bugs
3. If *bio* means life and *ology* means field of study, what does *biology* mean?
   study of life
4. If *thermo* means temperature and *meter* means a device for measuring, what does *thermometer* mean? _device for measuring temperature_
5. If *home* means place to live and *less* means without, what does *homeless* mean?
   without a place to live
6. If *tele* means at a distance and *scope* means an instrument for seeing, what does *telescope* mean? _instrument for seeing things at a distance_

Writing Practice: Write a persuasive paragraph to convince someone to not take drugs.

#3303 Daily Skills Practice–Grades 5-6   118   ©Teacher Created Materials, Inc.

Page 119

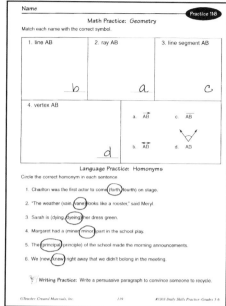

Name _____ Practice 116

Math Practice: Geometry
Match each name with the correct symbol.

1. line AB	2. ray AB	3. line segment AB
b	a	c

4. vertex AB	a. $\overrightarrow{AB}$ c. $\overline{AB}$
d	b. $\overleftrightarrow{AB}$ d. AB

Language Practice: Homonyms
Circle the correct homonym in each sentence.

1. Charlton was the first actor to come (forth, fourth) on stage.
2. "The weather (vain, vane) looks like a rooster," said Meryl.
3. Sarah is (dying, dyeing) her dress green.
4. Margaret had a (miner, minor) part in the school play.
5. The (principal, principle) of the school made the morning announcements.
6. We (new, knew) right away that we didn't belong in the meeting.

Writing Practice: Write a persuasive paragraph to convince someone to recycle.

©Teacher Created Materials, Inc.   119   #3303 Daily Skills Practice–Grades 5-6

Page 120

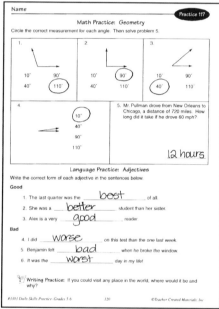

Name _____ Practice 117

Math Practice: Geometry
Circle the correct measurement for each angle. Then solve problem 5.

1.	2.	3.
10° / 90° / 40° / (110°)	10° / (90°) / 40° / 110°	10° / 90° / (40°) / 110°

4.	5. Mr. Pullman drove from New Orleans to Chicago, a distance of 720 miles. How long did it take if he drove 60 mph?
(10°) / 40° / 90° / 110°	12 hours

Language Practice: Adjectives
Write the correct form of each adjective in the sentences below.

Good
1. The last quarter was the _best_ of all.
2. She was a _better_ student than her sister.
3. Alex is a very _good_ reader.

Bad
4. I did _worse_ on this test than the one last week.
5. Benjamin felt _bad_ when he broke the window.
6. It was the _worst_ day in my life!

Writing Practice: If you could visit any place in the world, where would it be and why?

#3303 Daily Skills Practice–Grades 5-6   120   ©Teacher Created Materials, Inc.

Page 121

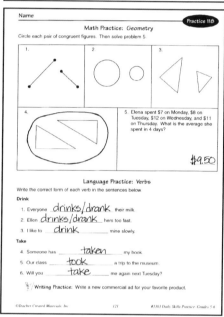

Name _____ Practice 118

Math Practice: Geometry
Circle each pair of congruent figures. Then solve problem 5.

1.	2.	3.

4.	5. Elena spent $7 on Monday, $8 on Tuesday, $12 on Wednesday, and $11 on Thursday. What is the average she spent in 4 days?
	$9.50

Language Practice: Verbs
Write the correct form of each verb in the sentences below

Drink
1. Everyone _drinks/drank_ their milk.
2. Ellen _drinks/drank_ hers too fast.
3. I like to _drink_ mine slowly.

Take
4. Someone has _taken_ my book.
5. Our class _took_ a trip to the museum.
6. Will you _take_ me again next Tuesday?

Writing Practice: Write a new commercial ad for your favorite product.

©Teacher Created Materials, Inc.   121   #3303 Daily Skills Practice–Grades 5-6

Page 122

Name _____ Practice 119

Math Practice: Geometry
Define the geometry terms listed below. Then solve problem 5.

1. parallel	2. segment	3. plane
straight lines lying in the same plane but never meeting, no matter how far extended	a finite section of a line	a flat or level surface

4. vertex	Raisins are sold in boxes of 12¢ each or in a package of 8 for $1.00. Which would be cheaper?
a point in a plane figure common to two or more sides	12¢ each

Language Practice: Syllables
Circle the word which is correctly divided into syllables.

1. member — me-mber / (mem-ber)
2. memory — (mem-o-ry) / memo-ry
3. measure — mea-sure / (meas-ure)
4. matron — mat-ron / (ma-tron)
5. mayor — ma-yor / (may-or)
6. meditate — (med-i-tate) / me-di-tate

Writing Practice: Write a "how-to" paragraph on how to make a banana split.

#3303 Daily Skills Practice–Grades 5-6   122   ©Teacher Created Materials, Inc.

Page 123

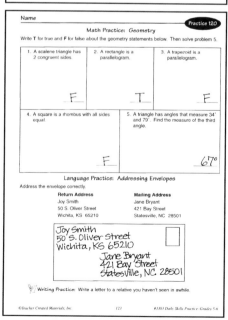

Name _____ Practice 120

Math Practice: Geometry
Write T for true and F for false about the geometry statements below. Then solve problem 5.

1. A scalene triangle has 2 congruent sides.	2. A rectangle is a parallelogram.	3. A trapezoid is a parallelogram.
F	T	F

4. A square is a rhombus with all sides equal.	5. A triangle has angles that measure 34° and 79°. Find the measure of the third angle.
F	67°

Language Practice: Addressing Envelopes
Address the envelope correctly.

Return Address
Joy Smith
50 S. Oliver Street
Wichita, KS 65210

Mailing Address
Jane Bryant
421 Bay Street
Statesville, NC 28501

Joy Smith
50 S. Oliver Street
Wichita, KS 65210

Jane Bryant
421 Bay Street
Statesville, NC 28501

Writing Practice: Write a letter to a relative you haven't seen in awhile.

©Teacher Created Materials, Inc.   123   #3303 Daily Skills Practice–Grades 5-6

Page 124

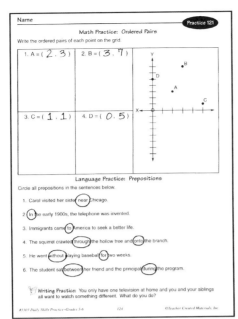

Name

Practice 121

Math Practice: Ordered Pairs

Write the ordered pairs of each point on the grid.

| 1. A = (2, 3) | 2. B = (3, 7) |
| 3. C = (1, 1) | 4. D = (0, 5) |

Language Practice: Prepositions

Circle all prepositions in the sentences below.

1. Carol visited her sister near Chicago.
2. In the early 1900s, the telephone was invented.
3. Immigrants came to America to seek a better life.
4. The squirrel crawled through the hollow tree and onto the branch.
5. He went without playing baseball for two weeks.
6. The student sat between her friend and the principal during the program.

✏️ **Writing Practice:** You only have one television at home and you and your siblings all want to watch something different. What do you do?

#3302 Daily Skills Practice—Grades 5-6   124   ©Teacher Created Materials, Inc.

Page 125

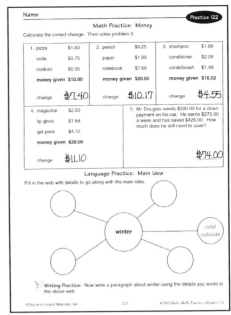

Name

Practice 122

Math Practice: Money

Calculate the correct change. Then solve problem 5.

1. pizza	$1.50	2. pencil	$0.25	3. shampoo	$1.89
soda	$0.75	paper	$1.89	conditioner	$2.09
cookies	$0.35	notebook	$7.69	comb/brush	$1.49
money given	$10.00	money given	$20.00	money given	$10.02
change	$7.40	change	$10.17	change	$4.55

4. magazine	$2.50	5. Mr. Douglas needs $500.00 for a down payment on his car. He earns $275.00 a week and has saved $426.00. How much does he still need to save?
lip gloss	$1.68	
gel pens	$4.72	
money given	$20.00	
change	$11.10	$74.00

Language Practice: Main Idea

Fill in the web with details to go along with the main idea.

winter   cold outside

✏️ **Writing Practice:** Now write a paragraph about winter using the details you wrote in the above web.

©Teacher Created Materials, Inc.   125   #3303 Daily Skills Practice—Grades 5-6

Page 126

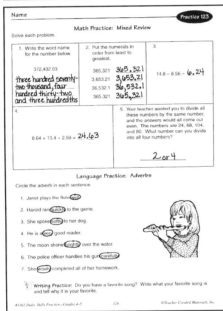

Name

Practice 123

Math Practice: Mixed Review

Solve each problem.

1. Write the word name for the number below.	2. Put the numerals in order from least to greatest.	3.
372,432.03	365,321 → 365,321	14.8 − 8.56 = 6.24
three hundred seventy-two thousand, four hundred thirty-two and three hundredths	3,653.21 → 3,653.21	
	36,532.1 → 36,532.1	
	365,321 → 365,321	

| 4. | 5. Your teacher wanted you to divide all these numbers by the same number, and the answers would all come out even. The numbers are 24, 68, 104, and 80. What number can you divide into all four numbers? |
| 8.64 + 13.4 + 2.59 = 24.63 | 2 or 4 |

Language Practice: Adverbs

Circle the adverb in each sentence.

1. Janet plays the flute well.
2. Harold ran quickly to the game.
3. She spoke softly to her dog.
4. He is a very good reader.
5. The moon shone brightly over the water.
6. The police officer handles his gun carefully.
7. She wisely completed all of her homework.

✏️ **Writing Practice:** Do you have a favorite song? Write what your favorite song is and why it is your favorite.

#3302 Daily Skills Practice—Grades 4-5   126   ©Teacher Created Materials, Inc.

Page 127

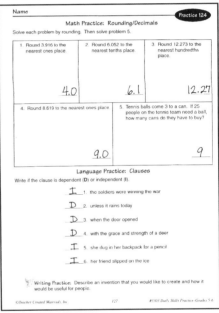

Name

Practice 124

Math Practice: Rounding/Decimals

Solve each problem by rounding. Then solve problem 5.

1. Round 3.916 to the nearest ones place.	2. Round 6.052 to the nearest tenths place.	3. Round 12.273 to the nearest hundredths place.
4.0	6.1	12.27
4. Round 8.619 to the nearest ones place	5. Tennis balls come 3 to a can. If 25 people on the tennis team need a ball, how many cans do they have to buy?
9.0	9

Language Practice: Clauses

Write if the clause is dependent (D) or independent (I).

I 1. the soldiers were winning the war
D 2. unless it rains today
D 3. when the door opened
D 4. with the grace and strength of a deer
I 5. she dug in her backpack for a pencil
I 6. her friend slipped on the ice

✏️ **Writing Practice:** Describe an invention that you would like to create and how it would be useful for people.

©Teacher Created Materials, Inc.   127   #3303 Daily Skills Practice—Grades 5-6

Page 128

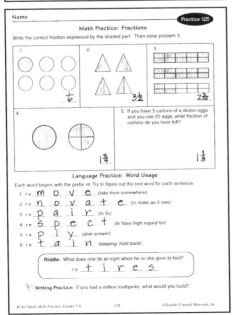

Name

Practice 125

Math Practice: Fractions

Write the correct fraction expressed by the shaded part. Then solve problem 5.

| 1. | 2. | 3. |
| $\frac{}{6}$ | $3\frac{1}{2}$ | $2\frac{1}{16}$ |

| 4. | 5. If you have 3 cartons of a dozen eggs and you use 20 eggs, what fraction of cartons do you have left? |
| $1\frac{3}{4}$ | $1\frac{1}{3}$ |

Language Practice: Word Usage

Each word begins with the prefix re. Try to figure out the root word for each sentence.

1. re m o v e (take from somewhere)
2. re n o v a t e (to make as if new)
3. re p a i r (to fix)
4. re s p e c t (to have high regard for)
5. re p l y (give answer)
6. re t a i n (keeping; hold back)

Riddle: What does one do at night when he or she goes to bed?
re t i r e s

✏️ **Writing Practice:** If you had a million toothpicks, what would you build?

#3303 Daily Skills Practice—Grades 5-6   128   ©Teacher Created Materials, Inc.

Page 129

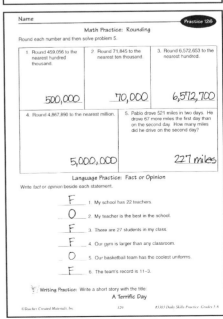

Name

Practice 126

Math Practice: Rounding

Round each number and then solve problem 5.

1. Round 459,056 to the nearest hundred thousand.	2. Round 71,845 to the nearest ten thousand.	3. Round 6,572,653 to the nearest hundred.
500,000	70,000	6,572,700
4. Round 4,867,890 to the nearest million.	5. Pablo drove 521 miles in two days. He drove 67 more miles the first day than on the second day. How many miles did he drive on the second day?
5,000,000	227 miles

Language Practice: Fact or Opinion

Write fact or opinion beside each statement.

F 1. My school has 22 teachers.
O 2. My teacher is the best in the school.
F 3. There are 27 students in my class.
F 4. Our gym is larger than any classroom.
O 5. Our basketball team has the coolest uniforms.
F 6. The team's record is 11–3.

✏️ **Writing Practice:** Write a short story with the title:
A Terrific Day

©Teacher Created Materials, Inc.   129   #3303 Daily Skills Practice—Grades 5-6

Page 130

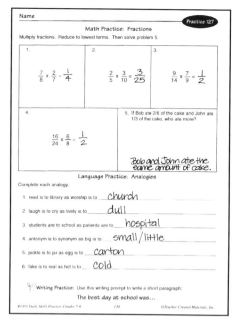

Name _____

Math Practice: Fractions
Multiply fractions. Reduce to lowest terms. Then solve problem 5.

1. $\frac{7}{8} \times \frac{2}{7} = \frac{1}{4}$	2. $\frac{2}{5} \times \frac{3}{10} = \frac{3}{25}$	3. $\frac{9}{14} \times \frac{7}{9} = \frac{1}{2}$
4. $\frac{16}{24} \times \frac{6}{8} = \frac{1}{2}$	5. If Bob ate 2/6 of the cake and John ate 1/3 of the cake, who ate more? *Bob and John ate the same amount of cake.*	

Language Practice: Analogies
Complete each analogy.

1. read is to library as worship is to _church_
2. laugh is to cry as lively is to _dull_
3. students are to school as patients are to _hospital_
4. antonym is to synonym as big is to _small/little_
5. pickle is to jar as egg is to _carton_
6. fake is to real as hot is to _cold_

Writing Practice: Use this writing prompt to write a short paragraph:
The best day at school was...

#3303 Daily Skills Practice–Grades 5-6   130   ©Teacher Created Materials, Inc.

Page 131

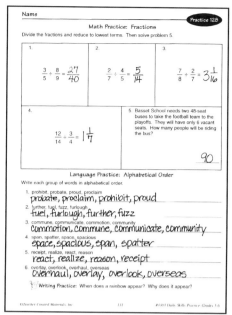

Name _____

Math Practice: Fractions
Divide the fractions and reduce to lowest terms. Then solve problem 5.

1. $\frac{3}{5} \div \frac{8}{9} = \frac{27}{40}$	2. $\frac{2}{7} \div \frac{4}{5} = \frac{5}{14}$	3. $\frac{7}{8} \div \frac{2}{7} = 3\frac{1}{16}$
4. $\frac{12}{14} \div \frac{3}{4} = 1\frac{1}{7}$	5. Basset School needs two 48-seat buses to take the football team to the playoffs. They will have only 6 vacant seats. How many people will be riding the bus? *90*	

Language Practice: Alphabetical Order
Write each group of words in alphabetical order.

1. prohibit, probate, proud, proclaim
 probate, proclaim, prohibit, proud
2. further, fuel, fuzz, furlough
 fuel, furlough, further, fuzz
3. commune, communicate, commotion, community
 commotion, commune, communicate, community
4. span, spatter, space, spacious
 space, spacious, span, spatter
5. receipt, realize, react, reason
 react, realize, reason, receipt
6. overlay, overlook, overhaul, overseas
 overhaul, overlay, overlook, overseas

Writing Practice: When does a rainbow appear? Why does it appear?

©Teacher Created Materials, Inc.   131   #3303 Daily Skills Practice–Grades 5-6

Page 132

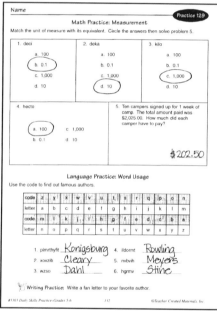

Name _____

Math Practice: Measurement
Match the unit of measure with its equivalent. Circle the answers then solve problem 5.

1. deci a. 100 (b. 0.1) c. 1,000 d. 10	2. deka a. 100 b. 0.1 c. 1,000 (d. 10)	3. kilo a. 100 b. 0.1 (c. 1,000) d. 10
4. hecto (a. 100) c. 1,000 b. 0.1 d. 10	5. Ten campers signed up for 1 week of camp. The total amount paid was $2,025.00. How much did each camper have to pay? *$202.50*	

Language Practice: Word Usage
Use the code to find out famous authors.

code	z	y	x	w	v	u	t	s	r	q	p	o	n
letter	a	b	c	d	e	f	g	h	i	j	k	l	m
code	m	l	k	j	i	h	g	f	e	d	c	b	a
letter	n	o	p	q	r	s	t	u	v	w	x	y	z

1. pimrthyfit _Konigsburg_
2. xovzib _Cleary_
3. wzso _Dahl_
4. ildormt _Rowling_
5. nvbvih _Meyers_
6. hgrmv _Stine_

Writing Practice: Write a fan letter to your favorite author.

#3303 Daily Skills Practice–Grades 5-6   132   ©Teacher Created Materials, Inc.

Page 133

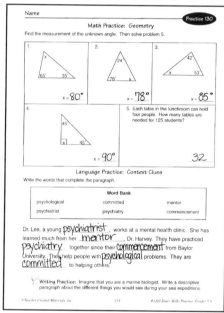

Name _____

Math Practice: Geometry
Find the measurement of the unknown angle. Then solve problem 5.

1. $65°$, $35°$, x — $x = 80°$	2. $24°$, $78°$, x — $x = 78°$	3. $42°$, $53°$, x — $x = 85°$
4. $45°$, $45°$, x — $x = 90°$	5. Each table in the lunchroom can hold four people. How many tables are needed for 125 students? *32*	

Language Practice: Context Clues
Write the words that complete the paragraph.

Word Bank		
psychological	committed	mentor
psychiatrist	psychiatry	commencement

Dr. Lee, a young _psychiatrist_, works at a mental health clinic. She has learned much from her _mentor_, Dr. Harvey. They have practiced _psychiatry_ together since their _commencement_ from Baylor University. They help people with _psychological_ problems. They are _committed_ to helping others.

Writing Practice: Imagine that you are a marine biologist. Write a descriptive paragraph about the different things you would see during your sea expeditions.

©Teacher Created Materials, Inc.   133   #3303 Daily Skills Practice–Grades 5-6

Page 134

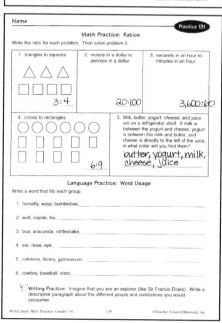

Name _____

Math Practice: Ratios
Write the ratio for each problem. Then solve problem 5.

1. triangles to squares *3:4*	2. nickels in a dollar to pennies in a dollar *20:100*	3. seconds in an hour to minutes in an hour *3,600:60*
4. circles to rectangles *6:9*	5. Milk, butter, yogurt, cheese, and juice are on a refrigerator shelf. If milk is between the yogurt and cheese, yogurt is between the milk and butter, and cheese is directly to the left of the juice, in what order will you find them? *butter, yogurt, milk, cheese, juice*	

Language Practice: Word Usage
Write a word that fits each group.

1. horsefly, wasp, bumblebee, _____
2. wolf, coyote, fox, _____
3. boa, anaconda, rattlesnake, _____
4. ear, nose, eye, _____
5. cafeteria, library, gymnasium, _____
6. cowboy, baseball, visor, _____

Writing Practice: Imagine that you are an explorer (like Sir Francis Drake). Write a descriptive paragraph about the different people and civilizations you would encounter.

#3303 Daily Skills Practice–Grades 5-6   134   ©Teacher Created Materials, Inc.

Page 135

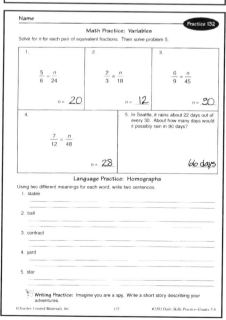

Name _____

Math Practice: Variables
Solve for n for each pair of equivalent fractions. Then solve problem 5.

1. $\frac{5}{6} = \frac{n}{24}$ $n = 20$	2. $\frac{2}{3} = \frac{n}{18}$ $n = 12$	3. $\frac{6}{9} = \frac{n}{45}$ $n = 30$
4. $\frac{7}{12} = \frac{n}{48}$ $n = 28$	5. In Seattle, it rains about 22 days out of every 30. About how many days would it possibly rain in 90 days? *66 days*	

Language Practice: Homographs
Using two different meanings for each word, write two sentences.

1. stable
2. ball
3. contract
4. yard
5. star

Writing Practice: Imagine you are a spy. Write a short story describing your adventures.

©Teacher Created Materials, Inc.   135   #3303 Daily Skills Practice–Grades 5-6

Page 136

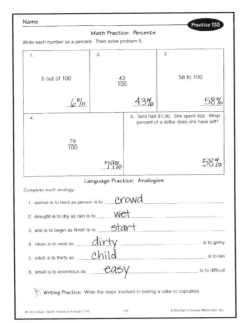

Name _____ Practice 133

Math Practice: Percents

Write each number as a percent. Then solve problem 5.

1.	2.	3.
6 out of 100	$\frac{43}{100}$	58 to 100
6%	43%	58%

4.	5. Tami had $1.00. She spent 42¢. What percent of a dollar does she have left?
$\frac{79}{100}$	
79%	58%

Language Practice: Analogies

Complete each analogy.

1. animal is to herd as person is to _crowd_
2. drought is to dry as rain is to _wet_
3. end is to begin as finish is to _start_
4. clean is to neat as _dirty_ is to grimy
5. adult is to thirty as _child_ is to ten
6. small is to enormous as _easy_ is to difficult

Writing Practice: Write the steps involved in baking a cake or cupcakes.

Page 137

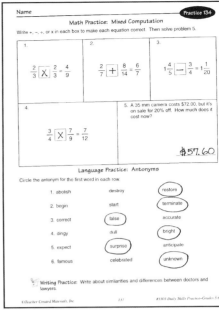

Name _____ Practice 134

Math Practice: Mixed Computation

Write +, −, ÷, or x in each box to make each equation correct. Then solve problem 5.

1.	2.	3.
$\frac{2}{3}$ ⊠ $\frac{2}{3}$ = $\frac{4}{9}$	$\frac{2}{7}$ ⊞ $\frac{8}{14}$ = $\frac{6}{7}$	$1\frac{4}{5}$ ⊟ $\frac{3}{4}$ = $1\frac{1}{20}$

4.	5. A 35 mm camera costs $72.00, but it's on sale for 20% off. How much does it cost now?
$\frac{3}{4}$ ⊠ $\frac{7}{9}$ = $\frac{7}{12}$	$57.60

Language Practice: Antonyms

Circle the antonym for the first word in each row.

1. abolish	destroy	(restore)
2. begin	start	(terminate)
3. correct	(false)	accurate
4. dingy	dull	(bright)
5. expect	(surprise)	anticipate
6. famous	celebrated	(unknown)

Writing Practice: Write about similarities and differences between doctors and lawyers.

Page 138

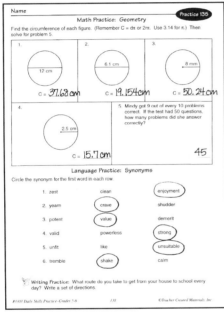

Name _____ Practice 135

Math Practice: Geometry

Find the circumference of each figure. (Remember C = dπ or 2rπ. Use 3.14 for π.) Then solve for problem 5.

1. (12 cm)	2. (6.1 cm)	3. (8 mm)
C = 37.68 cm	C = 19.154 cm	C = 50.24 cm

4. (2.5 cm)	5. Mindy got 9 out of every 10 problems correct. If the test had 50 questions, how many problems did she answer correctly?
C = 15.7 cm	45

Language Practice: Synonyms

Circle the synonym for the first word in each row.

1. zest	clean	(enjoyment)
2. yearn	(crave)	shudder
3. potent	(value)	demerit
4. valid	powerless	(strong)
5. unfit	like	(unsuitable)
6. tremble	(shake)	calm

Writing Practice: What route do you take to get from your house to school every day? Write a set of directions.

Page 139

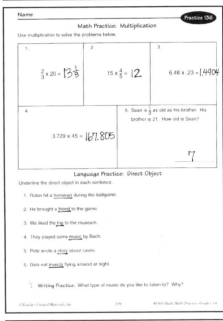

Name _____ Practice 136

Math Practice: Multiplication

Use multiplication to solve the problems below.

1.	2.	3.
$\frac{2}{3}$ x 20 = $13\frac{1}{3}$	15 x $\frac{4}{5}$ = 12	6.48 x .23 = 1.4904

4.	5. Sean is $\frac{1}{3}$ as old as his brother. His brother is 21. How old is Sean?
3.729 x 45 = 167.805	7

Language Practice: Direct Object

Underline the direct object in each sentence.

1. Robin hit a homerun during the ballgame.
2. He brought a friend to the game.
3. We liked the trip to the museum.
4. They played some music by Bach.
5. Pete wrote a story about caves.
6. Bats eat insects flying around at night.

Writing Practice: What type of music do you like to listen to? Why?

Page 140

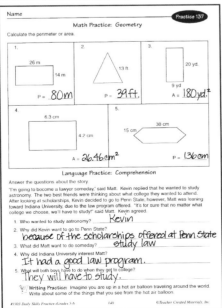

Name _____ Practice 137

Math Practice: Geometry

Calculate the perimeter or area.

1. (26 m x 14 m)	2. (triangle 13 ft)	3. (20 yd, 9 yd)
P = 80 m	P = 39 ft.	A = 180 yd.²

4. (6.3 cm x 4.2 cm)	5. (15 cm, 38 cm hexagon)
A = 26.46 cm²	P = 136 cm

Language Practice: Comprehension

Answer the questions about the story.

"I'm going to become a lawyer someday," said Matt. Kevin replied that he wanted to study astronomy. The two best friends were thinking about what college they wanted to attend. After looking at scholarships, Kevin decided to go to Penn State; however, Matt was leaning toward Indiana University, due to the law program offered. "It's for sure that no matter what college we choose, we'll have to study," said Matt. Kevin agreed.

1. Who wanted to study astronomy? _Kevin_
2. Why did Kevin want to go to Penn State? _because of the scholarships offered at Penn State_
3. What did Matt want to do someday? _study law_
4. Why did Indiana University interest Matt? _It had a good law program._
5. What will both boys have to do when they get to college? _They will have to study._

Writing Practice: Imagine you are up in a hot air balloon traveling around the world. Write about some of the things that you see from the hot air balloon.

Page 141

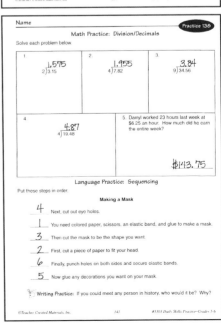

Name _____ Practice 138

Math Practice: Division/Decimals

Solve each problem below.

1. 1.575 / 2)3.15	2. 1.955 / 4)7.82	3. 3.84 / 9)34.56

4. 4.87 / 4)19.48	5. Darryl worked 23 hours last week at $6.25 an hour. How much did he earn the entire week?
	$143.75

Language Practice: Sequencing

Put these steps in order.

Making a Mask

4 Next, cut out eye holes.
1 You need colored paper, scissors, an elastic band, and glue to make a mask.
3 Then cut the mask to be the shape you want.
2 First, cut a piece of paper to fit your head.
6 Finally, punch holes on both sides and secure elastic bands.
5 Now glue any decorations you want on your mask.

Writing Practice: If you could meet any person in history, who would it be? Why?

Page 142

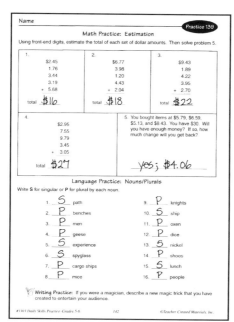

Page 143

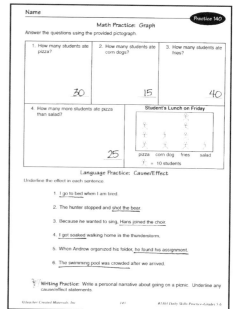

Page 144

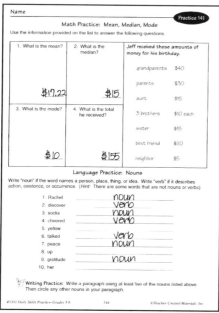

Page 145

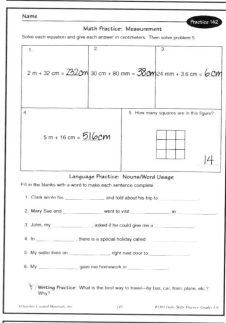

Page 146

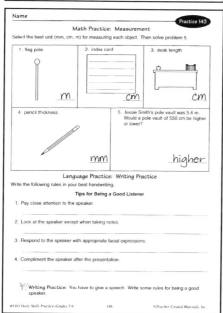

Page 147

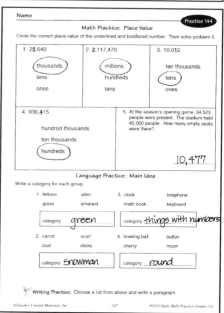

Page 148

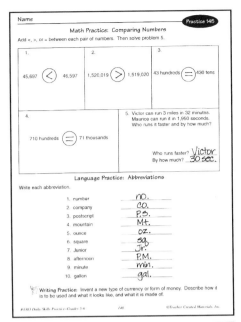

Name
Math Practice: Comparing Numbers — Practice 145
Add <, >, or = between each pair of numbers. Then solve problem 5.

1.	2.	3.
45,697 < 46,597	1,520,019 > 1,519,020	43 hundreds = 430 tens

4.	5. Victor can run 3 miles in 32 minutes. Maurice can run in 1,950 seconds. Who runs it faster and by how much?
710 hundreds = 71 thousands	Who runs faster? Victor By how much? 30 sec.

Language Practice: Abbreviations
Write each abbreviation.

1. number — no.
2. company — co.
3. postscript — P.S.
4. mountain — Mt.
5. ounce — oz.
6. square — sq.
7. Junior — Jr.
8. afternoon — P.M.
9. minute — min.
10. gallon — gal.

Writing Practice: Invent a new type of currency or form of money. Describe how it is to be used and what it looks like, and what it is made of.

Page 149

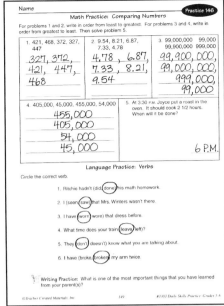

Name
Math Practice: Comparing Numbers — Practice 146
For problems 1 and 2, write in order from least to greatest. For problems 3 and 4, write in order from greatest to least. Then solve problem 5.

1. 421, 468, 372, 327, 447	2. 9.54, 8.21, 6.87, 7.33, 4.78	3. 99,000,000 99,000 99,900,000 999,000
327, 372, 421, 447, 468	4.78, 6.87, 7.33, 8.21, 9.54	99,900,000, 99,000,000, 999,000, 99,000

4. 405,000, 45,000, 455,000, 54,000	5. At 3:30 P.M. Joyce put a roast in the oven. It should cook 2 1/2 hours. When will it be done?
455,000 405,000 54,000 45,000	6 P.M.

Language Practice: Verbs
Circle the correct verb.

1. Ritchie hadn't (did, done) his math homework.
2. I (seen, saw) that Mrs. Winters wasn't there.
3. I have (worn, wore) that dress before.
4. What time does your train (leave, left)?
5. They (don't, doesn't) know what you are talking about.
6. I have (broke, broken) my arm twice.

Writing Practice: What is one of the most important things that you have learned from your parent(s)?

Page 150

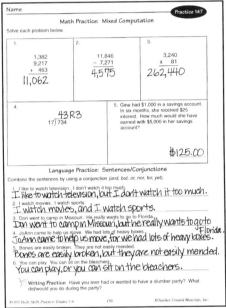

Name
Math Practice: Mixed Computation — Practice 147
Solve each problem below.

1.	2.	3.
1,382 9,217 + 463 11,062	11,846 − 7,271 4,575	3,240 x 81 262,440

4.	5. Gina had $1,000 in a savings account. In six months, she received $25 interest. How much would she have earned with $5,000 in her savings account?
43 R3 17⟌734	$125.00

Language Practice: Sentences/Conjunctions
Combine the sentences by using a conjunction (and, but, or, nor, for, yet).

1. I like to watch television. I don't watch it too much.
I like to watch television, but I don't watch it too much.
2. I watch movies. I watch sports.
I watch movies, and I watch sports.
3. Don went to camp in Missouri. He really wants to go to Florida.
Don went to camp in Missouri, but he really wants to go to Florida.
4. JoAnn came to help us move. We had lots of heavy boxes.
JoAnn came to help us move, for we had lots of heavy boxes.
5. Bones are easily broken. They are not easily mended.
Bones are easily broken, but they are not easily mended.
6. You can play. You can sit on the bleachers.
You can play, or you can sit on the bleachers.

Writing Practice: Have you ever had or wanted to have a slumber party? What did/would you do during the party?

Page 151

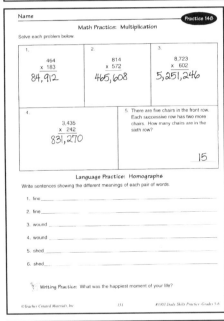

Name
Math Practice: Multiplication — Practice 148
Solve each problem below.

1.	2.	3.
464 x 183 84,912	814 x 572 465,608	8,723 x 602 5,251,246

4.	5. There are five chairs in the front row. Each successive row has two more chairs. How many chairs are in the sixth row?
3,435 x 242 831,270	15

Language Practice: Homographs
Write sentences showing the different meanings of each pair of words.

1. fine ___
2. fine ___
3. wound ___
4. wound ___
5. shed ___
6. shed ___

Writing Practice: What was the happiest moment of your life?

Page 152

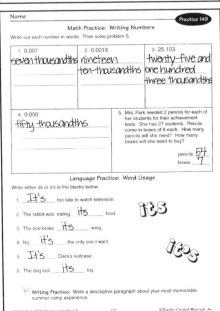

Name
Math Practice: Writing Numbers — Practice 149
Write out each number in words. Then solve problem 5.

1. 0.007	2. 0.0019	3. 25.103
seven thousandths	nineteen ten-thousandths	twenty-five and one hundred three thousandths

4. 0.050	5. Mrs. Park needed 2 pencils for each of her students for their achievement tests. She has 27 students. Pencils come in boxes of 8 each. How many pencils will she need? How many boxes will she need to buy?
fifty thousandths	pencils 54 boxes 7

Language Practice: Word Usage
Write either its or it's in the blanks below.

1. It's too late to watch television.
2. The rabbit was eating its food.
3. The bird broke its wing.
4. No, it's the only one I want.
5. It's Clara's suitcase.
6. The dog lost its toy.

Writing Practice: Write a descriptive paragraph about your most memorable summer camp experience.

Page 153

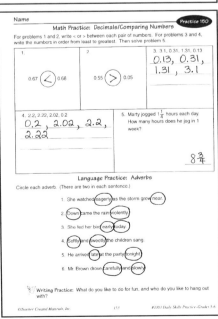

Name
Math Practice: Decimals/Comparing Numbers — Practice 150
For problems 1 and 2, write < or > between each pair of numbers. For problems 3 and 4, write the numbers in order from least to greatest. Then solve problem 5.

1.	2.	3. 3.1, 0.31, 1.31, 0.13
0.67 < 0.68	0.55 > 0.05	0.13, 0.31, 1.31, 3.1

4. 2.2, 2.22, 2.02, 0.2	5. Marty jogged 1 1/4 hours each day. How many hours does he jog in 1 week?
0.2, 2.02, 2.2, 2.22	8 3/4

Language Practice: Adverbs
Circle each adverb. (There are two in each sentence.)

1. She watched eagerly as the storm grew near.
2. Down came the rain violently.
3. She fed her bird early today.
4. Softly and sweetly the children sang.
5. He arrived late at the party tonight.
6. Mr. Brown drove carefully and slowly.

Writing Practice: What do you like to do for fun, and who do you like to hang out with?

Page 154

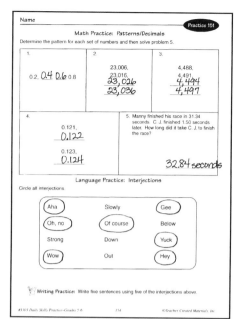

Name

Practice 151

Math Practice: Patterns/Decimals

Determine the pattern for each set of numbers and then solve problem 5.

1.	2.	3.
0.2, 0.4, 0.6, 0.8	23,006, 23,016, 23,026, 23,036	4,488, 4,491, 4,494, 4,497

4.	5. Manny finished his race in 31.34 seconds. C. J. finished 1.50 seconds later. How long did it take C. J. to finish the race?
0.121, 0.122, 0.123, 0.124	32.84 seconds

Language Practice: Interjections

Circle all interjections.

(Aha)	Slowly	(Gee)
(Oh, no)	(Of course)	Below
Strong	Down	(Yuck)
(Wow)	Out	(Hey)

✍ **Writing Practice:** Write five sentences using five of the interjections above.

#3303 Daily Skills Practice–Grades 5-6   154   ©Teacher Created Materials, Inc.

Page 155

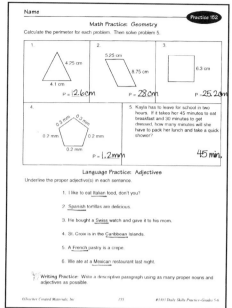

Name

Practice 152

Math Practice: Geometry

Calculate the perimeter for each problem. Then solve problem 5.

1.	2.	3.
4.25 cm, 4.1 cm P = 12.6 cm	5.25 cm, 8.75 cm P = 28 cm	6.3 cm P = 25.2 cm

4.	5. Kayla has to leave for school in two hours. If it takes her 45 minutes to eat breakfast and 30 minutes to get dressed, how many minutes will she have to pack her lunch and take a quick shower?
0.3 mm, 0.3 mm, 0.2 mm, 0.2 mm, 0.2 mm P = 1.2 mm	45 min.

Language Practice: Adjectives

Underline the proper adjective(s) in each sentence.

1. I like to eat Italian food, don't you?
2. Spanish tortillas are delicious.
3. He bought a Swiss watch and gave it to his mom.
4. St. Croix is in the Caribbean islands.
5. A French pastry is a crepe.
6. We ate at a Mexican restaurant last night.

✍ **Writing Practice:** Write a descriptive paragraph using as many proper nouns and adjectives as possible.

©Teacher Created Materials, Inc.   155   #3303 Daily Skills Practice–Grades 5-6

Page 156

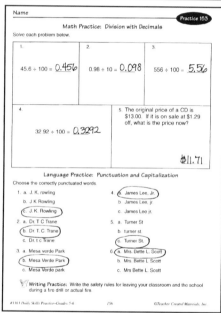

Name

Practice 153

Math Practice: Division with Decimals

Solve each problem below.

1.	2.	3.
45.6 ÷ 100 = 0.456	0.98 ÷ 10 = 0.098	556 ÷ 100 = 5.56

4.	5. The original price of a CD is $13.00. If it is on sale at $1.29 off, what is the price now?
32.92 ÷ 100 = 0.3292	$11.71

Language Practice: Punctuation and Capitalization

Choose the correctly punctuated words.

1. a. J.K. rowling
   b. J K Rowling
   c. J. K. Rowling ✓

2. a. Dr. T C Trane
   b. Dr. T. C. Trane ✓
   c. Dr. t c Trane

3. a. Mesa verde Park
   b. Mesa Verde Park ✓
   c. Mesa Verde park

4. a. James Lee, Jr. ✓
   b. James Lee, jr.
   c. James Lee jr.

5. a. Turner St
   b. turner st.
   c. Turner St. ✓

6. a. Mrs. Bette L. Scott ✓
   b. Mrs. Bette L Scott
   c. Mrs Bette L. Scott

✍ **Writing Practice:** Write the safety rules for leaving your classroom and the school during a fire drill or actual fire.

#3303 Daily Skills Practice–Grades 5-6   156   ©Teacher Created Materials, Inc.

Page 157

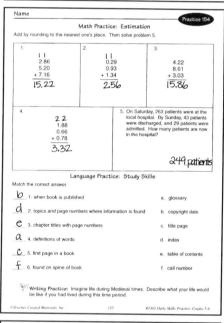

Name

Practice 154

Math Practice: Estimation

Add by rounding to the nearest one's place. Then solve problem 5.

1.	2.	3.
1 1 2.86 5.20 + 7.16 15.22	1 1 0.29 0.93 + 1.34 2.56	4.22 8.61 + 3.03 15.86

4.	5. On Saturday, 263 patients were at the local hospital. By Sunday, 43 patients were discharged, and 29 patients were admitted. How many patients are now in the hospital?
2.2 1.88 0.66 + 0.78 3.32	249 patients

Language Practice: Study Skills

Match the correct answer.

b 1. when book is published   a. glossary
d 2. topics and page numbers where information is found   b. copyright date
e 3. chapter titles with page numbers   c. title page
a 4. definitions of words   d. index
c 5. first page in a book   e. table of contents
f 6. found on spine of book   f. call number

✍ **Writing Practice:** Imagine life during Medieval times. Describe what your life would be like if you had lived during this time period.

©Teacher Created Materials, Inc.   157   #3303 Daily Skills Practice–Grades 5-6

Page 158

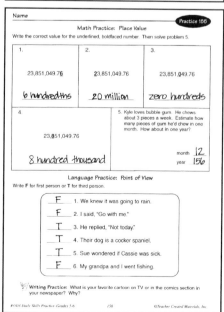

Name

Practice 155

Math Practice: Place Value

Write the correct value for the underlined, boldfaced number. Then solve problem 5.

1.	2.	3.
23,851,049.76 6 hundredths	23,851,049.76 20 million	23,851,049.76 zero hundreds

4.	5. Kyle loves bubble gum. He chews about 3 pieces a week. Estimate how many pieces of gum he'd chew in one month. How about in one year?
23,851,049.76 8 hundred thousand	month 12 year 156

Language Practice: Point of View

Write F for first person or T for third person.

F 1. We knew it was going to rain.
F 2. I said, "Go with me."
T 3. He replied, "Not today."
T 4. Their dog is a cocker spaniel.
T 5. Sue wondered if Cassie was sick.
F 6. My grandpa and I went fishing.

✍ **Writing Practice:** What is your favorite cartoon on TV or in the comics section in your newspaper? Why?

#3303 Daily Skills Practice–Grades 5-6   158   ©Teacher Created Materials, Inc.

Page 159

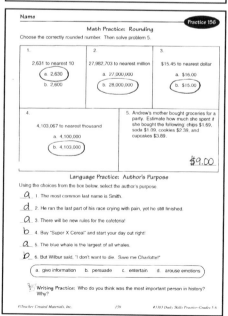

Name

Practice 156

Math Practice: Rounding

Choose the correctly rounded number. Then solve problem 5.

1.	2.	3.
2,631 to nearest 10 a. 2,630 ✓ b. 2,600	27,982,703 to nearest million a. 27,000,000 b. 28,000,000 ✓	$15.45 to nearest dollar a. $16.00 b. $15.00 ✓

4.	5. Andrew's mother bought groceries for a party. Estimate how much she spent if she bought the following: chips $1.69, soda $1.09, cookies $2.39, and cupcakes $3.89.
4,103,067 to nearest thousand a. 4,100,000 b. 4,103,000 ✓	$9.00

Language Practice: Author's Purpose

Using the choices from the box below, select the author's purpose.

a 1. The most common last name is Smith.
d 2. He ran the last part of his race crying with pain, yet he still finished.
a 3. There will be new rules for the cafeteria!
b 4. Buy "Super X Cereal" and start your day out right!
a 5. The blue whale is the largest of all whales.
b 6. But Wilbur said, "I don't want to die. Save me Charlotte!"

a. give information   b. persuade   c. entertain   d. arouse emotions

✍ **Writing Practice:** Who do you think was the most important person in history? Why?

©Teacher Created Materials, Inc.   159   #3303 Daily Skills Practice–Grades 5-6

Page 160

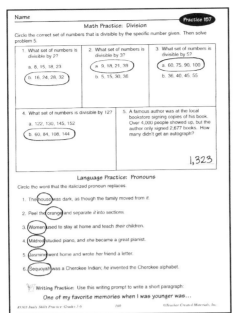

Math Practice: Division

Circle the correct set of numbers that is divisible by the specific number given. Then solve problem 5.

1. What set of numbers is divisible by 2?
   a. 8, 15, 18, 23
   b. 16, 24, 28, 32 ✓

2. What set of numbers is divisible by 3?
   a. 9, 18, 21, 39 ✓
   b. 5, 15, 30, 36

3. What set of numbers is divisible by 5?
   a. 60, 75, 90, 100 ✓
   b. 36, 40, 45, 55

4. What set of numbers is divisible by 12?
   a. 122, 130, 145, 152
   b. 60, 84, 108, 144 ✓

5. A famous author was at the local bookstore signing copies of his book. Over 4,000 people showed up, but the author only signed 2,677 books. How many didn't get an autograph?

1,323

Language Practice: Pronouns

Circle the word that the italicized pronoun replaces.

1. The house was dark, as though the family moved from *it*.
2. Peel the orange and separate *it* into sections.
3. Women used to stay at home and teach *their* children.
4. Mildred studied piano, and *she* became a great pianist.
5. Jasmine went home and wrote *her* friend a letter.
6. Sequoyah was a Cherokee Indian; *he* invented the Cherokee alphabet.

Writing Practice: Use this writing prompt to write a short paragraph:
One of my favorite memories when I was younger was...

Page 161

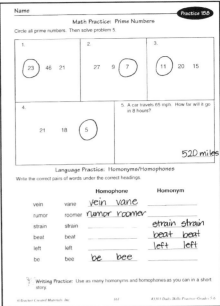

Math Practice: Prime Numbers

Circle all prime numbers. Then solve problem 5.

1. 23 (circled) 46 21
2. 27 9 7 (circled)
3. 11 (circled) 20 15
4. 21 18 5 (circled)
5. A car travels 65 mph. How far will it go in 8 hours?

520 miles

Language Practice: Homonyms/Homophones

Write the correct pairs of words under the correct headings.

		Homophone	Homonym
vein	vane	vein vane	
rumor	roomer	rumor roomer	
strain	strain		strain strain
beat	beat		beat beat
left	left		left left
be	bee	be bee	

Writing Practice: Use as many homonyms and homophones as you can in a short story.

Page 162

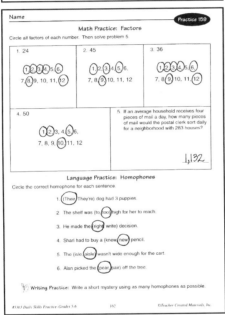

Math Practice: Factors

Circle all factors of each number. Then solve problem 5.

1. 24 → 1, 2, 3, 4, 6, 8, 12
2. 45 → 1, 3, 5, 9
3. 36 → 1, 2, 3, 4, 6, 9, 12
4. 50 → 1, 2, 5, 10

5. If an average household receives four pieces of mail a day, how many pieces of mail would the postal clerk sort daily for a neighborhood with 283 houses?

1,132

Language Practice: Homophones

Circle the correct homophone for each sentence.

1. (Their) They're dog had 3 puppies.
2. The shelf was (too) to high for her to reach.
3. He made the (right) write decision.
4. Shari had to buy a knew (new) pencil.
5. The isle (aisle) wasn't wide enough for the cart.
6. Alan picked the (pear) pair off the tree.

Writing Practice: Write a short mystery using as many homophones as possible.

Page 163

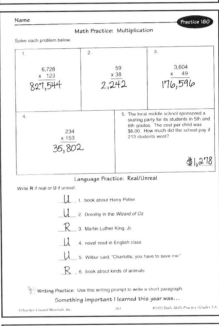

Math Practice: Multiplication

Solve each problem below.

1. 6,728 × 123 = 827,544
2. 59 × 38 = 2,242
3. 3,604 × 49 = 176,596
4. 234 × 153 = 35,802

5. The local middle school sponsored a skating party for its students in 5th and 6th grades. The cost per child was $6.00. How much did the school pay if 213 students went?

$1,278

Language Practice: Real/Unreal

Write R if real or U if unreal.

U 1. book about Harry Potter
U 2. Dorothy in the *Wizard of Oz*
R 3. Martin Luther King, Jr.
U 4. novel read in English class
U 5. Wilbur said, "Charlotte, you have to save me."
R 6. book about kinds of animals

Writing Practice: Use this writing prompt to write a short paragraph:
Something important I learned this year was...

Page 164

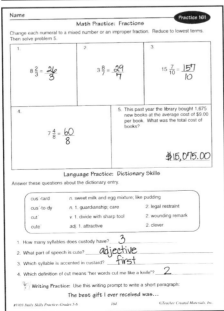

Math Practice: Fractions

Change each numeral to a mixed number or an improper fraction. Reduce to lowest terms. Then solve problem 5.

1. $8\frac{2}{3} = \frac{26}{3}$
2. $3\frac{8}{7} = \frac{29}{7}$
3. $15\frac{7}{10} = \frac{157}{10}$
4. $7\frac{4}{8} = \frac{60}{8}$

5. This past year the library bought 1,675 new books at the average cost of $9.00 per book. What was the total cost of books?

$15,075.00

Language Practice: Dictionary Skills

Answer these questions about the dictionary entry.

cus·tard   *n.* sweet milk and egg mixture; like pudding
cus·to·dy   *n.* 1. guardianship; care   2. legal restraint
cut   *v.* 1. divide with sharp tool   2. wounding remark
cute   *adj.* 1. attractive   2. clever

1. How many syllables does custody have? 3
2. What part of speech is cute? adjective
3. Which syllable is accented in custard? first
4. Which definition of cut means "her words cut me like a knife"? 2

Writing Practice: Use this writing prompt to write a short paragraph:
The best gift I ever received was...

Page 165

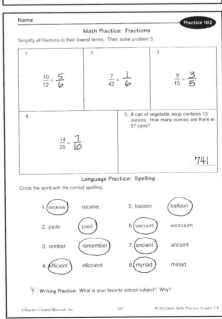

Math Practice: Fractions

Simplify all fractions to their lowest terms. Then solve problem 5.

1. $\frac{10}{12} = \frac{5}{6}$
2. $\frac{7}{42} = \frac{1}{6}$
3. $\frac{9}{15} = \frac{3}{5}$
4. $\frac{14}{20} = \frac{7}{10}$

5. A can of vegetable soup contains 13 ounces. How many ounces are there in 57 cans?

741

Language Practice: Spelling

Circle the word with the correct spelling.

1. (receive) recieve
2. pade (paid)
3. rember (remember)
4. (efficient) eficcient
5. baloon (balloon)
6. (vacuum) vaccuum
7. (ancient) anceint
8. (myriad) miriad

Writing Practice: What is your favorite school subject? Why?

Page 166

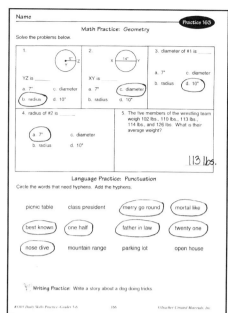

Page 167

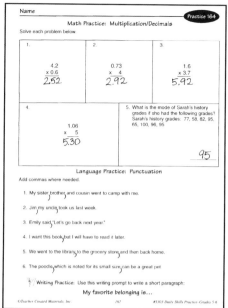

Page 168

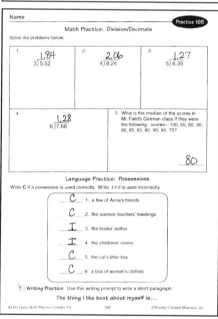

Page 169

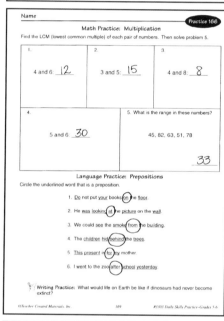

Page 170

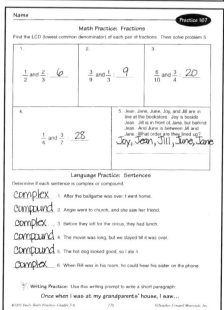

Page 171

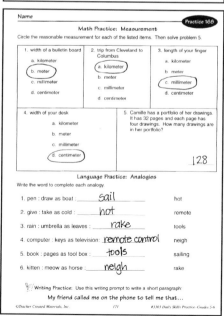

Page 172

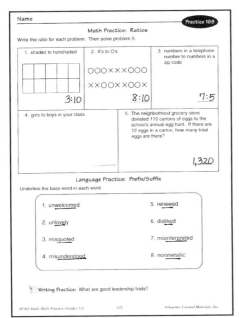

Page 173

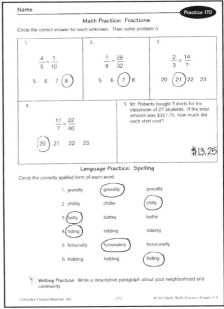

Page 174

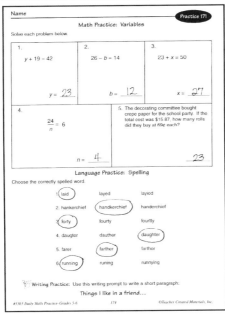

Page 175

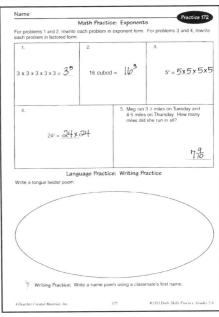

Page 176

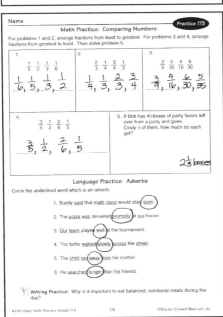

Page 177

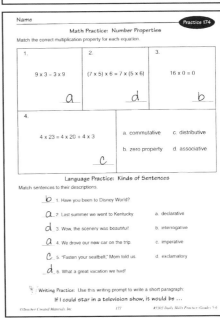

Page 178

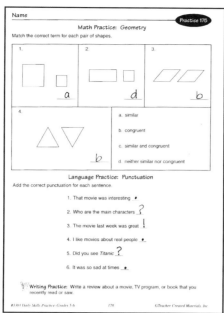

Page 179

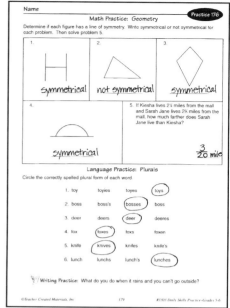

Page 180

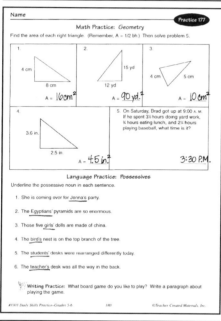

Page 181

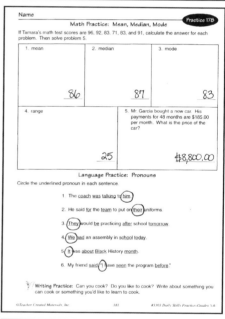

Page 182

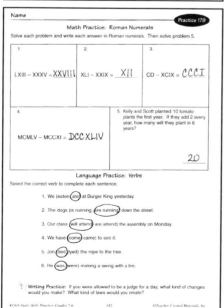

Page 183

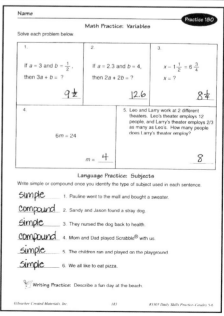

Page 184

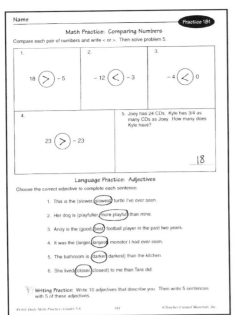

Name

Practice 181

Math Practice: Comparing Numbers

Compare each pair of numbers and write < or >. Then solve problem 5.

1.	2.	3.
18 $>$ – 5	– 12 $<$ – 3	– 4 $<$ 0

4.	5. Joey has 24 CDs. Kyle has 3/4 as many CDs as Joey. How many does Kyle have?
23 $>$ – 23	18

Language Practice: Adjectives

Choose the correct adjective to complete each sentence.

1. This is the (slower, slowest) turtle I've ever seen.
2. Her dog is (playfuller, more playful) than mine.
3. Andy is the (good, best) football player in the past two years.
4. It was the (larger, largest) monster I had ever seen.
5. The bathroom is (darker, darkest) than the kitchen.
6. She lived (closer, closest) to me than Tara did.

✎ **Writing Practice:** Write 10 adjectives that describe you. Then write 5 sentences with 5 of these adjectives.

#3303 Daily Skills Practice–Grades 5-6   184   ©Teacher Created Materials, Inc.

Page 185

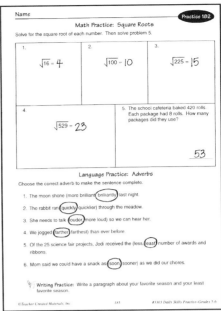

Name

Practice 182

Math Practice: Square Roots

Solve for the square root of each number. Then solve problem 5.

1.	2.	3.
$\sqrt{16}$ = 4	$\sqrt{100}$ = 10	$\sqrt{225}$ = 15

4.	5. The school cafeteria baked 420 rolls. Each package had 8 rolls. How many packages did they use?
$\sqrt{529}$ = 23	53

Language Practice: Adverbs

Choose the correct adverb to make the sentence complete.

1. The moon shone (more brilliant, brilliantly) last night.
2. The rabbit ran (quickly, quicklier) through the meadow.
3. She needs to talk (louder, more loud) so we can hear her.
4. We jogged (farther, farthest) than ever before.
5. Of the 25 science fair projects, Jodi received the (less, least) number of awards and ribbons.
6. Mom said we could have a snack as (soon, sooner) as we did our chores.

✎ **Writing Practice:** Write a paragraph about your favorite season and your least favorite season.

©Teacher Created Materials, Inc.   185   #3303 Daily Skills Practice–Grades 5-6

Page 186

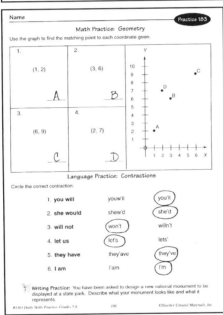

Name

Practice 183

Math Practice: Geometry

Use the graph to find the matching point to each coordinate given.

1.	2.
(1, 2) A	(3, 6) B

3.	4.
(6, 9) C	(2, 7) D

Language Practice: Contractions

Circle the correct contraction.

1. **you will** — youw'll / you'll
2. **she would** — shew'd / she'd
3. **will not** — won't / willn't
4. **let us** — let's / lets'
5. **they have** — they'ave / they've
6. **I am** — I'am / I'm

✎ **Writing Practice:** You have been asked to design a new national monument to be displayed at a state park. Describe what your monument looks like and what it represents.

#3303 Daily Skills Practice–Grades 5-6   186   ©Teacher Created Materials, Inc.

Page 187

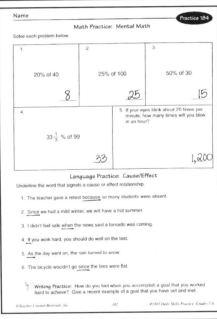

Name

Practice 184

Math Practice: Mental Math

Solve each problem below.

1.	2.	3.
20% of 40	25% of 100	50% of 30
8	25	15

4.	5. If your eyes blink about 20 times per minute, how many times will you blink in an hour?
$33\frac{1}{3}$ % of 99	
33	1,200

Language Practice: Cause/Effect

Underline the word that signals a cause or effect relationship.

1. The teacher gave a retest because so many students were absent.
2. Since we had a mild winter, we will have a hot summer.
3. I didn't feel safe when the news said a tornado was coming.
4. If you work hard, you should do well on the test.
5. As the day went on, the rain turned to snow.
6. The bicycle wouldn't go since the tires were flat.

✎ **Writing Practice:** How do you feel when you accomplish a goal that you worked hard to achieve? Give a recent example of a goal that you have set and met.

©Teacher Created Materials, Inc.   187   #3303 Daily Skills Practice–Grades 5-6

Page 188

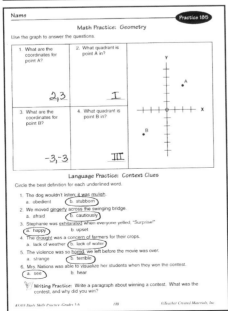

Name

Practice 185

Math Practice: Geometry

Use the graph to answer the questions.

1. What are the coordinates for point A?	2. What quadrant is point A in?
2,3	I

3. What are the coordinates for point B?	4. What quadrant is point B in?
–3,3	III

Language Practice: Context Clues

Circle the best definition for each underlined word.

1. The dog wouldn't listen; it was mulish.
   a. obedient   b. stubborn
2. We moved gingerly across the swinging bridge.
   a. afraid   b. cautiously
3. Stephanie was exhilarated when everyone yelled, "Surprise!"
   a. happy   b. upset
4. The drought was a concern of farmers for their crops.
   a. lack of weather   b. lack of water
5. The violence was so horrid, we left before the movie was over.
   a. strange   b. terrible
6. Mrs. Nations was able to visualize her students when they won the contest.
   a. see   b. hear

✎ **Writing Practice:** Write a paragraph about winning a contest. What was the contest, and why did you win?

#3303 Daily Skills Practice–Grades 5-6   188   ©Teacher Created Materials, Inc.

Page 189

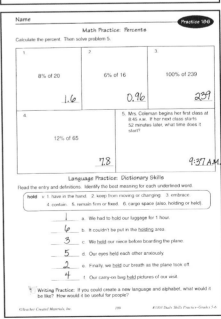

Name

Practice 186

Math Practice: Percents

Calculate the percent. Then solve problem 5.

1.	2.	3.
8% of 20	6% of 16	100% of 239
1.6	0.96	239

4.	5. Mrs. Coleman begins her first class at 8:45 A.M. If her next class starts 52 minutes later, what time does it start?
12% of 65	
7.8	9:37 A.M.

Language Practice: Dictionary Skills

Read the entry and definitions. Identify the best meaning for each underlined word.

hold v 1. have in the hand. 2. keep from moving or changing. 3. embrace. 4. contain. 5. remain firm or fixed. 6. cargo space (also, holding or held).

1 a. We had to hold our luggage for 1 hour.
6 b. It couldn't be put in the holding area.
3 c. We held our niece before boarding the plane.
5 d. Our eyes held each other anxiously.
2 e. Finally, we held our breath as the plane took off.
4 f. Our carry-on bag held pictures of our visit.

✎ **Writing Practice:** If you could create a new language and alphabet, what would it be like? How would it be useful for people?

©Teacher Created Materials, Inc.   189   #3303 Daily Skills Practice–Grades 5-6

Page 190

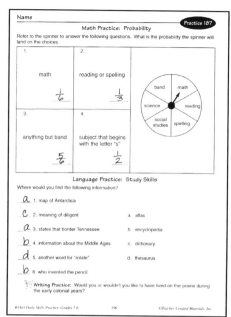

Name

Math Practice: Probability — Practice 187

Refer to the spinner to answer the following questions. What is the probability the spinner will land on the choices

1. math $\frac{1}{6}$

2. reading or spelling $\frac{1}{3}$

3. anything but band $\frac{5}{6}$

4. subject that begins with the letter "s" $\frac{1}{2}$

Language Practice: Study Skills

Where would you find the following information?

a 1. map of Antarctica
c 2. meaning of diligent
a 3. states that border Tennessee
b 4. information about the Middle Ages
d 5. another word for "rotate"
b 6. who invented the pencil

a. atlas
b. encyclopedia
c. dictionary
d. thesaurus

Writing Practice: Would you or wouldn't you like to have lived on the prairie during the early colonial years?

#3303 Daily Skills Practice–Grades 5-6   190   ©Teacher Created Materials, Inc.

Page 191

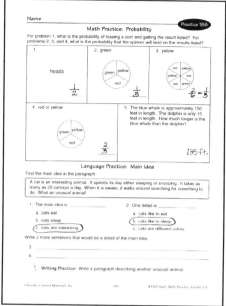

Name

Math Practice: Probability — Practice 188

For problem 1, what is the probability of tossing a coin and getting the result listed? For problems 2, 3, and 4, what is the probability that the spinner will land on the results listed?

1. heads $\frac{1}{2}$

2. green $\frac{1}{3}$

3. yellow $\frac{2}{6} = \frac{1}{3}$

4. red or yellow $\frac{2}{3}$

5. The blue whale is approximately 150 feet in length. The dolphin is only 15 feet in length. How much longer is the blue whale than the dolphin? 135 ft.

Language Practice: Main Idea

Find the main idea in the paragraph.

A cat is an interesting animal. It spends its day either sleeping or snooping. It takes as many as 20 catnaps a day. When it is awake, it walks around searching for something to do. What an unusual animal!

1. The main idea is
   a. cats eat
   b. cats sleep
   c. cats are interesting

2. One detail is
   a. cats like to eat
   b. cats like to sleep
   c. cats are different colors

Write 2 more sentences that would be a detail of the main idea.

3. _____
4. _____

Writing Practice: Write a paragraph describing another unusual animal.

©Teacher Created Materials, Inc.   191   #3303 Daily Skills Practice–Grades 5-6

Page 192

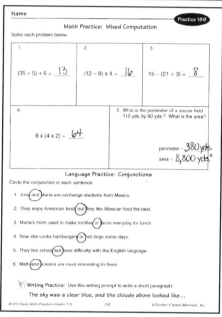

Name

Math Practice: Mixed Computation — Practice 189

Solve each problem below.

1. $(35 \div 5) + 6 = 13$
2. $(12 - 8) \times 4 = 16$
3. $15 - (21 \div 3) = 8$
4. $8 \times (4 \times 2) = 64$
5. What is the perimeter of a soccer field 110 yds. by 80 yds.? What is the area?
   perimeter = 380 yds.
   area = 8,800 yds²

Language Practice: Conjunctions

Circle the conjunction in each sentence.

1. Jose (and) Maria are exchange students from Mexico.
2. They enjoy American food (but) they like Mexican food the best.
3. Maria's mom used to make tortillas (or) tacos everyday for lunch.
4. Now she cooks hamburgers (or) hot dogs some days.
5. They like school (but) have difficulty with the English language.
6. Math (and) science are most interesting to them.

Writing Practice: Use this writing prompt to write a short paragraph.
The sky was a clear blue, and the clouds above looked like…

#3303 Daily Skills Practice–Grades 5-6   192   ©Teacher Created Materials, Inc.

Page 193

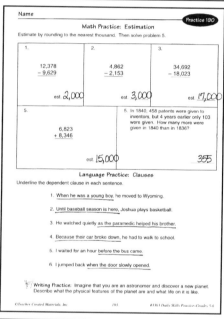

Name

Math Practice: Estimation — Practice 190

Estimate by rounding to the nearest thousand. Then solve problem 5.

1. 12,378 − 9,629   est. 2,000
2. 4,862 − 2,153   est. 3,000
3. 34,692 − 18,023   est. 17,000
4. 6,823 + 8,346   est. 15,000
5. In 1840, 458 patents were given to inventors, but 4 years earlier only 103 were given. How many more were given in 1840 than in 1836?   355

Language Practice: Clauses

Underline the dependent clause in each sentence.

1. When he was a young boy, he moved to Wyoming.
2. Until baseball season is here, Joshua plays basketball.
3. He watched quietly as the paramedic helped his brother.
4. Because their car broke down, he had to walk to school.
5. I waited for an hour before the bus came.
6. I jumped back when the door slowly opened.

Writing Practice: Imagine that you are an astronomer and discover a new planet. Describe what the physical features of the planet are and what life on it is like.

©Teacher Created Materials, Inc.   193   #3303 Daily Skills Practice–Grades 5-6

Page 194

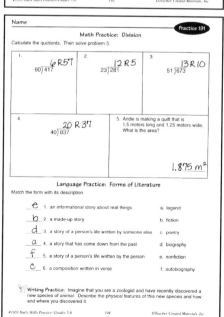

Name

Math Practice: Division — Practice 191

Calculate the quotients. Then solve problem 5.

1. $60\overline{)417}$ 6 R57
2. $23\overline{)281}$ 12 R5
3. $51\overline{)673}$ 13 R10
4. $40\overline{)837}$ 20 R37
5. Andie is making a quilt that is 1.5 meters long and 1.25 meters wide. What is the area?   1.875 m²

Language Practice: Forms of Literature

Match the form with its description.

e 1. an informational story about real things
b 2. a made-up story
d 3. a story of a person's life written by someone else
a 4. a story that has come down from the past
f 5. a story of a person's life written by the person
c 6. a composition written in verse

a. legend
b. fiction
c. poetry
d. biography
e. nonfiction
f. autobiography

Writing Practice: Imagine that you are a zoologist and have recently discovered a new species of animal. Describe the physical features of this new species and how and where you discovered it.

#3303 Daily Skills Practice–Grades 5-6   194   ©Teacher Created Materials, Inc.

Page 195

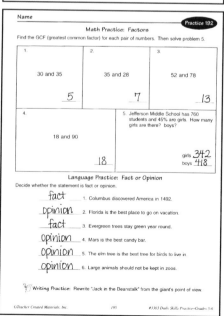

Name

Math Practice: Factors — Practice 192

Find the GCF (greatest common factor) for each pair of numbers. Then solve problem 5.

1. 30 and 35   5
2. 35 and 28   7
3. 52 and 78   13
4. 18 and 90   18
5. Jefferson Middle School has 760 students and 45% are girls. How many girls are there? boys?   girls 342 boys 418

Language Practice: Fact or Opinion

Decide whether the statement is fact or opinion.

fact 1. Columbus discovered America in 1492.
opinion 2. Florida is the best place to go on vacation.
fact 3. Evergreen trees stay green year round.
opinion 4. Mars is the best candy bar.
opinion 5. The elm tree is the best tree for birds to live in.
opinion 6. Large animals should not be kept in zoos.

Writing Practice: Rewrite "Jack in the Beanstalk" from the giant's point of view.

©Teacher Created Materials, Inc.   195   #3303 Daily Skills Practice–Grades 5-6

Page 196

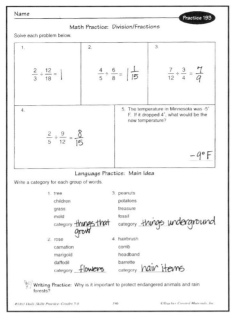

Name _____ Practice 193

Math Practice: Division/Fractions

Solve each problem below.

1.	2.	3.
$\frac{2}{3} \div \frac{12}{18} = 1$	$\frac{4}{5} \div \frac{6}{8} = 1\frac{1}{15}$	$\frac{7}{12} \div \frac{3}{4} = \frac{7}{9}$

4.	5. The temperature in Minnesota was -5° F. If it dropped 4°, what would be the new temperature?
$\frac{2}{5} \div \frac{9}{12} = \frac{8}{15}$	$-9°F$

Language Practice: Main Idea

Write a category for each group of words.

1. tree
   children
   grass
   mold
   category _things that grow_

3. peanuts
   potatoes
   treasure
   fossil
   category _things underground_

2. rose
   carnation
   marigold
   daffodil
   category _flowers_

4. hairbrush
   comb
   headband
   barrette
   category _hair items_

Writing Practice: Why is it important to protect endangered animals and rain forests?

#3303 Daily Skills Practice–Grades 5-6   196   ©Teacher Created Materials, Inc.

Page 197

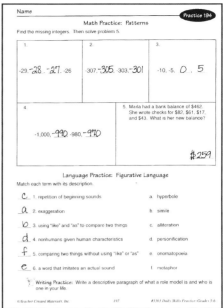

Name _____ Practice 194

Math Practice: Patterns

Find the missing integers. Then solve problem 5.

1.	2.	3.
-29, -28, -27, -26	-307, -305, -303, -301	-10, -5, 0, 5

4.	5. Marla had a bank balance of $462. She wrote checks for $82, $61, $17, and $43. What is her new balance?
-1,000, -990, -980, -970	$259

Language Practice: Figurative Language

Match each term with its description.

c 1. repetition of beginning sounds   a. hyperbole
a 2. exaggeration   b. simile
b 3. using "like" and "as" to compare two things   c. alliteration
d 4. nonhumans given human characteristics d. personification
f 5. comparing two things without using "like" or "as" e. onomatopoeia
e 6. a word that imitates an actual sound   f. metaphor

Writing Practice: Write a descriptive paragraph of what a role model is and who is one in your life.

©Teacher Created Materials, Inc.   197   #3303 Daily Skills Practice–Grades 5-6

Page 198

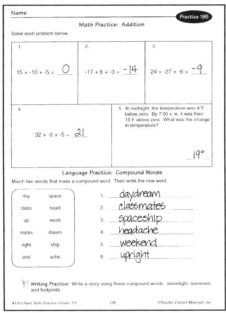

Name _____ Practice 195

Math Practice: Addition

Solve each problem below.

1.	2.	3.
$15 + -10 + -5 = 0$	$-17 + 6 + -3 = -14$	$24 + -27 + -6 = -9$

4.	5. At midnight, the temperature was 4°F below zero. By 7:00 A.M. it was then 15°F above zero. What was the change in temperature?
$32 + -6 + -5 = 21$	$19°$

Language Practice: Compound Words

Match two words that make a compound word. Then write the new word.

day	space
class	head
up	week
mates	dream
right	ship
end	ache

1. daydream
2. classmates
3. spaceship
4. headache
5. weekend
6. upright

Writing Practice: Write a story using these compound words: moonlight, someone, and footprints.

#3303 Daily Skills Practice–Grades 5-6   198   ©Teacher Created Materials, Inc.

Page 199

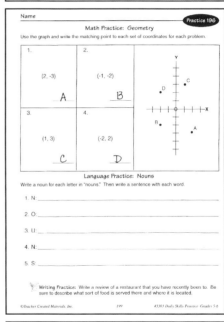

Name _____ Practice 196

Math Practice: Geometry

Use the graph and write the matching point to each set of coordinates for each problem.

1. (2, -3) A	2. (-1, -2) B
3. (1, 3) C	4. (-2, 2) D

Language Practice: Nouns

Write a noun for each letter in "nouns." Then write a sentence with each word.

1. N _____
2. O _____
3. U _____
4. N _____
5. S _____

Writing Practice: Write a review of a restaurant that you have recently been to. Be sure to describe what sort of food is served there and where it is located.

©Teacher Created Materials, Inc.   199   #3303 Daily Skills Practice–Grades 5-6

Page 200

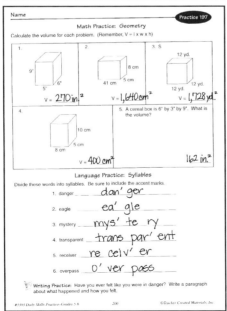

Name _____ Practice 197

Math Practice: Geometry

Calculate the volume for each problem. (Remember, V = l x w x h)

1.	2.	3. S
$V = 270 in.^2$	$V = 1,640 cm^2$	$V = 1,728 yd.^2$

4.	5. A cereal box is 6" by 3" by 9". What is the volume?
$V = 400 cm^3$	$162 in.^2$

Language Practice: Syllables

Divide these words into syllables. Be sure to include the accent marks.

1. danger _dan' ger_
2. eagle _ea' gle_
3. mystery _mys' te ry_
4. transparent _trans par' ent_
5. receiver _re ceiv' er_
6. overpass _o' ver pass_

Writing Practice: Have you ever felt like you were in danger? Write a paragraph about what happened and how you felt.

#3303 Daily Skills Practice–Grades 5-6   200   ©Teacher Created Materials, Inc.

Page 201

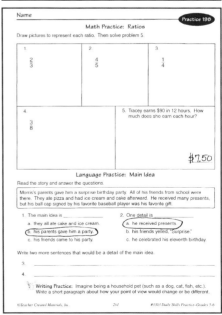

Name _____ Practice 198

Math Practice: Ratios

Draw pictures to represent each ratio. Then solve problem 5.

1. $\frac{2}{3}$	2. $\frac{4}{5}$	3. $\frac{1}{4}$

4. $\frac{3}{8}$	5. Tracey earns $90 in 12 hours. How much does she earn each hour?
	$7.50

Language Practice: Main Idea

Read the story and answer the questions.

Morris's parents gave him a surprise birthday party. All of his friends from school were there. They had pizza and had ice cream and cake afterward. He received many presents, but his ball cap signed by his favorite baseball player was his favorite gift.

1. The main idea is ___
   a. they all ate cake and ice cream.
   b. his parents gave him a party.
   c. his friends came to his party.

2. One detail is ___
   a. he received presents.
   b. his friends yelled, "Surprise."
   c. he celebrated his eleventh birthday.

Write two more sentences that would be a detail of the main idea.

3. _____
4. _____

Writing Practice: Imagine being a household pet (such as a dog, cat, fish, etc.). Write a short paragraph about how your point of view would change or be different.

©Teacher Created Materials, Inc.   201   #3303 Daily Skills Practice–Grades 5-6

Page 202

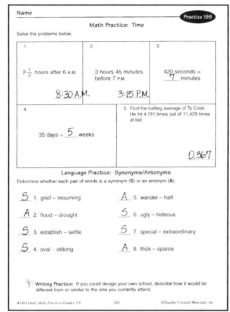

Math Practice: Time

Solve the problems below.

1.	2.	3.
$2\frac{1}{2}$ hours after 6 A.M. **8:30 A.M.**	3 hours 45 minutes before 7 P.M. **3:15 P.M.**	420 seconds = **7** minutes
4. 35 days = **5** weeks	5. Find the batting average of Ty Cobb. He hit 4,191 times out of 11,429 times at bat. **0.367**	

Language Practice: Synonyms/Antonyms

Determine whether each pair of words is a synonym (S) or an antonym (A).

S 1. grief – mourning   **A** 5. wander – halt

A 2. flood – drought   **S** 6. ugly – hideous

S 3. establish – settle   **S** 7. special – extraordinary

S 4. oval – oblong   **A** 8. thick – sparse

✐ **Writing Practice:** If you could design your own school, describe how it would be different from or similar to the one you currently attend.

#3303 Daily Skills Practice–Grades 5-6   202   ©Teacher Created Materials, Inc.

Page 203

Math Practice: Measurement

Solve the problems below.

1.	2.	3.
3 pecks = 24 quarts	20 pecks = **5** bushels	18 pints = **9** quarts
4. 80 pints = **5** pecks	5. Sheila's mom bought 4 candy bars for 69¢. How much would it cost if she bought enough for Sheila's class of 24 students? **$4.14**	

Language Practice: Proofreading

Rewrite the sentences correctly.

1. one of jeffs favorite movies is a bug's life
   One of Jeff's favorite movies is "A Bug's Life."
2. what is you favorite movie
   What is your favorite movie?
3. mom and i go for a walk threw yellowstone national park
   Mom and I went for a walk through Yellowstone National Park.
4. we seen too deers on the path
   We saw two deer on the path.
5. would you like to here my cousin terrys poem
   Would you like to hear my cousin Terry's poem?
6. the road less traveled are it's name
   "The Road Less Traveled" is its name.

✐ **Writing Practice:** What would life be like if you were two inches tall?

©Teacher Created Materials, Inc.   203   #3303 Daily Skills Practice–Grades 5-6

Page 204

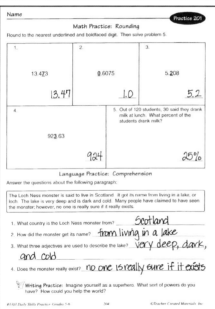

Math Practice: Rounding

Round to the nearest underlined and boldfaced digit. Then solve problem 5.

1.	2.	3.
13.4**7**3 **13.47**	**0**.6075 **1.0**	5.2**0**8 **5.2**
4. 92**3**.63 **924**	5. Out of 120 students, 30 said they drank milk at lunch. What percent of the students drank milk? **25%**	

Language Practice: Comprehension

Answer the questions about the following paragraph:

> The Loch Ness monster is said to live in Scotland. It got its name from living in a lake, or loch. The lake is very deep and is dark and cold. Many people have claimed to have seen the monster; however, no one is really sure if it really exists.

1. What country is the Loch Ness monster from? **Scotland**
2. How did the monster get its name? **from living in a lake**
3. What three adjectives are used to describe the lake? **very deep, dark, and cold**
4. Does the monster really exist? **no one is really sure if it exists**

✐ **Writing Practice:** Imagine yourself as a superhero. What sort of powers do you have? How could you help the world?

#3303 Daily Skills Practice–Grades 5-6   204   ©Teacher Created Materials, Inc.

Page 205

Math Practice: Comparing Numbers

For problems 1 and 2, order the numbers from least to greatest. For problems 3 and 4, order the numbers from greatest to least. Then solve problem 5.

1.	2.	3.
-7, 0, 17, -17, 7 **-17, -7, 0, 7, 17**	15, 0, -13, 3, -5 **-13, -5, 0, 3, 15**	15,000.01, 15,001.01, 15,001.10, 15,010.01 **15,010.10** **15,001.10** **15,001.01** **15,000.01**
4. 1,234.3, 12.343, 1.2343, 123.43 **1,234.3** **123.43** **12.343** **1.2343**	5. Hilda takes 20 minutes to type her three-page report. If she begins at 3:00 P.M., when will she be finished? **3:20 P.M.**	

Language Practice: Sentences

Circle yes if the words make a sentence or no if they do not.

(yes) no   1. Barry is a cute baby.
yes (no)   2. The blue and white car in the garage.
(yes) no   3. Candy is sweet.
yes (no)   4. A big bus in an accident.
yes (no)   5. Like a pizza.
(yes) no   6. See my pencil?

✐ **Writing Practice:** Some people say that all children need to eat a good breakfast before they come to school. Write a persuasive paragraph about this topic.

©Teacher Created Materials, Inc.   205   #3303 Daily Skills Practice–Grades 5-6
